"*Finding the Way* is an inspiring, informative story of the entrepreneurial journey. Filled with timeless lessons about the joys and challenges of building a business, this book is overflowing with insights that are missing from most entrepreneurial books and MBA classes. A single nugget from the book could save an entrepreneur untold time and money, and this book is full of them. The story format makes it interesting to read and less preachy than a textbook. Overall a great book and a great read!"

—**Ellie Byrd,** Business Coach and Advisor; Founder,
ForumSherpa and MachPoint; Author, *Eating Ramen:*
A Survival Guide for Tough Financial Times

"The most effective leaders inspire by crafting a vision, charting a path, and relentlessly pursuing it. The author's authenticity, management style, and commitment to the process of improvement shine through. Reading this book has compelled me to sustain focus on becoming a better communicator and a more pragmatic leader. Absolutely a must-read for every-level entrepreneur!"

—**Scott Roberts,** Founder and CEO, Pioneer Rubber & Gasket

"*Finding the Way* is an entertaining journey full of useful business advice that clearly comes from Ren's own personal experience. Practical, sound, and actionable life lessons for entrepreneurs and business people alike. It was emotional and felt like I was reading my own story in many ways."

—**Derek Elder,** CEO, Board Member, and Investor

"Cap Treeger truly pays it forward by sharing his experiences and the invaluable advice of his network of successful business mentors to provide an entertaining, lesson-filled story to guide any want-to-be entrepreneur. There are many essential experiences to live and learn from. For example, there is incredible wisdom on cost structure and understanding the cost of risk in *Finding the Way* that should be required reading for all entrepreneurs and small business leaders. Dive in and take your own inspiration from idea to reality!"

—**Jeff Taylor,** CEO, Dead River Ranch Materials, LLC

"*Finding the Way* captures the plight of the entrepreneur journey in a captivating, motivating way. From the ups and downs to the twists and turns, Cap Treeger acts as a sherpa guiding the reader through a founder's experience with grace and aplomb by way of the hero Ren. Every entrepreneur would do well to take their first step here."

—**David Cummings,** Entrepreneur; Investor; Founder, Pardot and Atlanta Tech Village; Author, *Startup Upstart*

"Climb aboard for a roller coaster ride! *Finding the Way* is not just for entrepreneurs and those around them, it is for leaders in all walks of life and anyone interested in personal development. The journey gets more enjoyable and the lessons more valuable as the book progresses. Cap Treeger's story leads you to live and learn through his experiences and wisdom from mentors and mistakes, emphasizing so many of the essential business and leadership lessons that are not taught elsewhere. There are no shortcuts to becoming a strong leader, but *Finding the Way* is as close to a road map as I've seen."

—**Russell Smith,** Entrepreneur; Angel Investor; Founder and CEO, RTS Associates

"*Finding the Way* is a must-read business development 'textbook' for all aspiring entrepreneurs. The unique, breezy style of this book, which involves family members, real-to-life business associates, and advisors dealing with real-life business opportunities, challenges, and learning experiences, is not only entertaining but also rewarding. The takeaway is a concise yet comprehensive checklist of things to consider along the road to success in an entrepreneurial endeavor."

—**Joe Bleser,** CFO, Board Member, and Advisor to many public and private companies

"Cap Treeger provides something that every entrepreneur—and every person—should crave: understanding gained from other people's experiences. He not only shares the lessons learned from the ups and downs of starting a business, but also relays tremendous wisdom learned from many amazing mentors in his life. There is something in this story for everyone."

—**Shane Jackson,** Speaker; President, Jackson Healthcare; Author, *Fostering Culture: A Leader's Guide to Purposefully Shaping Culture*

"*Finding the Way* is an easy read, as the author takes us down the road of starting and growing a business. And this is a great read for any kind of endeavor. While businesses are all different, entrepreneurs and their companies share many common problems and challenges. Being familiar with them before they occur will make the process of dealing with them easier."

—**Jim McDonald,** Former President and CEO (retired),
Scientific-Atlanta, Prime Computer, and Gould, Inc

"Starting a business and building momentum is hard. *Finding the Way* allows you, the reader, to be the proverbial fly on the wall as Ren the entrepreneur implements layer upon layer of sound advice from his mentors. A great read that makes an interesting story of some of the most important lessons in entrepreneurship."

—**Davis Knox,** Entrepreneur; Co-Founder, Outdoors By Owner;
Co-Founder and CEO, Fire & Flavor

"*Finding the Way* is a fantastic read, packed with lessons every aspiring entrepreneur should lean into. Each chapter is packed with real life experiences that occur in new enterprises each and every day. There are no shortcuts to success; however, this book offers many insights that can help pave the way."

—**Ernest L. Ellis,** Founder and CEO, FS360

"*Finding the Way* is a must read for individuals contemplating an entrepreneurial journey. This novel delivers the experience of the highs and lows involved in starting and growing a company."

—**Irv Grossman,** Logistics Founder and Entrepreneur

"This is an inspiring story; you will live through the author's dreams, visions, and actions of being an entrepreneur creating a business. His endless search for experience, knowledge, and advice while developing a company with all the ups and downs of clients, products, markets, personalities, and finances is a constant battle. Then he gets to go home to his family and that support system that you can't forget."

—**G. Niles Bolton,** Founder, Chairman, and CEO,
Niles Bolton Associates

"*Finding the Way* is a great read for anyone thinking of starting a business and wanting to learn from the experience of others. Hearing the story of the challenges and successes, understanding what worked and did not work, and learning from the first hand experiences of those that have been there are all enormously valuable for anyone thinking of starting out on a new venture! A great read!"

—**G. P. "Bud" Peterson,** PhD, President Emeritus,
Georgia Institute of Technology;
Chairman, Partnership for Inclusive Innovation

"This is a wonderful business parable that is packed with wisdom from end to end. You can tell that the author has both lived the roller coaster ride of business and thoroughly studied the subject. An aspiring entrepreneur would save countless dollars, headaches, and amount of time by taking to heart even just a handful of the lessons contained herein."

—**Steven Hong,** Serial Entrepreneur; Founder, Sylvane

"*Finding the Way* is a warm, thoughtful account of a young, aspiring CEO growing into the role. The story vividly and realistically chronicles Ren's struggles in addressing the changing structural and personnel needs of his business as it grows as well as the challenge of maintaining a healthy balance between family and work. Whether you are in the early stages of your journey as a business leader or nearing the end of the road reflecting back, *Finding the Way* will be a great read."

—**Joe Evans,** Banking Founder and CEO;
Chairman (retired), State Bank Financial Corporation;
Vice Chairman, Cadence Bancorporation

"Normally novels serve to provide engaging entertainment. Business books—insights, knowledge, and winning strategies. Cap Treeger's *Finding the Way* bridges the gap between the two approaches in a very unique fashion. Character interactions coupled with engaging dialogue take the reader on a journey filled with wisdom, grounded insights, and the guidance to help direct one's passion in the relentless quest for business success. I strongly recommend it as a must-read for aspiring entrepreneurs regardless of the stage in their journey. The book entertains while teaching, encouraging, and enlightening."

—**Clifford Schorer,** Entrepreneur in Residence,
Columbia Business School

"Parables have been used since the beginning of time, among all major cultures and religions, to teach important life lessons in a way that the reader or listener can easily relate to. *Finding the Way* is no exception and is a modern parable for every business owner. Following the story of Ren on his entrepreneurial journey, business owners and aspiring entrepreneurs can learn valuable lessons and save themselves years of headaches, time, and money. I highly recommend this book!"

—**Rebekah Barr,** CEO, Allyon, Inc

"*Finding the Way* is a fantastic journey, offering a comprehensive blueprint in company building. It shows the path from concept to execution. I wish I had read this 20 years earlier."

—**Brian Terrell,** Entrepreneur; Founder, VFXnow and
GPL Technologies

"I like this book. It is not formulaic. The author encounters problems, most of which he has not seen before. He asks for advice, listens, and deals with his problems, sometimes clearly, sometimes in a messy way . . . like life—with insightful and humble introspection along the way."

—**Jim Balloun,** retired CEO

"*Finding the Way* captures Cap Treeger's brilliant mind for starting and managing highly successful businesses. A truly riveting and educational experience, and written in the format of a page-turner novel, its teachings seek to inspire a new generation of startup entrepreneurs and unicorn operators."

—**Justin Chen Li,** CEO, Helio Genomics; Venture Advisor;
Director; *Forbes* Thought Leader

"A depiction of a young entrepreneur's journey in seeking direction and guidance toward his goal of establishing a successful startup, this book is a wonderful guidebook in coaching the journey for anyone who's interested in this courageous and exciting path in life. It provides details on different stages of strategic planning but more importantly, it highlights the charismatic characters of great entrepreneurs who value integrity, compassion, and respect for others at all stages of their lives."

—**Verna Meng,** Founder and CEO, VEE International

"My favorite concept from this book was the Villain—who lurks everywhere, ready, willing, and able to screw up my business and teaching me to be prepared. This book so uniquely labels critical concepts in an engaging manner that you can't help but remember them in your daily life. I'm going to provide a copy of this book to all my entrepreneurship students."

—**Samir Patel,** Entrepreneur;
Investor, Trophy Point Investment Group;
Instructor of Entrepreneurship, Georgia State University

"This tale is an excellent guide for first-time entrepreneurs. Cap Treeger takes the reader on an enjoyable, entertaining tale highlighting the pitfalls and opportunities of starting a business. *Finding the Way* is packed with useful information for entrepreneurs and potential investors. And it is very instructive for those who wish to be mentors of entrepreneurs."

—**Doug Johns,** Mentor; Former Senior Executive, Internet Security
Systems and Compaq; Former Chairman and CEO,
Monorail Computer Company and Nivis

"This outstanding business novel packs more value than any 'how-to' book on entrepreneurship. It's a very personalized story through all phases of the startup journey. The protagonist masters the art of building a company rather than just a successful product, and he puts to best use the practical advice he is given along the way by his advisors and mentors. Countless restaurant meetings bring to the story the daily practicalities of how such wisdom is often passed along. You'll develop an appetite for even more!"

—**Ben J Dyer,** Entrepreneur; Investor; CEO; Entrepreneur in Residence,
Advanced Technology Development Center

"You don't need to be a die-hard entrepreneur to enjoy and benefit from *Finding the Way*. Its compelling lessons, folded into a terrific and heartfelt narrative, may help you manage your own business, whatever it may be, and your own life more effectively. This may give you insight into those hyper-driven business starters you know and will certainly remind you of the value of deep relationships and great mentors. And if you catch the bug yourself, you'll find a road map to building a successful business without losing what's most important. So, dive on in!"

—**Alvin Townley**, Best-selling *New York Times*–reviewed Author; Senior
Leadership Fellow, United States Naval Academy

"This book is an excellent guide for every aspiring or established entrepreneur. Cap Treeger does a wonderful job of guiding the readers through a roller coaster journey, overcoming challenges and taking advantage of various opportunities in a fun and easily readable fable. This entrepreneurial journey is an excellent example of achieving the peak of success through clearly articulated vision, plan, perseverance, self-belief, continuous learning, and persistence. *Finding the Way* is a must-have guide for anyone who wants to build a prosperous organization."

—**Dr. Srikanth Gaddam,** President and CEO, ERPA; Entrepreneur; Angel Investor; Author, *The Future of Disruptive Technologies, The Entrepreneurial Guide, The Leadership Guide,* and *Destination Success*

"*Finding the Way* is a journey through the early life of a business and is packed with wisdom for the business, personal, and family life of every entrepreneur. Whether you are an entrepreneur or you are in a relationship with an entrepreneur, this book will give you a new perspective on the ups and downs of the founder's life. You will want to dog ear, highlight, and scribble in the margins."

—**David McMullen,** Co-Founder, redpepper; Entrepreneur; Consultant; Investor in creative organizations

"This story is one that many entrepreneurs live time and again. Not looking at their repeat missteps, they then wonder why they are not experiencing the success that they were expecting. This book allows you to travel the entrepreneur's journey from a birds eye view first, without having to make those same miscalculations yourself. It's like having a mentor to guide you through your journey but in a book - educational and entertaining!"

—**Kashi Sehgal,** Founder of Retaaza

"*Finding the Way* spoke to me! This novel emphasizes one of the most important lessons for aspiring entrepreneurs: starting, launching, and growing a business is never a straight line. Every entrepreneur's journey is a roller coaster with surprises at every turn. This book should become required reading for founders or anyone who has wondered 'What is it really like to start a business?' Whether it's employee drama, late-night crazy stories, or software bugs that create problems you never expect, there is never a dull moment. The stories and lessons included in *Finding the Way* are invaluable for entrepreneurs at every stage and scale."

—**Johnson Cook,** Co-founder, Greenlight Financial Technology

Finding
the
Way

THE ENTREPRENEUR'S TALE

Finding the Way

CAP TREEGER

GREENLEAF
BOOK GROUP PRESS

Published by Greenleaf Book Group Press
Austin, Texas
www.gbgpress.com

Distributed by Greenleaf Book Group

For ordering information or special discounts for bulk purchases, please contact Greenleaf Book Group at PO Box 91869, Austin, TX 78709, 512.891.6100.

Design and composition by Greenleaf Book Group
Cover design by Greenleaf Book Group
Cover images used under license from ©Shutterstock.com/Antonov Maxim;
©Shutterstock.com/Manon_Labe; ©Shutterstock.com/Zenzen;
©Shutterstock.com/dedMazay;

Publisher's Cataloging-in-Publication data is available.

Print ISBN: 978-1-62634-911-7

eBook ISBN: 978-1-62634-912-4

To offset the number of trees consumed in the printing of our books, Greenleaf donates a portion of the proceeds from each printing to the Arbor Day Foundation. Greenleaf Book Group has replaced over 50,000 trees since 2007.

Printed in the United States of America on acid-free paper

22 23 24 25 26 27   10 9 8 7 6 5 4 3 2 1

First Edition

A Way of Life

Go placidly amid the noise and the haste, and remember what peace there may be in silence. As far as possible, without surrender, be on good terms with all persons.

Speak your truth quietly and clearly, and listen to others, even to the dull and the ignorant; they too have their story.

Avoid loud and aggressive persons; they are vexatious to the spirit. If you compare yourself with others, you may become vain or bitter, for always there will be greater and lesser persons than yourself.

Enjoy your achievements as well as your plans. Keep interested in your own career, however humble; it is a real possession in the changing fortunes of time.

Exercise caution in your business affairs, for the world is full of trickery. But let this not blind you to what virtue there is; many persons strive for high ideals, and everywhere life is full of heroism.

Be yourself. Especially, do not feign affection. Neither be cynical about love; for in the face of all aridity and disenchantment it is as perennial as the grass.

Take kindly the counsel of the years, gracefully surrendering the things of youth.

Nurture strength of spirit to shield you in sudden misfortune. But do not distress yourself with dark imaginings. Many fears are born of fatigue and loneliness.

Beyond a wholesome discipline, be gentle with yourself. You are a child of the universe no less than the trees and the stars; you have a right to be here.

And whether or not it is clear to you, no doubt the universe is unfolding as it should. Therefore be at peace with God, whatever you conceive Him to be.

And whatever your labors and aspirations, in the noisy confusion of life, keep peace in your soul. With all its sham, drudgery and broken dreams, it is still a beautiful world. Be cheerful. Strive to be happy.

—Max Ehrmann, "Desiderata," 1927

Experience Sharing

Failure Assured

"Too many prefer gentle lies to hard truths."

—Shane Parrish

"You're not going to make it." The older man's words were simple and direct, delivered in a comfortable, matter-of-fact tone that contrasted sharply with the harsh message.

His fork frozen in midair, Ren didn't know whether to be insulted or just surprised.

Before he could respond, the wise man continued, still in an even tone, with a deliberate pace and a bit of a Southern drawl. "In fact, the only thing you would be less qualified to do is maybe if you decided to become a brain surgeon."

Putting down his fork, Ren squinted and opened his mouth slightly in surprise. After a pause that stretched well into the zone of discomfort, he settled into feeling curious. He needed to know more.

This was the rather unconventional start to what would become one of the most essential relationships of Ren Hatcher's professional and personal life. He would often reflect back on this fateful lunch meeting on a bright Wednesday, at a Taco Mac restaurant in Cobb County, in the northern suburbs of Atlanta. You see, when he shared the beginnings of his new business plan, he expected the older man to be impressed. After all, Ren, now twenty-seven, had found prior success as one of the first employees in a successful venture. He had helped grow Standard Link from a startup through implementation and into a solid exit. Before that, he'd had good jobs in high-profile businesses. Some even regarded him as a prodigy. He'd made some mistakes during his career—who hadn't? But he had learned from them, and he felt sure he would be a winner.

Ren had met with a lot of successful business leaders over the previous weeks, floating his startup idea by each of them. Without fail, they all told him that he was destined to succeed. He had all the right stuff. His ideas were superb. Unique. His business plan was flawless. He knew the right people. He was smart and experienced. He had been part of a prior winner. In a world where success was measured by how much money you raised from investors, funding this new venture would be a no-brainer. He was a golden boy.

Then, a mutual friend suggested that he talk to David Olden, the older gentleman who was now sitting across from him and delivering this unexpected message.

As a rule, Ren always checked people out before meeting with them. Prior to their first in-person connection, he learned that David was well known in business circles for his acumen and successful ventures. David had apparently been around the block a few times, and from what Ren could tell, he must have known what he was talking about. He estimated David to be in his early fifties, maybe a few years younger than Ren's father. His résumé was impressive, sporting decades of experience and the wisdom that comes with it.

One well-informed mutual friend even described David as *the* most accomplished visionary in healthcare information technology, the sector Ren was hoping to enter. Everyone described him as very smart.

After so many recent meetings with so many bright, successful people, Ren felt exhausted. They all were encouraging, but every meeting seemed the same. After introductions, he would share his concept. The other person would express enthusiasm and confidence in his success, giving him some version of a congratulatory pep talk. They would then offer to help and perhaps recommend a book he should read or someone else that he should meet. All of the meetings felt like slight variations of a now-predictable script. There was little new feedback.

So, as relevant and intriguing as David's background was, he had scheduled this meeting with David because he felt appreciative of—and somewhat obligated to—the mutual friend who had made the introduction. Ren wasn't expecting to hear anything new, but he was glad enough to expand his network and meet a business legend. He felt sure he'd get additional confirmation of what he already knew: He was destined to succeed.

What he found instead was the seemingly modest David Olden. And, after Ren shared his background and the new business idea, David was so unimpressed that he had just flatly told him in no uncertain terms that he would not succeed.

David's words were like a slap in the face, and he certainly caught Ren's attention. As time stood still for him, Ren had the sensation of sinking slowly through water. After what was less than ten seconds but felt like an eternity, the conversation resumed.

"From your story, I know you feel like your last company was a success," David continued. "I understand that y'all had an innovative solution and were very good with technology and great at sales. It was the right time to be in that particular business. That may be a really good way to start a new venture, but it's not a sustainable, replicable business in itself. Even if you have great ideas, do you want to depend on bringing them to the market at the right place at the right time, when you have so much on the line? You may not deserve to be so cocky about being this genius business leader just yet. If y'all hadn't sold that company when you did, you would have needed to evolve into a real, sustainable model, or the wheels would've eventually come off."

Feeling a pressure in his shoulders and temples, Ren's face may have gone through a few different shades of color, from an initial red to a light ashen. This moment felt surreal.

Why did this bother him so much? Could the triumph of Standard Link have depended on luck, on being at the right place at the right time, as much as skill and expertise and hard work? Was there more to leadership and giving a business a better chance that he needed to learn? If so, did that make him . . . well, some sort of a fraud?

David tempered his comments slightly. "Look, it's not that you can't learn how to get there. I expect that you're very capable," he went on. "But I can tell you that you are not prepared to give yourself the best chance to make it. You haven't yet grown into the kind of purposeful leader that you could be. You've never really had to learn about business models, product positioning, or even putting the right team together in the right position to succeed in an ongoing way. Having been through those things before and having learned them the hard way myself—as a lot of entrepreneurs and business leaders have had to—I almost feel them like scars on my back.

"You don't have any idea of what you are up against and how much you don't know," David said deliberately. "Ninety percent of startups fail. Less than four percent of companies ever make it to over a million dollars in revenue. And only a tiny percentage of those become the kind of high-flying success that you want to build. You will face adversity that you couldn't possibly be prepared for now. And you don't even understand the industry that you're planning to get into, which is a big deal in this case."

The numbers David presented were nothing new. Ren had seen the statistics and knew that the odds were nearly insurmountable. It was the "nearly" that he held on to and that made successful entrepreneurship, in his mind, a game that could be learned. But what made Ren very uncomfortable was that, up until this moment, sitting across the table from David, he had felt certain that his prior round of the entrepreneur game with Standard Link had made him an advanced-level player. Yet here was David, telling him there was more to it and that winning one game didn't automatically mean as much—not that you were a good player, and definitely not that you were going to win your next game.

I know we worked hard at Standard Link! We had some really smart people and great ideas there. What else is there?

In the wake of the unexpected direction of this conversation, Ren had forgotten to eat his lunch. He fumbled a bit through his salad and burger and wings, mostly just to have something to do with his hands. He wasn't sure whether to respond or take another bite. His first instinct was self-defense. *Who did this guy think he* was *to challenge him? Why would he do this?* His thoughts were racing.

"Well, I was just part of a great exit. Over the past couple of months, I've shared my accomplishments and this idea with a number of seriously successful people," Ren said, feeling a little insecure and exposed and trying to recapture control over the conversation. "Everyone told me it's a winner. I learned a lot from being a part of these businesses that did very well. The timing is exactly right now, and this is a huge opportunity."

David sipped his coffee without breaking eye contact with Ren—and still not looking impressed.

Stopping himself, Ren ran a hand through his thick, sandy hair and took a fortifying deep breath. Maybe this wasn't the right approach. Maybe he shouldn't be talking about what other people said or about his past successes.

"David," he said, "I've always prided myself in appreciating people who talk straight, people who tell me what I need to hear, rather than what I *want* to hear. I appreciate your honesty and openness.

"But, please understand," Ren continued, "this isn't the response I'm used to getting. I think you've just caught me off guard. I'm interested to hear more." He hoped he truly meant the last part.

David's expression softened. "Well," he said, "I'm not sure you're as far along toward wise and purposeful leadership, or knowing how to build a sustainable business, as you seem to think you are. But a lot of successful people started out as impostors. And you seem to have the persistence and determination. If you're crazy enough to pursue this, I'm willing to try to help you."

CHAPTER 1

Entrepreneurial Genesis

"Our need will be the real creator."

—Plato, from *The Republic*

Most entrepreneurs can recall the moment when they made their "go or no go" decision: the point where they either walked away or fully committed—at great personal risk—to move forward on a new venture.

Some people quit their jobs to pursue this new opportunity or mortgaged their homes or borrowed from a family member. No matter the specifics, it was always a terrifying and exhilarating step driven by opportunity, by a desire to do something meaningful or perhaps live the dream. For others, it was born of necessity or even desperation.

In Ren Hatcher's case, there were significant elements of all of this.

He would never put himself forward as particularly special. He didn't enter the workforce post-college with a single-minded drive to become an innovator, but he had many of the characteristics of a successful entrepreneur. He was persistent, focused, could be detail obsessive, and had an innate need to build and construct. He loved to learn and he loved to teach. Ren's bookshelves were overflowing. If you ever got him started on a rant about any of a myriad of subjects, you might be in it for a time. His best friend once told Ren that he had never met anyone that was so caught up with always improving himself. Ren would often say, "I don't care how good or bad I am today, as long as I'm better tomorrow."

About three months before that first pivotal lunch meeting with David Olden, Ren's prospects were well short of what he had hoped. The job market was good, but none of the offers were on par with his inflated expectations and identity.

Ren had been fortunate to be one of the early employees of a technology startup company, Standard Link Systems, founded by a few of his friends. The startup had taken off like a rocket, and he had helped guide it to the top. Hailed as a tremendous success in many publications, the company had sold to a bigger business just before the acquiring company filed to go public.

When the ink was dry on the deal, Ren found that his position was not likely to be what he thought it should be, and so he decided it was best to move on. Technically, he wasn't fired or "let go," but he may as well have been when the acquiring company told him that they didn't need him in executive leadership and didn't know of a meaningful role where he might fit. When he left without another opportunity waiting in the wings, he found himself trapped between his needs for challenge and development and his family's needs for security and stability.

Those were interesting times. Ren and his wife, Tiffany, lived very frugally with their young son, RJ, in the northern outskirts of Atlanta. Ren had some potentially valuable stock in the parent company that bought Standard Link. But the acquiring company was closely held, with no opportunity for him to cash in at the time. He knew he'd have a great shot at walking away with plenty of cash once the company went public. But without a job and the regular paycheck that came with it, he needed to figure out a way to pay his bills and support his family—and fast.

While he wouldn't have been too proud to clean toilets or to take out the trash, Ren felt completely uninterested in doing it for someone else's company. After Standard Link's meteoric rise to the top, "tech startup guy" had become an identity he enjoyed. He wore it like a badge of honor, and his friends and family seemed proud by association. Who doesn't enjoy being admired? He was willing to go to great lengths to validate those expectations.

The few job opportunities that he was offered felt like a letdown after his ostensible success at Standard Link. He just couldn't bring himself to take any of them. One opportunity did seem promising, with an early stage, rapid-growth company. Ren had a warm introduction to the opportunity by a good friend, an established partner at the company. He did his homework and spent hours researching the company, then went through an intensive recruiting process with three interviews, only to receive The Call: "Sorry. We went with another candidate." Ren felt stuck.

Running out of time and options—with his mortgage to pay and a family depending on him—he had to pick a path and get moving.

Then, one day, as he was visiting his old college campus near downtown, Ren bumped into an old friend, Cary Kraus, who had hit it big with an internet company he started in college. Cary had rapidly become a local legend and was making a name for himself in the wider world now.

Ren had never been close with Cary, but he had always liked him. And he was blown away by all that the new tech-tycoon was doing in the community, including having just made a huge donation to their mutual alma mater.

He asked Cary to lunch, hoping to catch up and hear his story. When they finally got together a few weeks later over steaks at Joey D's Oak Room in the northern metro Atlanta suburb of Dunwoody, Cary was modest and, after his colossal success, still remained as genuine and humble as ever.

As Cary shared more about what he was accomplishing in the world in the wake of his success, Ren became increasingly excited. During that conversation, he firmly recognized that he needed to start his own business, and he knew he needed to be an entrepreneur. He was inspired by who Cary was and what he was doing more than by anything he said. *If he can do it, so can I!*

———

Once he decided to throw himself into this new direction, Ren was all in. The big question was, what business to start?

He knew that many of the best businesses are started by a specialist—someone who sees a specific need and knows how to create value for a customer. Perhaps it's a technician or a solution provider or salesperson who innovates a better way to position or deliver a product. And of course, from the work where they derived their proficiency, many of these specialists start out already having a very important little thing called "customers."

Ren didn't have any of that. He was like many people who wanted to be an entrepreneur but didn't even know what the business would be. The more he considered it, however, the more he realized that he *did* have an idea and that he had believed in it for many years.

He would build a better software solution—easier to use and understand— to enable better business decisions. The idea had really started in college, as a student at Georgia Tech. Ren had studied industrial engineering, something one of his favorite professors described as "like getting a technical degree in common sense." Essentially, it entailed finding better ways of doing things using proven, empirical methods and technologies. With their flexible techniques, industrial engineers often worked in logistics and supply chain management, quality control, production planning and control, plant layout or safety, or many other areas as well.

During his first couple of years at Georgia Tech, Ren hadn't been a great student. He had somehow been accepted to this leading engineering and tech-nology university, known for turning out highly successful graduates. Perhaps it was his test scores. But he had been immature, unmotivated, undisciplined— and most of all hated to do what he thought of as "busy work." He didn't go to class often enough or put effort into homework or lab assignments. He drank too much beer, went on too many dates, and found plenty of enjoyment in fraternity living.

But, when push came to shove and he did invest any time in his courses, Ren "got it" regarding the coursework and subject matter. He made good grades on his exams, which partly offset the bad grades on homework and labs. It wasn't unusual for other students to come to him to ask for help with their work. He had always been up for that, since helping could open the door for an opportu-nity to "study" with a cute girl or to exchange notes over a beer at the pub next to campus.

As college progressed and he got more into his major courses, Ren embraced learning and became more studious. The subject matter felt more practical and interesting in a way that the more general courses hadn't. He came to really love his major and what he could do with it. What industrial engineers did was cool!

Industrial engineering was more than the methodologies. To Ren, it was a way of thinking. There was always a way to improve processes and solutions for everything. From the very beginning of his studies, he realized that the software and tools available to industrial engineers were powerful, but that many of them weren't very functional or user-friendly. That seemed odd, since the intention of industrial engineering was to make things more efficient and functional. It seemed like the solutions they used should be more intuitive and clear.

A lightbulb had gone off one day as Ren was daydreaming during a core class, when everyone, even the professor, was struggling to make use of the software they had. Why hadn't someone created software to empower people to better use and understand these tools that industrial engineers utilized?

The question would surface again after graduation. In his first job, at a technology hardware manufacturing company called Innovation Atlanta, Ren worked on projects that implemented a program for Total Quality Management and to earn an International Standards Organization certification. With these efforts, the management of the company wanted to improve quality and consistency in the company's processes and output. But it seemed that many of the people that were working on implementation didn't fully understand what the tools were trying to accomplish. And the software and solutions they used seemed unnecessarily complicated.

The lightbulb had flared brighter a few weeks later while working on his annual tax return. Ren was using software with an intuitive interface to complete his taxes. He knew the tax software was doing some complex things behind the scenes, but the user interface was very clear and simple. It illustrated where it was going as he went along, and this made the process user-friendly.

He knew there had to be something there that would be applicable to the work he was pursuing professionally. *What if I could simplify and clarify how to use the powerful tools and methodologies we use? What if there was a way to empirically see what was underlying any decisions and test and explore better ways to do things? What if I could take the user-friendliness of the tax software and apply it to the more complicated methods I'm using to improve manufacturing or logistics practices?*

Ren inquired among his professors and friends working in the industry for such a solution. "If you find one, let me know, because it'll make my life a whole lot easier" was the staple answer. It seemed so obvious, but the software didn't exist. A few of the people he spoke with encouraged his idea as promising and needed. Two friends at manufacturing companies even suggested they would like to buy such a solution if he could provide it.

He thought it *had* to be possible to integrate the powerful tools that industrial engineers use—solutions with big-sounding names like statistical process

CHAPTER 2

Tulip in a Tornado

"Your purpose in life is to find your purpose and
give your whole heart and soul to it."

—Buddha

Once Ren made the decision to start his own business, he felt more committed than he had ever been before. He threw himself completely into the process.

The next few months were a blur. Ren felt like a tulip in a tornado. It was like powerful forces—potential opportunities, an upturn in the economy, new information and ideas—were swirling all around him, faster and more intensely than he could keep up with. And even though he had what he thought (no—he *knew!*) was a winning idea, he didn't have the right direction.

Feeling almost manic, Ren downloaded some templates for business planning, financial modeling, and software design. And he surprised himself by enjoying working through them, molding and developing them to his purposes. He would often get lost in his work for hours, forgetting to eat or sleep. The time for such things came and went as he worked through various scenarios.

He was wearing himself out with his efforts and researching opportunities. And he was also researching people: hungry to meet with just about anyone who would take the time to visit with him. From fear of missing out on what could potentially turn out to be useful advice or a valuable new contact, he wasn't particularly picky about who he sat down with. And he didn't take the time to step back and look at the big picture, as he was so involved with discussing his ideas with anybody he felt might be helpful or have constructive feedback.

All of the work, pressure, worry, and even guilt for where he was with his career and family had led to sleeplessness. After one particularly laborious day, Ren was really dragging. As he put his son, RJ, to bed, he noticed his hand shaking. He did the quick math and calculated that he had had at least ten cups of coffee between the time he woke up and his last meeting.

Maybe exhausted wasn't the right word to describe Ren's state of being. Did he need more sleep? Sure. Did both his mind and body crave actual rest? Desperately. But more than anything, he felt drained.

He lay on his bed, listening to the sound of crickets through the open window. The air conditioner was out and, for lack of money, he was trying to delay getting a new one for as long as he could. The cool May air blowing in made it tolerable, but Ren knew that the hot days and nights were only a few short weeks away. He felt like he was competing against time on so many frontiers. He needed to get as much advice and help as he could, as quickly as possible. He needed to get his idea up and running before there was a competitor on the market, but while making sure he had enough data to launch successfully. He was doing the hard work and putting in the hours now when RJ was young, so he could give his son more of his time and attention later on. Yet he wrestled with not wanting to completely miss out on his son's life during these early years. Ren didn't feel like he had a chance to win any of his fights.

To ease his mind toward sleep, Ren began to imagine doing yardwork. He visualized himself walking out in the garden and looking around. He installed new plants and manicured the lawn. He pictured going stem by stem, just above each bud, catching on up his roses that were past due for pruning. Then he carefully edged the driveway and began to place some stones that were coming out of a little decorative wall that he had built. Ren took each stone in his hands and then meticulously put it in its place in the wall. Once the wall was done, he began to count the stones.

The yardwork exercise, though, soon brought him to think of the numbers he had forgotten to add for a testing solution in his prospective development budget. Bam! All hope of sleep was lost. He knew that if he didn't go add it now, he would lay awake for a very long time and probably forget it again.

He got up and quietly felt his way across the room to avoid waking Tiffany, who was sound asleep, and made his way downstairs to his home office to huddle over his desk once again.

Succumbing to his restless thoughts, Ren began to use his nights as opportunities to read and learn about every possible subject he thought might be relevant to his business. Many of the successful people he met gave him—along with affirmation and well-meaning advice—a "great" book or recommendation for yet another insightful article. Those added up. It became apparent to him that many successful people read a lot and loved to swap books and articles. Ren learned a little bit about a lot of things: leadership, communication, personality typing, sales, marketing, product development, reading people, financial management, productivity hacks, managing employees, and anything else that seemed relevant.

He also tried to train himself, with a sort of Pavlovian association, to sleep whenever he got in bed. He would work and study until exhausted, only going to bed when he felt absolutely ready to crash. Of course, all it took was one troubling thought or one arising question to rob him of sleep and get him back to his office desk.

Just about everyone Ren met was very encouraging and seemed glad to take time to meet with him. He appreciated when successful people would carve out an hour or more from their busy schedules for him. Ren wondered whether that revealed some sort of common success factor. Were they gracious and helpful to him because they were successful? Or were they successful because they were the sort of people who wanted to do more and pay it forward?

He also noticed how many of them were just nice, genuine people. And some of his conversations turned into a small, friendly competition to determine who was cheapest. The majority of the wealthiest people Ren met up with drove practical vehicles: maybe a Toyota Camry or a Ford Explorer, rather than the Bentley or Ferrari some might have expected. And it seemed that many of them were also tight in other ways. "I bought all my plastic shaving razors in a bulk pack, where they end up costing less than 10 cents each," one uber-wealthy business leader told him. "And I carefully dry them after each use, so I can utilize each one for a year. That's a lifetime supply of shaving for less than $5," he exclaimed victoriously. Another wealthy former entrepreneur boasted that he re-used a paper towel until it seemed like it had too much mustard on it.

Increasingly, Ren felt there could be a connection between what initially felt like extreme frugality and business success. He wondered if watching your pennies really did encourage the dollars to take better care of themselves. One older gentleman explained that the fastidiousness and discipline of doing so can carry throughout other practices in the business.

Consideration and kindness were always a priority in Ren's life. He vowed that, even after he found success, he would try to emulate these good people. He would always try to make time for anyone who legitimately wanted to work hard and build a business. He thought, *Once I'm a huge success, I want to stay humble and respectful, and prioritize others' efforts. Rather than making people accommodate me, I'll be willing to meet with them according to their schedule, and I'll even drive to them to make it easier. My success will allow me to pay it forward, just like all my mentors have done for me.*

This was a pivotal season in his life and business. Hungry for wisdom and knowledge, he tried to absorb as much as possible. Each day, he felt more convinced that he was destined to be an entrepreneur. That recognition and taking action in that direction felt good. But while his heart was in the right place, Ren didn't have a clear strategy or path forward. Where he didn't have direction or discipline yet, he increasingly became aware of the need for those things and purposefully set out to attain them.

One of Ren's early mentors, Joe Chapman, used to tell him, "Always keep moving forward." All in all, the months quickly rushed by as he did just that. He invested a lot of time in market research, including prospective competition and the size of the opportunity. He spoke with business leaders and studied about planning and strategy for a new company. He discovered that there were a lot of books, and sometimes conflicting opinions, on such matters. It was mostly encouraging but sometimes confusing. And he found a broad market that probably needed to be narrowed at first, without any competitive solutions that he could identify.

———

Joe Chapman was a lean, fit, gray-haired sixty-something, with creases at the corners of his eyes from decades of genuine smiles and laughter, as well as plenty of lines on his face from hours spent awake when he should have been asleep. Joe spoke slowly, choosing his words carefully, but making each of them count.

He had built a great services company with deep, loyal customer relationships and thousands of devoted employees. And Ren liked it that he still signed every check that went out the door from that business.

Joe had been very gracious, helpful, and patient with his time over a period of many years. He and Ren had made it a habit to meet up at Waffle House, usually the same one, located near Joe's home, where they preferred to sit at the exact same table, in their usual spots. Ren would face the room and the door. And the well-known Joe could be a little less recognizable, looking toward the back wall.

At one of their early meetings, Ren shared his determination for entrepreneurship and his plan for a new business. He told Joe what he was doing daily and what he planned as his next moves. Then he began to list the names of people he had consulted and the advice he had received when Joe lifted his palm up.

"What are you looking to accomplish?"

Ren stared at Joe.

"I mean," Joe continued, "what, in the simplest terms possible, do you want to do? And why?"

Ren felt he knew the answer well, but heard his voice hesitate when he responded.

"I want to . . . build a business with my software."

Joe nodded barely noticeably, visibly not sold on Ren's response.

"It helps to have a strong idea of what you want to accomplish. You need to think through some considerations. For one, do you want to build a growth business or a lifestyle business?

"There's not a right or wrong. But it's worth a lot to have a clear idea of your expectations," Joe continued. "With a young family, many people would be happy with setting up a lifestyle business to provide income for their family, without as much investment or the risk of trying to grow aggressively.

"But, for me, I usually feel like a growth business is less risky. It used to be that people would go into a new venture, maybe a restaurant or a plumbing or other services company, or even a specialty manufacturing business, and they could make a decent living for themselves and their families with a good lifestyle business."

Processing this while Joe paused to take another bite of his grilled chicken, Ren looked from the anemic pieces of chicken across the way to the Texas melt and loaded hash browns on his own plate and suspected that he'd gotten the better end of the culinary stick.

Joe took a sip of his coffee. "The world is changing so fast, Ren. You have two options. You either get better or you get worse."

As Joe continued, Ren thought he recalled once hearing the same thing from a football coach.

"So there can be real risk in not pursuing growth. Your employees and customers and, really, you will feed off the energy of a rapidly growing company more now than in the world we used to live in.

"It is hard to grow your business—and have employees—and live with the risk and drama of all that. But you are deciding between one set of problems and another. I also think it's risky not to have depth and to have little or no safety net or slack. Without the depth that comes from growth and employees, I even think there is a cost when you have to go a long time without taking a vacation yourself.

"If you, say, start with a sole-proprietorship-type business and grow hand-to-mouth from there with few or no employees for a long time, everything then comes down to you. There is no depth and no scalability: nothing to replicate and grow with. Your margin of error is even more razor-thin," he continued. "Either way, depending on what you want to do, you may basically want to go ahead and pick one course or the other."

Ren purposefully pushed his hash browns, crumbled extra-crispy bacon, scrambled eggs with cheese, and steak sauce against his Texas melt, the sandwich making a decent backstop to contain the mixing process, before methodically lifting each bite to his mouth.

"You need to look at what you want to do. If your business is going to need significant capital, scale or critical mass, or to evolve, as these technology companies often do now, you just about have to be a growth business," Joe said. "Growing gives you more margin for error. You have more capital, more breadth and depth, and more ability to evolve as you learn and position to do so."

Of course, before Joe had gone very far, Ren knew his answer—rapid growth. But he had let Joe keep going, with good reason, and he left that conversation more inspired than ever.

CHAPTER 3

The First Investor

"Don't mix business and family. Or, you may lose both."

—Unattributed wisdom

M ark Hatcher, Ren's dad, was a titan in his son's life. He wasn't perfect—what parent is?—but he modeled values like character and integrity, as well as frugality and a great work ethic. Mark had built a solid family enterprise providing local telephone service and cable television, and he had eventually gone into other small business endeavors in their rural community.

Growing up working summers, school breaks, and weekends in that family business, Ren had always assumed he would return to his hometown one day to run it. But he also carried a chip on his shoulder about making it on his own, first, as opposed to benefiting from nepotism. He felt an existential, immutable imperative to prove to himself, his dad, and the world that he could succeed on his own merit first. Though Mark never vocalized or even implied any expectations to that effect, Ren always felt that his independent success was important to his dad, as well.

In fact, his heart had swelled with pride when he once overheard his dad, not the sort to brag to his face, refer to him as a "self-made success," after his earlier opportunities and being a part of building and selling Standard Link. For Ren, there was nothing like making his pop proud, especially because he felt such deep reverence for the man. His appreciation for both his parents had come into sharp focus with the birth of his son, RJ, a couple of years earlier. Becoming a parent himself had made him recognize how he wanted to make his own parents proud. And he also knew that his father could bring decades of valuable business insights to the new venture.

He knew that he needed to talk to his dad about his company, but he kept putting it off. Would his dad want to be involved? Would he want to be an advisor? In a world where it seemed that all startups expected to raise money to get going, everyone kept telling him to go to friends and family for his initial funding. But he felt conflicted and reticent about the prospect.

Ren felt very strongly that, as a capable, grown man with a family of his own, he should be able to carry his own weight, relying only on himself. Maybe he had a sense of pride about that, but was that sort of pride even a bad thing? But he also thought that his dad might be able to give him some sage advice and would possibly offer investment without him having to ask. While he didn't *want* to want it, he probably would be glad to have it.

And he owed his dad the chance, right? A venture capitalist friend had explained to Ren that many startups would do an informal "friends and family" financing round to get enough capital to get their concept off the ground. Not only did he feel an uncanny sense that his success was inevitable, but he also felt, as other entrepreneurs often genuinely do, that he was being gracious and generous when he allowed others to be a part of that success. So, if he let his dad invest or join as an advisor, he would be doing him a favor, right? If he didn't at least offer this great investment opportunity to the person who had done the most for him while he was growing up, that would hardly be fair. Of course, this was still a month or so *before* that eye-opening first meeting with David.

Maybe Ren was just talking himself into something he found horrifying: wanting something from his dad. At the very least, it felt uncomfortable and challenging to even think about approaching his dad about his business, much less with anything that might seem like a request for help.

Finally feeling ready enough, he went back to his hometown, with conflicted feelings, to have a face-to-face talk with his dad. Of course, he had already told his parents that he was planning to start a new business, and his father had already given some of his own thought to Ren's intentions. So when he had asked for a chance to meet up, he expected that his dad would guess that it would be about the new business.

One sunny Wednesday afternoon, Ren drove to the rural community where he had grown up. He pulled up to the comfortable two-story ranch home. It was built into a hillside in a heavily wooded area, where his parents had lived since before he was born. His mom, Carol, was still a youthful and vibrant blondish-brunette, who had shown Ren the power of empathy, warmth, and genuine consideration of others' perspectives and feelings. She opened the door and gave him a warm hug. She was always thrilled to see her baby boy.

After catching up and asking about Tiffany and RJ, Carol ushered Ren back to his father's home office. His dad also greeted him warmly while his mom slipped out to prepare the evening meal.

The room was dark and serious, setting an almost somber mood. A big window looked out on a beautiful view from the hillside, but much of the light was lost in the subdued curtains, cabinets, and furnishings. The built-in bookshelves were full of heavy tomes about business and world affairs, and the room had a measure of gravitas, a product of years of weighty discussions. This was where Mark had delivered a number of stern talks and meted out well-deserved punishments for Ren's assorted misbehaviors throughout his youth.

After reading so many books about subconscious factors in sales and decision-making, it now occurred to Ren that this room was an unfavorable venue for this conversation with his dad. Although he didn't necessarily feel like he was trying to make a sale here, he at least wanted to sense how his father felt about his new endeavor. He had learned that, depending on circumstances, particular times of day were better for getting a "yes" or making a sale, when the existing answer that he had to overcome was a "no." Right after breakfast or right after lunch—when people tended to be nourished—were prime times. This meeting was happening during the late afternoon, not long before the dinner hour. It was not a particularly favorable time of day to persuade anyone away from an existing expectation and into supporting new ideas.

Ren had been studying such matters, not to optimize his own circumstances in negotiations, but rather to recognize when others sought to manipulate him. He liked to believe that convincing someone to invest or buy or engage through what he saw as parlor tricks would not last and would ultimately not work out well for anyone. When dealing with his father, it seemed even more important that his case stand on its own merit, rather than on sales tricks or smoke and mirrors.

After exchanging a few niceties and catching up about family, Ren shared more with his dad about his business ideas. "I want to marry an intuitive user interface with predictive technology and the tools that industrial engineers regularly use," he said. "I know this innovative idea could revolutionize the world."

Ren paused, inspecting his father's face and noting signs of interest and support. He wasn't sure if he wanted to ask for involvement or investment—or how much—but presumed some level of support and affirmation. "Dad," he began, "would you like to be a part of this? Perhaps as an advisor or board member or even an investor?"

Mark looked at Ren with sincere affection. After only the briefest hesitation, he said, "Son, we've had such a great relationship. Let's keep it that way."

After another pause of several seconds that allowed Ren to process that statement, his father continued, "I don't see myself being an advisor to or actively involved in your company. I know from growing up in my own family business that working with family members can be hard, particularly when your livelihood and self-worth are tied up in your business. Feedback always seems more critical when it comes from your dad. With that being said, if this is the path you are going to follow, I do want to show my belief in you—and to be supportive in the healthiest way possible."

Ren let out the breath he'd been holding. "Thanks, Dad," he said. "I appreciate you putting our relationship first. You know how much I appreciate you and Mom. I wouldn't want anything to come between us."

"I would be open to investing a bit of seed capital to help you get started," Mark continued. "I really like what you're talking about doing, and I'm excited for all of the lessons you will surely learn along the way."

"But," he continued with a slightly grave expression, "I don't want you to learn to get things from your dad. You need to discover more about building a good business—and that means getting money from your customers and not just investors. If I put in a little cash to help you get started, I want you to think of that as a one-time thing and not expect to come back later."

It seemed to hurt Mark a little to say that last part, but Ren honestly felt relieved. He could immediately see the wisdom in his father's statement. The line about "having a great relationship and keeping it that way" stayed with Ren as one of the wisest and best bits of relationship perspective he had ever heard.

He realized that what he had sought in meeting with his father was exactly what Mark had just offered: his support and encouragement. That felt tremendously empowering. He made a firm mental note to provide the same message and tone to his own children when it was their turn, no matter what path they decided to pursue.

Ren's father ended up making a generous investment to help get the company up and going. And although he had firmly declined the role of an advisor, he ended up being one, unofficial but invaluable, who never imposed his views on Ren but was willing to share them when his son requested his opinion.

CHAPTER 4

Searching for Focus

"Focus is a matter of deciding what things you're not going to do."

—John Carmack

O ver the course of the next few weeks, Ren made steady progress toward creating a business plan for his idea, but he was still thinking about it in very general terms. He knew he wanted to create a new, more usable software solution for combining intuitive predictive technology with the existing programs that industrial engineers used regularly. And he felt it could be done in a way that could apply to any industry: manufacturing, transportation, telecommunications, and just about anything else. Why not cast a wide net? He figured, "If big is good, then bigger must be better."

A breakfast with an old fraternity brother proved pivotal in changing his thinking. Since their first meeting in college years ago, Tom Strong had been somewhat of a role model figure in Ren's life. Tom was only a couple of years older, but Ren had always looked up to him. Tom was a tall, heavyset guy with sandy blond hair and piercing eyes. He wasn't your first guess for the most popular guy, and there was nothing flashy about him. But if Ren had polled their college friends about who was the most respected person, Tom would likely have been at the top of the list. He was a smart, stand-up guy. It also happened that Ren followed Tom in a few courses—and occasionally ended up leaning on him for help.

Throughout their college years, Tom had given Ren a hard time for not applying himself. Once, over too many beers, Ren got an angry lecture about "the evil of wasted potential." Tom was really mad at him for not making more of himself and his abilities. Pretty soon, he had Ren studying more and becoming a better student, as well as reading and working more on self-improvement. He had even convinced Ren to get up early in the morning to do push-ups, something Ren hadn't done regularly since his wrestling days—although that hadn't lasted long after Tom wasn't around anymore.

Following graduation, Tom had taken a job in a local hospital as a management engineer, which, for some reason, is what they called industrial engineers in hospitals. Ever a diligent worker, he had risen through the ranks quickly and became the hospital's chief operating officer at a relatively young age. Tom had already built a solid career and been made comfortable by the fruits of his labor.

Though Ren and Tom didn't catch up as often as either would've liked, they stayed in touch. Even though his career had been nothing like being an entrepreneur, Tom was still near the top of Ren's list of people to connect with, to hear his thoughts on the new venture.

With memories of shared Waffle House breakfasts in the wee hours of the morning during college, the greasy and carb-filled dishes soaking up a night's worth of partying, Ren suggested a meeting with his old friend at a Waffle House near Tom's home. Tom was now a family man, with a wife and two young kids, so he could only meet early. What a change it was from their college years! The pair set a meeting at 5:30 a.m. so Tom could then help get his kids off to school before heading to work that windy winter day.

They greeted each other with a warm hug—they were both huggers—and settled into a booth in the back corner, where they first caught up on family and funny stories. Anyone eavesdropping on the stories might have blushed or looked at them with shame. Tom ordered bacon, eggs, and a much-needed cup of black coffee, and Ren got his usual: two eggs scrambled with cheese, a large order of extra-crispy bacon, and hash browns scattered with everything except gravy and tomatoes. He would devour it all with Heinz 57 steak sauce on top. And he would down it with his usual iced sweet tea. As long as the service could keep up, he would often go through eight to ten glasses through each breakfast and lunch, no matter how low the temperature outside dropped.

As they ate, Ren shared his idea and what he wanted to do, explaining the void he saw in the market. He told Tom about his epiphany with the intuitive tax software and how he felt certain his idea was primed to take any industry by storm when he got it out there.

"You know the power of measuring processes and performance and using data to make better and more proactive decisions," said Ren. "You also remember the cumbersome software we used in college and are familiar with what many businesses use now. And when I work with managers, they want the acronyms, like TQM, ISO certification, and so forth. And they want to do things more efficiently and more functionally and consistently.

"But they could do it so much better if they could understand the principles behind those concepts. And when we work with people on the floor, it's hard for them to buy in at all because they don't understand where they're going and have to work hard just to get there properly. It's the people on the floor that run the machines or manage the production lines. They wear hard hats, safety glasses, and steel-toed boots and are so much more important than some managers realize.

"I think the managers sometimes see them as necessary commodities," Ren continued. "Pushing a button or placing and removing items from a belt. But the good ones could make a difference, if empowered and enabled to do so. I want people to more easily use these powerful tools, to better interact and understand what they are doing."

Tom was considerate and thoughtful, interrupting with a lot of questions and comments. "So, why does this work better than the software packages we used in college or what I have on my desk now?" Or "But if others haven't done that, how are you going to do it? Any idea how hard it is to get good data? Do you realize the consequences in healthcare? When hospitals make mistakes, people can die."

Ren was more than a little caught off guard when Tom said, "You should look at doing this for hospitals." And he really grabbed Ren's attention as he continued, "I think it could be hard as a startup to serve too many masters, so to speak, in the broadest markets. I've heard it said that, at some point, a small company can't be a shotgun. You need to be a laser. You should pick a specific vertical and target a specific sort of customer. And I think there is a real opportunity in hospitals."

"Really?" Ren asked, intrigued. "I think of healthcare providers as not being very progressive in their use of information technology. Even hospitals leading in new techniques to embrace information management for clinical practices aren't very good at using it for operational improvement. And treating people seems almost impossible to standardize. Why do you think that would be a smart move?"

"You're right about a lot of that," Tom replied. "But there's a big need and opportunity. For one thing, hospitals are now being mandated to use statistical process control to measure certain processes for their accreditation." He paused to take a fortifying sip of black coffee. "As you might expect, they struggle with it. At the highest level, most of them know it could be useful but have no idea how to get there. To your points, they're often terrible at doing this sort of thing. In fact, I know some progressive, big-time organizations that are investing in doing this right and struggling to do so. I think they might buy your concept."

Ren had been speaking with some friends at a couple of large, high-tech manufacturing companies about building the solution for them. Both friends seemed very interested and could probably get deals done with him and their companies. But, as Tom spoke, this idea increasingly grabbed his attention.

He left the early morning meeting just as the sun was peeking above the trees, turning the skyline hopeful shades of pink and orange. It felt like a good omen: Tom's insight could be a turning point in focusing Ren's broad idea onto a specific industry. Ren was determined to investigate how his concept could make a difference for the healthcare world. And it would be a huge relief to finally have a definitive market and direction.

———

Through some cursory research, Ren discovered that healthcare was one of the nation's largest industries, with trillions of dollars spent every year on healthcare costs. There were over 6,000 hospitals in the United States, with millions of provider organizations, including doctor's offices and specialists like physical therapists.

After a breakfast meeting, a healthcare industry consultant friend had sent Ren a book called *Healthcare Is Killing Us: The Power of Disruptive Innovation to Create a System That Cares More and Costs Less* by Terry Howell and Aaron Fausz. He was so startled to learn more about the issues in the industry that it took doing some of his own research to believe what the book taught him. Once Ren verified the information for himself, he had to read the book again, taking copious notes and using a marker to highlight a number of passages—blue for noteworthy, yellow for points to research or challenge for himself.

The industry was a behemoth but extraordinarily inefficient. Studies showed that hospitals waste hundreds of millions of dollars each year through ineffi-cient processes and operations—unnecessarily killing tens of thousands of people annually through inadequate care, misdiagnosis, accidental introduction of infec-tions or exposures, misguided care management, and other factors.

The healthcare industry was largely full of well-meaning, smart people who had dedicated their careers to helping others and saving lives. But Ren learned that it was also impractical, impeded by bureaucracy and challenges associated with so many disparate patient circumstances and needs. Every expert he spoke with, each from different facets of the industry, highlighted that sometimes misguided and often-changing reimbursement policies were the force driving treatment and delivery.

While Ren didn't yet realize just how messed up the industry was, he knew that it had a bigger need and opportunity than anywhere else he could go. The technology he wanted to create could help streamline many of the tools that already existed in healthcare administration, management, and operations.

Aside from the obvious business opportunity in healthcare, he realized that the nameless, faceless industry was made up of millions of very real individuals who could be helped or hurt by their experiences with doctors and hospitals. He loved the idea of being able to help people more directly, supporting life-saving decisions and ultimately helping organizations get to clinical best practices. The more he learned, the more interested he became.

Though he wasn't, as yet, ready to step away from the conversations he was having with his friends in other industry sectors, Ren knew he was inexorably moving toward decision time.

It wasn't long before he figured out that pursuing a healthcare technology solution would be an exclusive proposition because that industry was so special-ized—it was unlike any other sector. Not only would the solution need to be different, but the healthcare industry was so disparate that it would be challeng-ing to sell solutions to them while also selling to other industries at the same time, at least as a startup.

Ren also discovered that the healthcare IT business was littered with out-side companies that had struggled to get in, many of which had failed pretty spectacularly in trying to reform the way things were done in the sector. Some of the more successful forays from outside businesses had been from companies that bought health IT firms and largely allowed them to continue to operate differently.

Over the coming weeks, as he continued to explore his opportunity—either in healthcare or outside for the manufacturing companies—Ren continued to read and learn from anyone who could offer insights to nudge him toward his decision.

CHAPTER 5

A Sound Learning Investment

"The only thing worse than being blind is having sight and no vision."

—Helen Keller

S ome of the people that Ren met during this period became friends, mentors, and advisors. He felt that many of the essential character traits—not just success factors in his entrepreneurial journey but of who he became as a person—were what he learned or modeled from them. He would regularly invite those wise individuals for a meeting, treating them for breakfast or lunch or coffee at their convenience, over which they could share insights. Some were one-offs or, more often, occasional ongoing conversations, while others would become lifelong counselors who would leave an indelible mark on how Ren approached business and life.

Ever since reading *How to Win Friends and Influence People* by Dale Carnegie when he was in middle school, Ren had sought to emulate and learn from characteristics he admired in others. He also enjoyed cultivating relationships with people he respected and felt that even just regularly being around such people was worth something. There was a long list of them, with a few who stood out in particular.

He recalled how he had fumbled through many of his early meetings with these important figures in his life. It had seemed harder, at first, to get successful people to take time from their schedule to visit with him. Many of the people Ren wanted to meet were incredibly busy and prioritized their time. Some had a "gatekeeper" assistant to screen calls and protect them. Getting them for lunch or office hours was hard, at least until they knew and trusted him. So he had learned to start with a warm introduction from a college professor, friend, coworker, or other connection they might know and respect. And he found decent success when he offered to treat them for breakfast or coffee at any location and time of their convenience. People had to eat. And they were more likely to be available at breakfast. With the right introduction and endorsement from a mutual connection, most everyone would eventually accommodate an introductory breakfast.

And Ren could see that they appreciated it when they recognized that he was not looking for money or favors from them but genuinely wanted their wisdom and to learn from their successes and characteristics. He also found that once he had earned credibility and a more trusted relationship with an accomplished leader, they would connect him with others in a way that opened doors much better than he ever could with a cold call.

———

As he began his entrepreneurial journey, Ren began to recall many of the best lessons from mentors who had educated him and role models whom he had learned from through observation.

From a former neighbor, Daniel Barrow, he had learned the power of focusing on the positive and not disparaging others, except to be honest for a necessary purpose. He also learned to treat everyone, in all walks of life, with the same respect and consideration. And he loved how the plainspoken Barrow always meant what he said and said what he meant.

From Joe Chapman, he had learned a great deal about paying attention, both to other people and to details in the business. Thanks to Joe, he learned to listen better. And he learned to delegate better, a hard thing for Ren to do at first.

Belinda Harden didn't lecture or try to instruct him like Barrow or Joe. But she inspired and educated him as effectively as anyone by her actions and how she treated him and others. An inspiring high-profile CEO, she was a great role model for empathy, consideration, and respect for others. She made Ren better by believing in him and encouraging him.

There were others that he met through his journey, such as Doug Banister and Sid Richardson, that he modeled himself on and learned from about business and industry acumen, community involvement, innovating in smarter ways, and so much more.

He got a lot from just watching all of them work, effectively, with dedication and diligence. Ren was able to observe their character in action, in so many examples: like when Joe took the high road with a troubled employee, or when Barrow helped local families in need without anyone else knowing. All were big on anonymous philanthropy and volunteer work that really made a difference. It was remarkable how often Ren was reminded of the quote from John Wooden that said, "The true test of a man's character is what he does when no one is watching."

And he learned from observing the imperative, foundational importance of integrity and honesty that was essential to all of his mentors. Joe had told him that he could build a career around being trusted.

———

As he started this new venture, another great learning opportunity for Ren came from Charlie Frank, a well-known local venture capitalist, a big-time guy in the community. Whenever Ren told someone he was "doing a tech startup," it seemed like they wanted to talk about venture capital. So finding a mentor wearing that hat seemed worthwhile. And even if he never raised any outside money, he thought he might learn perspectives in how they look at companies that might make him a better business.

Ren sort of knew Charlie through some volunteer activities at their mutual alma mater. He reached out to him through shared friends. Charlie was gracious and seemed more than willing to make time to meet. Ren would have preferred to meet over breakfast or lunch, but when trying to schedule with Charlie, he found that the venture capitalist wanted an afternoon meeting in his office. Given that Charlie was doing him a big favor, Ren was only happy to oblige.

So it was that he pulled up to Charlie's address on a cool, sunny Tuesday afternoon, about twenty minutes early for their two o'clock meeting. He caught up on a few things in his car before walking into the modest but nicely appointed lobby at 1:57 p.m.

Charlie personally walked out into the reception area, greeted him warmly, and offered coffee or water. A sharp, fit-looking fifty-something of average height, with gray hair at the temples, he led Ren into his corner office and, as he sat down, welcomed him to sit in a comfortable chair in front of his desk. Ren had noticed before that Charlie spoke with a lot of authority. But what also stood out now was that he addressed him with humble and friendly gestures and tone, rather than the sort of inflated manner of speaking that might be expected of such a figure.

After a friendly exchange and inquiries about family health and such, as was customary for professionals in Atlanta, Charlie encouraged him to share more about the business that he was building.

Ren quickly related that he was nowhere near ready to connect about raising money yet. He just wanted to learn a bit. And Charlie seemed to appreciate that.

"So tell me about your business," said Charlie in a flat tone but with a seriously interested expression. "What is the size of the opportunity? What do companies spend each year on those solutions? What are their IT budgets? And who is the decision maker you will be selling to?"

Charlie also offered some guidance in case Ren ever wanted to raise venture capital. He shared that his fund tended to make Series B equity investments, where they already had previously raised some capital.

"We typically invest in businesses that have already proven their concept with existing customers and revenues. Sometimes they already have those pie-in-the-sky things called earnings."

Charlie explained that many startups might do small family or angel investment rounds to get going. These investments could often range anywhere from several hundred thousand dollars or even to a million dollars—or sometimes much more. And they might, in some cases, be in the form of a convertible loan that would convert at a discounted valuation to the later investment that Charlie would then participate in.

"Everything in any kind of investment tends to come back to risk-adjusted return on invested capital," offered Charlie. "The bigger the risk, the bigger the potential return we need to expect to justify it."

For Charlie and his fund, he would typically invest several million dollars in a company. What he liked to see was strong leadership, coupled with a large opportunity and a detailed plan that made a strong case for why the business would succeed.

Charlie confessed to following entrepreneurs and their businesses from early stages until they were ready for him. "For one matter," he noted, "I like to see if you did what you told me you were going to do.

"Almost every business plan I see has a 'hockey stick' of projected rapid growth. I don't necessarily believe the numbers you show me," he added. "But I like to see a detailed plan and what's behind it and your financials. It helps me to know how the entrepreneur thinks, how much they have thought it through, and how well they can justify themselves."

This feedback was interesting because Ren also connected with another venture capitalist friend—investing in the same deals, at the same stage—who gave very different guidance. Where Charlie felt that it was worthwhile for his companies to invest a great deal of time and thought into their business plan, the other friend suggested that he wanted businesses to just do a good pitch deck—"at least a few PowerPoint slides to show the business, its leadership, financial and market highlights, and so on, with solid, high-level numbers"—and to spend more time in actually building their business than on their business plan.

Ren appreciated where both of those venture capitalists were coming from in their disparate perspectives. In fact, he continued to get conflicting feedback from others on business plans and pitch decks. And, as he later engaged with other VCs, his takeaway on the matter was that he would never please everyone. He just needed to come up with the plan or deck that best suited his purpose, one that was as simple and clear as could possibly serve the complexity of what he was doing at the time.

There were a few consistencies, though, that Ren took from all of the venture capitalists and advisors regarding his deck. It should, as Charlie put it, "help me to clearly, quickly understand who you are and what you are doing, as well as what you plan to do with my investment and why I should bet on you. If I have to look hard to try to figure that out, I might never give it a fair chance."

Ren also learned more about the good, and the bad, of how venture capitalists invest in, and help, their companies. In many cases, the venture capitalists gave their companies a better chance to succeed when they acted as board members or advisors or in connecting other resources. In some cases, the entrepreneurs felt that the venture capitalists were shortsighted in their guidance to the businesses, but, even in those circumstances, he felt that the VCs might have been a net positive contributor to success.

Ren's take-home from the meeting with Charlie and others in those early days was that a good VC could be very helpful, beyond their investment, in building a business. He also learned that, if he wanted to raise venture capital, it would help to be able to show a large and compelling opportunity, a strong leadership team, and a clearly articulated plan. He felt like the right introduction and relationships could help to get their attention. And while many businesses seemed to think of raising venture capital as their goal, his dad liked to remind him that it was more of a means to an end, and that in many cases, he might be more likely to become a better business without it.

Of course, there were a great number of others that Ren learned from. And it came together forcefully when he arrived at his fateful meeting with David Olden.

CHAPTER 6

Best Made Plan

"Plan for what is difficult while it is easy.
Do what is great while it is small."

—Sun Tzu

After David Olden delivered his "you're not going to make it" speech over wings, fries, and burgers at Taco Mac, Ren became more and more intrigued by the older gentleman and his story. He was able to piece together more information about David—from the man himself as well as from mutual friends. Ren found that he always understated himself, but those mutual friends would help to fill in the blanks.

In a career that spanned more than two decades, David had first spent a few years as a psychologist in the Army. From there he had built two very successful public companies in the health information technology space. David had truly driven the foundational vision for that entire industry. And he had advised, and in some cases invested in, dozens of other companies in many different fields. What Ren was most impressed by, though, was how he felt like he learned something just about every time he watched David interact with someone. He began to recognize that David's years as a psychologist must have also taught the man a lot about dealing with people.

David was what many might term distinguished, standing at 5' 11" with salt-and-pepper hair that had receded considerably. He was reasonably fit and healthy for his age, with the sort of slightly protruding, soft midsection that revealed his wife was an avid, skillful baker.

David reminded Ren of his dad at times, in that it took a while to catch up to his wisdom. When they worked on anything together, it was hard at first for Ren to go on for as long as David did. *How can a guy that old keep at it like that?* And while the frankness caught him by surprise, he really appreciated David's honesty. Ren increasingly recognized the power of being able to trust him, noting that he modeled integrity in all facets of his life. That must have been a big part of making him a leader that people wanted to follow. As Ren's dad had put it, "The best way to get people to trust you is to just always *be* trustworthy!"

David was the kind of friend who would tell you the way things were, rather than how you wanted to see them. If he respected you and thought you were listening, he was willing to invest time and effort in helping you succeed.

As they were wrapping up their initial fateful lunch where David told Ren he was not going to make it, then for whatever reason offered to help out—the offer that Ren accepted—David stated his conditions.

"You are going to start doing homework," David said. "One of the most important things you'll do for your company is a business plan. But that doesn't come out of nowhere. Before you put pen to paper and start writing, you have to have some things clear as day in your head. You need to have a purpose—a reason for what you do—and you must know what your company stands for. Knowing who you are, what your company represents, and where you are going with it doesn't just empower you and your employees, but it also gives a sense of purpose to your customers and potential investors. And purpose is powerful, because it helps everyone know who and what they are dealing with. It will also help you find the right employees, which is key. The ones who are a great fit for the company will immediately be attracted to your purpose—to what you stand for."

David paused and looked at Ren to see if he understood. Ren nodded in assent.

"If this all makes sense to you, then you can begin with your first assignment. Your job is to draft three identity statements for your company. Number one: What is your company's mission? Number two: What is your vision for the company? And number three: What values will your company represent? You can think of the last one as defining company culture. What is the essence of your company; the thing that permeates everything in how the company operates?"

"Thank you, David!" Ren already felt buoyed by the idea of having these clear statements to guide him as he was processing the work to do.

David smiled. "Don't thank me yet. Let's see what you can do. Start with your mission statement," he said as he slid out of the booth. "What is the purpose behind your company?"

Over the next week, Ren wrote down identity statements that eventually became this mission statement:

COMPANY MISSION

Our mission is to enable healthcare organizations to maximize clinical, financial, and operational performance by providing user-friendly, scientifically sound management solutions.

We will always exceed our customers' expectations.

Our ultimate goal is to give our clients tools that allow them to improve their value to their customers by maintaining and improving clinical outcomes and operational results, and controlling costs.

At their next meeting, Ren and David discussed the mission and continued the exercise.

"Next," David said, "I want you to list the fundamental, non-negotiable values of your company. Serving that mission, create a vision and a list of values that you want. These lists are a big deal. By writing them down now, you're fighting a lot of your battles up front. If you and your stakeholders know what you want and expect, you'll all be able to see whether you're living up to those values and working toward that vision. If your company at any point veers off course, your values will serve as a compass to get you back on the right track."

After this conversation, Ren toiled away, caught up in the process. And after a good deal of notes and refinement—and some painfully direct advice from David on how to revise and clarify—he shared his full vision statement:

COMPANY VISION

Employees: We will create a positive and rewarding work environment and culture that is characterized by teamwork, passion, respect, and tolerance. The employees are the most important assets of the company, and supporting them in terms of resources and personal growth is the primary focus of management. We are creating an atmosphere where passion, excellence, and effort are rewarded.

Customer: Success is a happy customer who gets a compelling return on the money they pay us. Our products will help healthcare organizations make better decisions, thereby achieving results. We will provide a total solution to our clients, providing the assistance and training necessary to implement these concepts.

Speed: We are a fast company. Decisions are made quickly and at the lowest appropriate level. We trust our team to do their best.

Over another few weeks, Ren hacked away at his keyboard and, with guidance from David and others, worked through drafts and critiques to create the company values. This process turned out to be the hardest one of all. He came up with big, ethical statements, but then always started asking himself, "Well, what does this mean *in practice*, in a business?" He felt inspired when writing his sentiments, but every time he read them out loud, they ended up sounding like a bunch of lofty talk and nothing else. Finally, Ren told himself to just unpack the values, one by one. He sat at the kitchen table, a little cold because he refused to raise the thermostat, and just wrote some words out by hand on a piece of paper. Then he went down to his office and pecked away at his laptop, taking the words from the handwritten paper and evolving them. He looked up and realized that hours had passed. He was never going to be happy with anything, but this was a pretty good start.

COMPANY VALUES

Customer first: Success is achieved with a happy customer. We focus on providing value, exceeding expectations, and creating win-win situations.

Integrity: Honesty and integrity are the cornerstones of everything we do.

Leadership: Management leads by example and focuses on getting employees the resources they need to do their job.

Diversity: We value diversity and believe it makes us stronger. Our customers are diverse. And we need to be diverse to better serve them.

Financial: We understand that in order to accomplish the objectives of the business, we must always remain cognizant of financial performance and that, in the long term, this is a complement to providing value and satisfying the customer and enables us to make the world a better place.

100 percent effort: We strive to do our best for the customer, the company, and our fellow employees. Pushing ourselves to do better leads to personal growth.

Speed: Speed is a competitive advantage. Decisions are made quickly. Non-value-added controls are minimized. We make realistic promises and keep them.

Mistakes: We accept mistakes made when people are making their best efforts, meeting aggressive timelines, and exploring new territory as a sign of progress. We do not accept those caused by sloppiness or lack of effort.

Have fun: We maintain a sense of humor and have fun while working to achieve our goals and objectives.

Frugality: We strive to be prudent and wise in the use of company resources.

Teamwork: We extend a helping hand to those who need it to achieve a win for the team. We always treat others with dignity and respect.

Results: We are a company of people who deliver tangible results, both internally and for our customers.

When David read the first version, he pulled a pen from his pocket and started swiping through some of Ren's points, writing commentary here and there, like: "You have to put integrity first. Without that, you don't really have anything," or "Your company's values will reflect that of its leadership. You need to move this one up." Although he didn't really change the values so much as he emphasized the order and statement, it felt pretty harsh to Ren, who only then realized how important and personal these statements were. This might have rubbed him the wrong way, if he were not getting used to David's tough love. The older man sometimes hurt his feelings, but his insights were always delivered with empathy and affection. He found it hugely rewarding to have someone who cared enough to tell him the truth, even if it stung. Most of the time, David provided insights that Ren wasn't getting anywhere else. *You can't put a price tag on that kind of wisdom or on a true friend who cared enough to be honest.*

Ren used to wonder why a man as successful as David was willing to invest so much of his precious time in somebody like himself—a stranger wanting David's advice and mentoring. What could David possibly get out of the relationship? A lot, Ren later learned. He realized that helping young entrepreneurs was rewarding and even energizing to David. "It keeps me young!" David said.

The relationship between the two started out as an occasional coffee here and a lunch there, but it gradually developed into something much more: a personal, close connection between two likeminded individuals. The openness and trust developed relatively quickly, and those qualities only strengthened over time. What began as conversations strictly on business and entrepreneurship gradually came to include other aspects of life, too. Although Ren had suspected as much earlier, it was really only through David that he learned that entrepreneurship wasn't just a job, but a way of living. And that with the goals and mindset Ren had, he would never be just a business owner. In a way, or, in truth, he *was* his business.

When he looked at David, he saw a mentor and friend. Ren sometimes wondered what David saw in him.

CHAPTER 7

Cauliflower and Truth

"Better a comfortable truth than a cruel delusion."

—Edward Abbey

A little gray blur flashed in the corner of Ren's eyes, darting into the road from the edge of a yard across the street, streaking in front of an oncoming car and then in front of his own older-model Dodge Durango. Tires screeching, he swerved as he slammed on the brakes.

Somehow Ren's evenings had fallen into a pattern. No matter who he was meeting or whatever he was working on, he did his best to be home for dinner at six o'clock. Afterwards, he would put RJ to bed and read to him before getting back to work until late into each night. Family time had become important. It was hard to explain how rewarding it was just being around his young son. And it was his "sane time" in each frantic, inconsistent day of meeting people and building toward a new business.

The drive home this particular Wednesday night was brutal. He had a lot on his mind. It felt important to be there for dinner by six. Rush-hour traffic in North Atlanta had worn him out. And the light rain on the gray evening didn't help.

Ren thought about how he was wearing himself out with the drive. He realized that he was somehow trying to *will* himself through traffic. It was almost like if he wanted through enough, his mind or willpower or some magical force would somehow move the car in front of him. The sea of cars would part and let him through. Only that never seemed to work. At all. So by the time he was almost home, he was exhausted from working way too hard and not seeing any benefit.

Now driving too fast as he approached his driveway, before slamming on the brakes to avoid the blur that passed in front of his car, he could feel the bouncing of the antilock system as he came to a stop. The cars behind, and coming from the other direction in front of him, were also screeching to a halt. But there was no noise or bump from a fender bender. *What was that little gray blur that passed in front of my car?*

At home now, he pulled into his driveway and walked back toward where the streaking apparition had arrived near the street. Cautiously he walked over and gently picked up the small, soaking bundle that had been the blur.

A few minutes later, Ren came into the side door, from the open garage into his house.

"What have you done?" Tiffany's face betrayed strong feelings. Her shoulders shrugged as her posture opened. She moved quickly toward Ren, as he came through the door.

"You never cease to surprise me," she said, voice rising as she reached for the little fuzzy gray and brown ball that he held. "Where did you find this little guy?"

With a concerned half smile and bright eyes, Tiffany cradled the bundle. Scraggly. Soaked. Scared. Shaking. She walked briskly down the short hallway and into the bathroom, Ren following.

Waiting for the water to warm up a little, she began to clean the small ball of fur in the sink as it became a frightened puppy. Cleaned up, it was a light off-white color, with some light brown and gray splotches. Some sort of young poodle-terrier mix. It was thin and seemed to have a few ticks. A quick check verified that it was female.

As much as Ren had ever seen her do so, Tiffany took charge.

"Go to Kroger and get some flea and tick shampoo and some puppy food. The good kind from a can. Get some treats, and a small collar. She's obviously a stray. I'll take her to a vet tomorrow and start looking for a home for her." Ren took his marching orders, turning abruptly and heading out on his mission.

When he got back home, RJ had awakened. Past his bedtime, he seemed enraptured by the puppy. She had already devoured a small amount of cold cuts and cheese. Now clean and having eaten a bit, she looked less like a big, fuzzy rat. And she seemed thrilled with the treats that Ren produced.

Ren took a reluctant RJ back to bed and eventually got him to sleep, reading an extra chapter of *Watership Down* along the way. When he rejoined Tiffany and the puppy, he was expecting a conversation about perhaps putting up flyers in the neighborhood. About looking for a home for the rescue puppy, and taking care of it until they found one.

But Tiffany had already decided they had a new family member and seemed resolved to the name "Cauliflower." Ren didn't love the name. But her basic color was the same sort of off-white, and from a distance the light blotches might have looked a little like the sort of shading you might see from the texture of cauliflower. And pretty soon they were all calling her "Caulie."

"I was really surprised when you walked in with her," Tiffany said. And Ren was surprised by what she said next: "That is the first *human* thing I have seen you do in months."

Mistaking where she was going with that, Ren said, "Look, I had to do something. She was going to get run over or who knows? She was out on the street at the edge of the yard as I got home. She looked so scared. I couldn't possibly leave her out there."

Tiffany just looked at him for a bit.

"That's not what I mean," she said. "I mean . . . Look, we don't even really talk much anymore! Not about anything meaningful. We talk a lot about RJ and paying bills." Her expression turned and her voice rose as she said, "But you never open up and you never let me in."

Caught off guard and not processing this very well, Ren's questioning look and pause encouraged her to continue.

"I think the same warm guy is in there somewhere. But you never share or even seem to care as much about anything human anymore. Really since y'all decided to sell Standard Link. And especially since you left there. I watch you be nice and considerate to others. But when you walk into the house and talk to me, it feels like I'm just something in your way."

Ren realized it must have taken a lot for Tiffany to say this. This was completely unlike her. But reflecting on his behavior recently, he could see where she was coming from. *Was I protecting her from my problems?*

And he could see her frustration and concern as she let go, "You never talk to me very much about what you are doing and these big decisions you are making."

By now, her voice was trembling, and she had tears in the corners of her eyes. This was well outside of her comfort zone.

"I don't know if it is some kind of macho testosterone thing. Or pride. Or even shame about not having the opportunities you want. But you don't talk to me in any meaningful way. You know these decisions you make are affecting me and RJ. I could have had a great career! Just being honest, my job prospects might have been better than yours coming out of college. But we agreed that I would stay at home with RJ. And that puts all of us at the mercy of your decisions. But I don't seem to have any say. Or even to be included!"

"What do you want me to say?" Caught off guard and still processing, Ren responded, sounding a bit defensive. "I'm really focused now. I have a lot on my mind." His tone was rising. "And I don't have anything to be ashamed about. We just sold our company."

Seeing that she had touched a nerve, Tiffany softened her voice. "Look, Ren," she said, as she took him by the hand and led him back up to their room. "I'm not looking for a fight. Take tonight off from work and come to bed,"

Later, as they were lying in bed, trying to sleep, Tiffany spoke again. "I'm sorry. I really wasn't looking to upset you. I'm just frustrated."

Feeling disarmed, Ren responded, "You know I've never been very good at being sappy. I don't know if it's testosterone or pride or whatever. I just . . . I just am not in touch with my feelings at times. Maybe the only feelings I've ever really been completely in touch with are about RJ. But honestly, a lot of it is this business. I just get really focused and locked in sometimes. And I guess I don't see any reason to burden you with my problems."

"Well, sometimes it feels like you're being a jerk to me!" This time Tiffany somehow managed to seem warmer, less accusatory. Ren couldn't see her face in the dark. But it was easy to tell that she was trying to break through.

"Try it!" she said. "Try sharing with me a little. What has you so worked up these days anyway?"

"Well . . ." Ren paused as he sifted through what was bothering him most. "Money is going to be really tight, at least until the Standard Link exit pays off when they go public—hopefully soon. And I need to get things moving fast to get some cash coming in."

It felt strange to speak about this. He was not sure that he liked being so vulnerable. Mollified by Tiffany's warmth and a little reconciliation with his feelings, he shared, "But it's more than that . . . what really got me is this guy I met recently. David. I know I am going to hit it big and raise a lot of money and sell this company fast for twenty or fifty million dollars or more. And I know we did great at Standard Link. But this old guy I just met kind of got my attention."

Tiffany's patient silence in the dark encouraged him to continue.

"David told me, straight out, that I wasn't going to make it. To be honest, I think he must have hurt my feelings. He actually called me *cocky*. He basically called me a fraud." Ren was speaking faster now. "And he thought I don't deserve to be too proud about our success at Standard Link and the exit. He really questioned my leadership. And what I know about building a business. And he said I am not the right kind of purposeful leader and don't know how to give my business the best chance to succeed.

"It makes me wonder, Tiffany. Is that how people see me? How do *you* think others see me?"

Tiffany's voice was soft now in the darkness. "You're the one who said if someone says something that hurts your feelings, you should treat it like it's true. And maybe people *do* see you as a little cocky when you start to talk about this business.

"You know," she went on, "I get to see you be considerate to others all the time. But you could see my frustration earlier. You really haven't been empathetic toward me, at all. I spend all my days with RJ. I don't get much adult interaction. I try to be really supportive. But this is hard on me. And it is terrible to feel so affected by you but to not even know what is going on."

Ren frowned in the dark. But Tiffany wasn't done.

"And as far as how people see you," she said, "it seems like he must have touched a nerve. You're also the one who always says, show me someone who's cocky or arrogant, and I'll show you someone who's insecure. Just being truthful, I think you are insecure about this business. I was there for Standard Link . . . " Her voice trailed off.

In a moment she spoke again, softly. "Look, you are the most trustworthy, hardworking, smartest guy I know. Everyone loves you and trusts you. And those things can take you a long way. You are really considerate and respectful of others. But you're sure not that way to me these days. And it sure seems to me like you're being insecure because something is bothering you. Maybe you know he is right. And I kind of wonder how you are treating others around you at times, with that."

Lying there quietly thinking until he realized he was not going to be able to sleep again for now, Ren reached in the dark and lightly patted the head of the now-sleeping Tiffany, then got up and padded off into his office in the basement to get a little work done.

CHAPTER 8

Unequal Partners

"Victorious warriors win first and then go to war, while
defeated warriors go to war first and then seek to win."

—Sun Tzu

N ow that he was focused on the idea of building a solution for the healthcare industry and had a workable start on his business plan, Ren began mining his personal network for people who might offer wisdom, experience, or any other contribution to the journey. He discovered that—even beyond Tom Strong—people he had known in college were a veritable treasure trove of healthcare and technology connections. Two of these included Trey Bremen and Sam Parr, guys who Ren remembered and respected from his days at Georgia Tech.

Trey and Sam had already been working as highest-level developers for the leading business in the health information technology industry. They were good guys: smart, honest, hardworking, and focused. Trey and Sam had remained connected since Georgia Tech and were working together now, as their careers took off. Their sought-after technical proficiency was unparalleled.

While most of Ren's friends earned themselves at least one great nickname during their college years, Sam and Trey were the kind of guys that you didn't really give nicknames to. Blending in rather than standing out, they were somewhat nondescript, predictable, and constant, but in a way that let you know you could count on them under any and all circumstances. Trey and Sam had spent countless hours together as they had been through numerous escapades during their years at Georgia Tech, in the classroom, in the football stadium, at a favorite local burger joint called The Varsity, and at many of the college bars around campus.

Sam and Trey had, for years, harbored daydreams of one day starting a business together and riding the entrepreneurial wave to success. With their college years in the rearview mirror, the guys had gone their separate ways and until recently had been working at different companies to earn a paycheck. Yet the dream had never died. Now they were employed together and gathered on a regular basis to brainstorm and imagine possibilities to make their dream a reality.

By the time Ren connected with Trey and Sam again, they were already working toward their new business in creating an online collaboration tool for developers—a great solution that was probably ahead of its time. But when Ren invited the two to meet and presented them with his idea, he could see them get excited. They asked good questions and listened very intently.

"I can see where this could be a huge opportunity," said Sam.

"That type of solution would be a great fit for the technologies we have been working with. We could build a prototype to test the market pretty quickly," Trey added. Ren noticed the "we."

That meeting started a series of conversations about possibly starting a business together. At first, the talks were high level and conceptual, full of ifs and maybes. But in a matter of weeks, the conversations grew more serious. It seemed like a great fit. Trey and Sam were strong with healthcare information technology and software development, while Ren had experience with business and sales at Standard Link and elsewhere. Among the three of them, they had the skills, knowledge, and drive to turn the idea into a winner.

A couple of weeks in, over another breakfast conversation at a diner in midtown near Georgia Tech called The Silver Skillet, they fell into the requisite discussion about the corporate structure, ownership percentages, and salaries. As the talk between the three got more and more serious, this was a conversation that needed to happen. But it still caught Ren off guard and unprepared.

The first one to speak up was Sam. "We're all in this together, so we should be equal partners. We're all going to sacrifice our time and energy and contribute one hundred percent to make it successful." Sam paused and looked at the other two sitting at the table.

"I say, all for one and one for all! The dream team!" he exclaimed, with a raised fist and a smile. He was the high-energy cheerleader of the group. He could find the silver lining in every cloud, not that there was a cloud in sight at this point.

"We're all taking a big risk," continued Trey. "We're going to have to leave our current jobs and put all our energy into this, so we'll need to draw a full salary too."

Sam nodded in agreement, but Ren felt troubled. Something didn't feel right. The old college camaraderie was great, and there was plenty of excitement at the table, but something didn't add up.

Unenthusiastically nibbling at his corned-beef hash and breakfast, Ren's buttered-and-jellied toast felt like cardboard in his mouth as he tried to digest what had transpired in the past few minutes.

He didn't say much during the rest of the breakfast. On his drive home, he felt deflated. Maybe even a bit angry. Equal partners? Sure, if the three were sharing the risks and burdens equally, too. But while Trey and Sam would put their time and effort, and perhaps some of their reputation, on the line, what Ren was bringing to the endeavor was his *everything*. This was *his* idea. It was *his* relationships and contacts that would be used to get the thing off the ground. It was *his* plan and vision that they would all follow.

The thought wouldn't let Ren be. He tried to justify to himself why Trey and Sam deserved to be equal owners and why that was the right way to go about things. But he never managed to convince himself. He knew he needed someone to talk to—an outsider to the situation but an insider to the world of entrepreneurship.

The couple of days to Ren's next lunch date with David felt long. When the awaited time finally came, he could barely contain himself enough to look at the lengthy menu—which at LongHorn was more like a book than a simple sheet of options—and order before unloading all his concerns. David, as usual dressed like he was headed straight for the golf course, looked at the impatient Ren, appearing almost amused.

After briefly explaining to David who Sam and Trey were, how he knew them, and what their expertise and skills were, Ren got to the heart of the matter.

"Essentially, Sam and Trey want equal shares for all three. And they need a market salary. But," he said, "they want me to come up with the starting money. Once I've gotten that, we would then build out my idea together."

Ren paused, half-expecting David to have an immediate reaction, but David seemed content with listening and learning more.

"It's not like I can't see where they are coming from. I do. I really do. But this doesn't seem right. It doesn't seem just, considering what we each put into it."

David pointed his striped plastic straw at Ren before putting it in his iced tea.

"Let me get this straight. This business is your idea. You are putting up the startup capital. You are taking most of the initial risk. And they want market salaries *and* they want equal ownership?"

Only after a long exhale did Ren realize he had been holding his breath. "Well . . . yes, sir."

David's furrowed brow told the story even before he began speaking. "I realize that when people start a business with partners, they don't always arrive at things from the same perspective. That's absolutely understandable," he said slowly. "If you ever start a business with a partner, there are some things that need to happen up front.

"Look, Ren, my bottom line is: What you are doing is great. It's important for prospective partners to be able to speak frankly with one another before moving forward. You should not want to be in business with anyone that you can't have direct, honest conversations with. Because if you can't communicate with them now, you think it'll be easier further down the line, when the stakes are higher and everybody's more involved? You can learn a lot about people's communication styles and, most importantly, their character when they are in a tight spot. You gotta know how these guys deal with tricky situations before you get more involved."

Listening to David, Ren felt enormous gratitude. What had at first seemed mainly like a pesky negotiation and communication issue had now, within a matter of minutes, transformed into a golden opportunity to find out some essential things about his potential future business partners.

"For a number of reasons, fight as many battles up front as possible," David said. "It is more friendly and less personal to address—and agree on how to handle—problems and circumstances before they happen. Now is the time to write the rules.

"Let me ask you this, Ren. What happens if you get into the venture and someone's not pulling their weight? They might have a good reason, like a family health problem or something equally big and understandable, but it is nevertheless very problematic for the business. How do you act? What if one of you wants to sell the business, but the others want to continue to grow it? What if the original goal was to build a rapid-growth business but one of the partners has an emergency and needs to pull money from the business? What if the business, against all plans, evolves into a lifestyle business? What happens when someone thinks it's time to rethink the organization and wants to hire a new CEO, but the others disagree?"

Ren's lips were tight, his eyebrows up and eyes wide open as he listened to David. Although a little conflicted, he mostly felt relieved and found himself starting to understand how best to address this with Sam and Trey.

"There's not a right or wrong answer for any of those considerations," David noted. "But these—or other comparable things—are almost certain to happen at some point. And the more those issues are addressed before moving forward—or at least the more you understand how you will address them when they arise—the better served you will be going into the business."

Ren looked at the man, trying to find the words to express the gratitude he felt. Failing to find them, he said only what he most strongly felt. "David, thank you."

David nodded. "You bet. Good luck."

———

At home that night, Tiffany asked Ren about his work. Instead of the usual dismissive "It's good," Ren looked at her and told her the latest. He shared how he was at a critical point with his old friends in possibly being in business together and indicated that he was wrestling with whether and how to move forward.

While it was clear from the look on Tiffany's face that she would have been glad to hear more, the fact that he was actually sharing with her seemed to go a long way. And she gave up when he seemed to ignore her question about it.

Later that night, sitting by his desk, Ren heard Tiffany's words again in his head. "Are Trey and Sam good guys that you would want to be in business with?"

It was a good question. He genuinely liked the two. But was liking them enough to justify making the kinds of compromises he felt they asked of him?

They were really nice people. Ren acknowledged the want in himself to do almost whatever was necessary to have Trey and Sam be on board with him. But, there was more to it. He even wondered, would he grow resentful if he felt like he was setting up an unfair deal?

He spent the better part of the night sitting there, first making different kinds of lists—everything from pros and cons to simple whys and why-nots—but finally just thinking back to David's words. To Ren, some aspects seemed decisive. First, he was the one taking all the financial risk by funding the business costs for the startup. The equity needed to reflect that. Second, he was the who had come up with the concept and who had already put in several months of unpaid research and development to get the business off the ground. This, too, was something he felt needed to show in the division of equity.

What Trey and Sam would bring to the business was absolutely of value—something that would be hard to find elsewhere. But they also had all of the huge upside potential and much less downside risk. The risk-to-reward equation didn't seem to be in balance.

He wondered if the conversation was going to be a difficult one. *What would he do if the guys became combative? How would he defend his point of view if they strongly disagreed?*

Always wanting to be more prepared than anyone else in any meaningful negotiation, Ren had a habit of writing down his thoughts ahead of time and working through various scenarios. This time, being prepared felt especially important. By the time he got in bed the night before his next meeting with Sam and Trey, he had not only rehearsed and memorized his speech down to every word and utterance, but also managed to make himself very anxious about the meeting. He reminded himself that Sam and Trey were good guys, and they were as likely as anyone to be reasonable and rational. But sometimes people—even friends with whom you share a long history—can get a little weird and touchy when discussing things like business, finances, and partnerships. Also, there were two of them and only one of Ren. He worried that it might be harder to discuss his concerns while at this disadvantage.

He got up and paced around. The thing he was most worried about was that the situation and the potential pressure would get him to forget what he wanted to say, and exactly how he wanted to say it. Ren hoped he could just write down his thoughts, exactly as they were, and deliver them to Trey and Sam. And then he realized he could—by writing them a letter. He took all the notes he had already made, wrote down the thoughts and phrases he had played in his head for hours, and put them all on paper.

In his letter, Ren first told Trey and Sam how deeply appreciative he was to know them and how happy he had been to learn about their desire to be part of his business. But, Ren said, he felt that as things were coming together to this point, it was *his* business, and one that he had worked on for quite some time. He explained how, in his view, the risks, too, were ultimately his, and how these things made him feel firm about his position on the equity. Ultimately, he wrote, the guys could contribute more to the risk for more ownership, if they wanted to. But they could also opt not to. The bottom line, Ren wrote, was that under the current circumstances, this was not an equal partnership deal.

It was after 4:30 a.m. when Ren collapsed on the living room sofa for a couple of hours of sleep. Though the time was short, he slept restfully now, knowing that he had organized his thoughts clearly and concisely. He felt confident that he was handling this in the best way possible.

He shot up with the sun, in time to make a few tweaks to the letter and in plenty of time to head to the meeting at Sam's home, twenty minutes away.

Not seeing a doorbell, Ren knocked directly on the door. Sam's wife, Fran, answered. Smiling and balancing a toddler on her hip, she welcomed him and escorted him to the living room in the back of the home, where the meeting could proceed undisturbed.

He entered to find Sam and Trey talking away, as usual. They looked up and said their hellos. For a fleeting moment, Ren wondered if he detected a bit of apprehension in their mannerisms but quickly brushed it off.

Aside from preparing notes, he had learned that practicing in advance for a potentially nerve-racking conversation, like the one he was about to have, could turn out to be lifesaving. But when Ren saw Trey and Sam, all he managed was, "Hey, guys, I'm really struggling here."

Both heads looked up in unison, as if they were part of a coordinated dance. "I mean about the equity structure . . . I've been thinking about this a lot, and I'm just not comfortable about the direction we're heading," he said, his voice faltering ever so slightly but gaining strength as he made a conscious effort to push words out more firmly.

"You know I have the utmost respect for you guys. And if it makes sense for all of us, I would love to partner in this business with you. But the way you were looking at this the other day just doesn't work for me."

Ren realized he was looking down and avoiding eye contact with his friends, perhaps to miss seeing disappointment or concern on their faces. He intentionally tried to show a more confident posture and deeper voice to project more confidence than he felt, as he nodded down at the green nylon notebook in his hand. He opened the zipper and pulled out the loose pages inside, for a moment wondering what he looked like to the two sitting on the couch.

He nodded at the letters. "I've written down my thoughts about how, at least from my perspective, this needs to play out. I'll leave these with you. When you've read them, we should talk."

With that, Ren handed Trey and Sam copies of his early morning thoughts. When he finally looked the two in the eye, he couldn't quite decipher how to interpret the looks on their faces.

"As *Ahnold* would say, 'Ah'll be bock,'" he feebly tried to joke. Trey and Sam didn't seem to notice.

Ren went to a nearby Cracker Barrel for breakfast. The restaurant's comfort food seemed particularly appealing today. He hardly noticed the merchandise and confections that usually slowed him down, much less the busy crowd milling about in the store. With the hard part of broaching a difficult topic in his rearview mirror, he was feeling ravenous for the first time in a couple of days. He ordered his favorite breakfast and mixed it all—the scrambled eggs, bacon, ham, hash browns, grits, biscuits, and gravy—into a big, appetizing-looking pile which resembled the mountain in *Close Encounters of the Third Kind*. Ren began eating away at the pile in large spoonfuls. He methodically worked his way through the meal and then ordered some extra biscuits and a side of extra-crisp bacon and honey, to combine into a honey-bacon biscuit.

All the sweet tea and breakfast and lunch meetings were starting to catch up to Ren. At some point, he knew it might be worth worrying about his expanding waistline. But he had plenty of other concerns on his mind for now.

It gave him some solace that he had handled this situation as decently as he knew how. If the guys were real friends and the sort of people he should start a business with, hopefully they would get it. And, if it didn't work out, at least he had done what he could, as well as he could, in a good spirit of fairness. If that didn't get it done, he felt at this point it was on them.

Feeling comfortably full and at peace, he left a generous tip for the waitress, paid the bill, and headed back to Sam's house to discover what awaited him.

This time, he didn't hear as much talking from outside the door as he arrived. The mood seemed decidedly more serious.

Ren walked inside and sat down to face his friends. To his surprise, Trey was the one who led the conversation. Trey was a man of few words, but when he spoke, you always wanted to hear what he had to say, because every word mattered.

"We get it," Trey said with a matter-of-fact voice. "We honestly hadn't looked at this from your perspective. We want you to succeed, and I think I speak for both of us in saying that we aren't in a position to contribute on the sweat equity side. With our families, we just can't afford to work without market salaries for now."

This was the most likely response that Ren had expected. More importantly, it was the sort of response he may have needed at the time.

Sam chimed in, making an obvious effort at levity, "So we're all going to keep our day jobs!"

They all chuckled, breaking the heaviness of the moment and alleviating some of Ren's concerns that he might have damaged their friendship.

"Seriously, Ren," Sam interjected, "we all wish you the best, and we'll do anything we can to help you from afar. We look forward to your success!" They stood, shook hands, and clapped Ren on the back as he made for the door.

And with that, the trio ended its shared entrepreneurial pursuit.

Over the coming years, Ren would see several other friends form partnerships on a napkin without addressing important considerations before moving forward and without fully understanding the concept of risk and how it could significantly impact equity and compensation in a startup. Sometimes these ventures worked out, to varying degrees, at least for a time. But in more cases than not, they eventually dissolved into chaos, broken partnerships, and even broken friendships, as big decision and evolution points arose. Ren felt blessed to have avoided those potential pitfalls. When it came down to it, he was glad to have learned these lessons and to have left the exchange with those friendships intact.

CHAPTER 9

Contemplation Comes Home

"When Chekhov saw the long winter, he saw a winter
bleak and dark and bereft of hope. Yet we know that
winter is just another step in the cycle of life."

—Phil Connors, *Groundhog Day*

Ren spent way too much time in traffic, too much of it wondering why some drivers had to go slow in the left lane. But he also used the time to wonder about a lot of other things.

He realized that he was still trying to "will" cars out of the way with his mind. It never came close to working. The idea was so ridiculous that it made him smile a little. And that brought recognition that it was nice to smile—something he didn't seem to do as much lately. *When had life become so serious?*

He also thought about how obsessed he had become with his idea and business. It seemed that everything came back to it. All day. All the time.

Ren was glad to be in a big SUV, where he could see over many of the cars in front of him. And he often thought about how driving was a metaphor for building a business in some ways. It was an advantage to be able to see over the other cars. To see which lanes were moving faster. And he felt like it helped to have a car with better acceleration and brakes, if you wanted to change lanes. *Wasn't it an advantage if your business was better at seeing what was happening in its industry? Wasn't it worth a lot to be able to move fast?* The lost prospect of working with Trey and Sam had worked out in as friendly a way as possible. Now, going at it alone, he would collect the fruits of his labor, but he also needed to make all the decisions. After investing so much hope in working with them, he felt a good deal of frustration over the lost time and the personal weight of everything.

The internal debate raged on. And with so much on the line for him and his family, it seemed like every week Ren's perspective changed from certainty to concern and back again. He had some big decisions to make. Soon. The sort of challenges and risks he was going to face were starting to get *real.* He was plagued more and more with thoughts about his first conversation with David. *Am I the right person to build this business? Do I know how to give it the best chance?* He had even found himself wondering if it was too late to back out. It's not like he had better options. *Were there even* any *other options, at this point?*

———

When Ren finally made it home and walked in the door, he was greeted by Caulie. Now growing and looking healthier, she had turned into the happiest, most excitable puppy he had ever seen, only a few weeks into her time in the family. It always brightened his day when she yipped and ran around in excited circles. Sometimes she seemed so thrilled just to see him that he worried she might injure herself. He felt a little happier, even as he took the time to get her to calm down.

It never failed. Whatever challenges he faced, and whatever seemed wrong in the world, at least this enthusiastic little ball of fuzz was always thrilled to see him. *If I were one-tenth as great as she thinks I am, I would be all right.*

Cheered up by Caulie's enthusiasm, he realized he needed a little break and a laugh, and wanting to try to be a little warmer to his wife, he invited Tiffany to join him in watching his favorite movie, *Groundhog Day*, after RJ fell asleep.

By 8 p.m., he was in front of the television, ready to start the movie. Caulie, exhausted from an earlier walk and all the excitement of Ren's homecoming for the evening, lay sleeping at their feet.

"Wait a minute before you hit start,'" said Tiffany. A couple of minutes later, she walked in in her pajamas and produced one of his favorite snacks for them to "share." It was a big bowl of popcorn with extra salt and butter melted on it, a few chunks of sharp cheddar cheese cut into rectangular sticks, and a big, cold glass of orange juice to wash it all down. They both knew she might nibble a little but that Ren would devour most of it.

"Thank you," said Tiffany.

Seeing his questioning expression, she continued, "This is the first time we've watched a movie or done much of anything together since well before y'all sold Standard Link. This seems like one of the few times you've really even taken a break like this, particularly with me. Maybe you don't understand, but it means something to me."

Ren looked at her warmly and said, "Yeah. Whatever." And he turned back to the movie with a little smirk. He was grateful that Tiffany knew him well enough to take that as intended, as weak but friendly humor.

And watching *Groundhog Day* always inspired Ren to make the most of every day. To take action. It was exactly the positivity and motivation he needed. Adding a little humor helped. He was still struggling and questioning. But at least he was doing *something*.

CHAPTER 10

Hero and Villain

"Challenges are what makes life interesting.
Overcoming them is what makes life meaningful."

—Joshua Marine

"If you are going to build a business, you need to believe in what you are doing and feel good about it in order to make the kind of commitment and sacrifice you need," said David, looking up from his steaming cup of coffee during another Waffle House breakfast session.

"Startups drive innovation, create millions of new jobs every year, and even serve to keep the larger businesses more competitive and inventive, before eventually becoming bigger companies, or parts of bigger companies, themselves. New businesses, like yours, drive our economy and make the world better in many ways."

David's words registered with how Ren wanted to think of himself as an entrepreneur—as a person wanting to change the world in some way, to somehow make it better. But the man's sentiment was also far from where Ren was at, trying to figure out the very basics of his business. He was searching for the right building blocks and then assembling them to form some kind of a foundation for the new venture. But he also knew that moral and ethical values were essential as a guiding star to go in the right direction.

David shook his head and chuckled. "You know, sometimes I think of building a business as almost an act of heroism. I mean, here you are as an entrepreneur: You fight through all these challenges, overcome obstacles and face barriers, and then one fine day you come out on the other side. And if you've done things the right way, you can look back and go, 'I think I just did something meaningful!'"

Ren's meetings with David had now become a regular occurrence. Sometimes it would be Ren doing most of the talking and David egging him on by asking questions or simply nodding. Other times, it felt like David was giving him a lecture on some aspect of his business philosophy. This particular morning, the sermon was unusually passionate. It felt to Ren like David had transitioned from being tough and cautionary to encouraging and reassuring.

"I really believe one of the best things an individual can do for the world is to build a strong business." David seemed inspired. "And I think maybe the best thing that *I* can do is to help them do that."

He paused briefly, seemingly for effect, before proceeding. "When I exited some prior businesses, I started doing some philanthropy. It felt good to go into a hospital and expect that our contributions were helping them save babies' lives—or to go to a ministry or a shelter and feel a part of providing new opportunities to people who were having a hard time.

"But, in many cases, I ended up wondering how much I was really helping," he continued. "Often, organizations would use our contributions for something like hiring a new administrator, building a new garden, or sprucing up a building. I honestly don't know if those were the right things to do. I usually gave them the benefit of the doubt that it was good for them. But in just about every case, it felt that each donation only served to make them more dependent on me. It felt almost like they needed me to continue to write the checks just to stay afloat. I could only have done that for so long, until I ran out of money to give. Then we'd all have a problem."

David paused again with an acknowledging nod to accept a coffee refill, no cream or sugar, from their waitress, who had tactfully waited for David to finish before offering to pour. David smiled at Ren in the way you do when you want to be polite but also really want to continue your conversation. The waitress took the cue.

"Don't get me wrong. I still enjoy philanthropy and still do more than my share of it," David continued. "But, after becoming cynical from my experience with so many causes, I honestly believe, in most cases, I'm making more of a difference when I help someone to innovate and build a business. And the value those businesses create is often very meaningful in itself."

Ren realized that while he and David had had a number of lengthy, detailed conversations about entrepreneurship from many different angles, this was the closest he had ever come to knowing David as a person. The more he listened to the older man, the more he learned about both David and himself, too. Ren realized that this want, or even need, he had to help others would ultimately come to fruition by doing what he was already planning on doing: by slowly and methodically building a solid, ethical business.

"Take, for example, another company that I've been really involved with," David said, gesturing in a broad swipe with his hands, a sure sign that he was on fire about a topic. "I'm a partner in a construction company. My partners run it, but I started it with them and invested alongside them. I like to meet with them regularly and feel like a part of building that business. They are still a small business. But they are growing rapidly and now have hundreds of employees and full-time equivalents, most as full-time contractors.

"That construction company pays their taxes and engages in the community in many ways. Their employees also pay their taxes and—even better—utilize the hospitals (where they pay their bills), send their children to the schools and get involved, and engage in their churches and mosques and synagogues and ministries and make their own donations. They get directly involved in helping more causes than I ever could. All of that does more—and particularly does a more sustainable job of making the world a better place—than any number of checks I could ever write.

"The construction company also innovates better methods and solutions, and this helps their customers in many ways. And those customers and their own employees, in turn, also pay taxes and engage in hospitals and schools and the community in constructive ways."

Ren's expression encouraged him to continue.

"Just know that while this may sound great and inspiring, it sure the heck isn't easy. In fact, a lot of us old, cynical guys won't do it anymore because of what we have learned. And if you had my experiences, it'd be hard for you to do it, too.

"I also don't think people understand how much risk they are taking on," David continued. "In most cases, small businesses are one car wreck or lawsuit away from losing everything. But that's okay. I even think it's a good thing that you don't understand what you are up against. You have a better chance of succeeding because you don't know any better. You'll be committed and hopefully you'll find a way. And you're willing to try it because you don't know enough to be afraid of all the hard times and challenges and risks that you're signing up for.

"And it's worth remembering that there is risk in anything, including working for any business or institution. I just need to highlight to you how precarious all startups are before you move forward. In fact, sometimes it's as simple as a well-meaning employee making a single decision that ends up becoming devastating, sometimes even when they're not really doing anything wrong. And that could hurt your customers and all of your other employees and their livelihoods. Startups are not for the faint of heart."

"I hear you, David," Ren responded. "And trust me, I feel it. I have plenty of excitement *and* fear in me about all of this."

"Well, hopefully you have just a little more excitement than fear," David said, winking. "Otherwise, you may never get going.

"What you will find, Ren, is that everything that happens in your business will be really personal to you. You'll feel like you carry the weight of your employees and their livelihoods and families. Even when the employees do wrong and very clearly need to be let go, you still feel pain and hurt for their families, who probably didn't do anything to deserve any tough decisions you have to make.

"When you and I first met, you described yourself as feeling like a tulip in a tornado—as all of these huge forces were blowing all around you. I've been there.

"But now, as you start your business, an analogy that you will hear a lot with startups is that of a roller coaster—because of all the ups and downs and staying on track through everything. In fact, most businesses, even bigger ones over time, do feel like they rise and fall and are surrounded by a thunderstorm of other forces all around you. I have been a part of companies well into the billions in revenues, and it's always an adventure. The problems and their scale may change, but they never go away. They are never easy. And you are recognizing that they are always risky," David continued. "So the roller coaster analogy is spot on—just add lightning, heavy rain, and strong winds to the image, and then you're close to what it really feels like.

"All of those forces around you are what you battle through, daily, as you build your business. You will be bludgeoned constantly, as your customers' needs and the market evolve; technology and the economy change; regulatory and other barriers rise and fall; competitors emerge and vary; different employee issues arise regularly that you would never have expected—most of this, you could say, is outside of your influence."

David made wild, illustrative gestures with his arms as he spoke of the ups and downs, and the storm gathered around them.

Feeling a little disarmed, Ren surprised himself by opening up. "Look. I totally get the roller coaster example. That's how I feel about everything, for sure. Everything seems so different about the business and opportunity from day to day with each new turn.

"I worry a lot about that stuff and more. It feels like my reputation is on the line. Really, I already feel the pressure that my family is depending on this and that others will be depending more and more on it over time. And there is so much that can go wrong. In fact, it is really only a matter of time until something does go wrong. There is so much to do. And, I do still remember in the early days at Standard Link when one of our key customers just quit paying their bills for a time. It almost put us out of business. There is no way to prepare for all the things that will happen."

"What you are describing is The Villain," David said.

"The Villain?"

David nodded.

"The Villain is a creature made up of all the problems you, as an entrepreneur, face every day and all the issues that keep you up at night, or at least stop you from sleeping well. It's the big beast lurking in every corner of every entrepreneur's office. Whether they recognize it by that name, every single entrepreneur I know of is scared of it. And they should be. Knowing The Villain is there is what keeps you trying harder and ultimately what helps you succeed. No, I take that back. It's what *enables* you to succeed. I even think that knowing this beast is out there helps some of us fight it. It keeps us alert and on our toes.

"Maybe the best thing I can tell you, though, is that once you succeed, you are always glad you did it. Every one of my businesses that I have been involved in—even the ones that became very successful—all went through some hard times when some of us didn't think we would make it, when we thought the wheels could have come off. Thinking back, they all taught us something we desperately needed to learn. And from where I am now, I'm glad we faced those hardships. But let me tell you, it sure didn't feel like it at the time.

"And of course," he added, "if you are passionate about what you do and believe in it, you'll always do it better!"

CHAPTER 11

Married to the Business

*"We need to have a purpose in this life. I'm pleading
with you, I'm begging with you to do the right thing.
And do it not for the sake of how it will impact your own
lives, but only for the sake of doing the right thing."*

—James McGreevey

For the first time in his life, Ren felt lonely.

Here he was, surrounded by caring, helpful people like David and Tiffany with whom he shared meals and thoughts, who listened to him and offered feedback, and who, he knew, all wished him well. And it seemed like he was meeting with everyone and their brother. Nonetheless, it seemed that he had stepped into a space where he was all by himself, and where he spent most of his days. Much later he understood that this was the space he had created for himself—where there was only room for him and for the business that was on his mind around the clock. This loneliness wasn't significant enough and didn't last long enough to be a real problem. But for the first time, Ren understood how isolated entrepreneurs can feel.

The early days of his business were interesting times for Ren and his family.

Armed with a civil engineering degree and having had some career interest, Tiffany had still not gone back to employment after RJ's birth. She made the household work and did almost all of the cleaning and meal preparation. She eventually would become a terrific cook, though her meals were not very good at the time. Sometimes Ren found himself wondering how it was even possible to mess up making a Pop-Tart. Then he heard his own thoughts and realized that, besides toasting the pastry, Tiffany probably had twelve other things she was preoccupied with—things he didn't see or even know existed.

In their very frugal life, the most common staple meal that Tiffany presented for dinner, often a couple of times a week, was something that looked, and unfortunately very much tasted, like a light-brown hockey puck made of leather. Eventually, Ren discovered that the puck was a fish patty of sorts, acquired from Wal-Mart in big bags that cost relatively little money, which Tiffany then simply thawed and warmed for dinner.

Tiffany must have assumed Ren enjoyed the dish, since the puck became a regular dinner entree. He didn't have the heart to tell her otherwise and quietly slathered the patty in packets of three-pepper sauce left over from Arby's.

Keeping "startup hours," Ren was at a breakfast meeting—or in the office in advance of his breakfast meeting—at least by 6:30 a.m. every weekday, most Saturdays, and even some Sundays. He would get home by 6:00 p.m. most days, maybe let Caulie out after she greeted him excitedly, eat a distracted dinner, spend a little time with RJ and read to him before putting him to bed, and then usually go back into the office until after midnight, or however long it took to get so exhausted he wasn't capable of staying awake.

Weekends were sometimes better. He really wanted to save his Sundays, in particular, for family and any small amount of personal time. And when he did manage to dedicate the day for his family, the days were simple but great. Looking back at it later, Ren realized that a part of it might have been exactly that: They didn't have the means to go out and do a lot of things, so instead they focused on each other and what was immediately around them.

Ren loved to find an hour here and there to walk with RJ, and sometimes Caulie, down to the creek behind the house and play in the water and mud. They made little rafts or boats from sticks, dropped them in the creek, and then just watched them bounce around in the rocks and turbulence as they made their way down. Sometimes RJ and Ren would each throw a stick in and treat it like a race to see which one made it farther or faster in the creek. When the weather cooperated, the two would work together in the yard, Ren in the lead, RJ following close by, helping out with whatever task at hand using the little plastic tool set—rake, shovel, and saw—that Tiffany had bought him.

But there were more days when the creek just wasn't an option, when Ren sat by his desk and RJ peered into the office, hoping for another raft race or shoveling session. In these moments, all Ren had for him was a "maybe later" or "not right now." Each time he heard RJ's footsteps fading, he felt the burn in his chest and reminded himself that ultimately, the reason he couldn't go was for his son: to ensure that he would have what he needed in life to make it good. But the irony of the situation wasn't lost on Ren, nor was the look on RJ's face when he backed out of the office.

When Ren got really hyper-focused sometimes, that came with its own set of problems and benefits. And underneath, he still carried plenty of guilt about where his career and family involvement was.

———

About two hours after dark on a cool Thursday evening in early November, Ren eased tentatively into the open garage at his older split-level ranch-style brick home, as his old blue Dodge Durango barely fit. As always, he had to pull forward just the right amount, so his door didn't open into one of the varied-shades-of-red brick columns that held up the roof over the garage.

It had been another long day of calls and meetings, including two breakfasts, two "coffees," and a dinner with potential advisors, possible future customers, and friends that wanted to help. And through all of that, he was really struggling with some big directional decisions. He was locked into healthcare now but had some big, critical moves to make with a couple of prospective opportunities and product positioning. He had to make a call to move forward on multiple fronts, right away.

Ren was so deep in thought that he didn't notice the lights were out in the house, nor that Tiffany's car was not there, in her usual spot. He had already started to pay less attention to Caulie's still-uber-excited greetings when he entered. But if he hadn't been too distracted to notice her absence this evening, he would have realized that she must have been in their fenced-in backyard. Normally, Tiffany would have the lights on and the dinner ready by now.

Fumbling for the right key to unlock the side door from the garage into the kitchen, Ren walked in. And he didn't think much at all about the lights being out or Tiffany seemingly not being home—until he emerged into the room next to the kitchen and they came on suddenly. Tiffany jumped out and yelled, "SURPRISE!!"

She had a warm, happy smile. And she lit candles that she had put out and came over to hug him.

That was when Ren got really worried. What had he missed? An anniversary? *I don't think so.* A birthday? Maybe Tiffany's? *I think we celebrated RJ's birthday a few weeks ago and can't think of another. So what did I forget or screw up this time?*

He was incredibly relieved when Tiffany said, "I am just trying to spend a little quality time with you. I was shocked when you asked me to watch a movie with you recently. And the last time we had a real conversation was when you first met David and were worried about how he challenged you. And that was months ago. RJ was exhausted tonight, so I put him to bed early. And you've been working so hard that I was hoping we could have a nice dinner together, just us.

"I made your favorite: a Chef Boyardee pepperoni pizza kit, with the crust spread super thin, extra grated cheese, baked until crunchy and brown on top. And I made a dessert you love: I took frosted brown sugar and cinnamon Pop-Tarts, spread a little butter on them, and will toast them in the oven and serve hot with a big, cold glass of milk. I even got the real Pop-Tart brand instead of the generics this time!"

Ren really appreciated Tiffany's warm intentions. But his thoughts of gratitude never found their way to words as he stared blankly at the frosted treat on his plate, brow furrowed, not seeming to process the delicious and thoughtful kindness represented in front of him.

"How was your day?" Tiffany inquired, trying to inspire any sort of conversation, as they sat down. "What's the latest with your business? I know you were worried about the retaining wall in the front yard. What did you decide to do about that?"

"Everything with the business is just pretty complicated right now. Lots of factors affecting everything, multiple variables, and a whole lot of decision-making with what seems like not enough information," Ren said, inadvertently letting out a sigh.

Tiffany reached for his hand across the table. Ren attempted a smile.

"I'm not saying it's impossible. It's just . . . a lot."

Tiffany nodded.

"That's why I think you need . . . Pop-Tarts!" She exclaimed.

When Tiffany brought out the warm pastries and milk, he looked at her and said, "Tiffany, I really appreciate this, but I have to return a couple of calls and emails. Do you mind if I take these to my office?"

Tiffany nodded quickly and turned back to the kitchen.

"Thanks again, this was really nice," Ren repeated as he headed downstairs.

As he worked diligently, hunched over at his solid oak desk, Ren was so locked in that he forgot to finish his Pop-Tarts until they were cold and didn't finish his milk at all, as it sat, hardly touched, until warm. In addition to the tough, big decisions that were looming so urgently, there was another pressure. With RJ's birth, he had felt a motivation and urgency that he never had before. He realized, much more than ever, how responsible he was for the lives of others, for both Tiffany's and RJ's. He felt up for the task. He embraced the challenge. But its magnitude worked as a magnet, pulling him to his work for most of his waking hours.

By the time Ren got through his emails, did some financial modeling on a couple of possible scenarios that he needed to make commitments on, and finally put pen to paper in articulating and initiating his plans, it was early morning. He poured the milk down the drain and walked to bed, where he found Tiffany fast asleep. She lay in the middle of the bed and Ren realized she had hoped to wake up when he joined her. Instead, he carefully slid under the blanket on the sliver of bed left for him and fell asleep.

There were times when Ren felt he didn't live up to Tiffany's expectations, which, he realized, weren't even unreasonable. He noticed the times when his hasty exit from a dinner party or his early departure from a family get-together gave Tiffany's face a certain sadness. He realized that when he canceled a planned trip or his participation in an event at the last minute, he forced her to either attend alone or cancel her own attendance. And he really wasn't helping much with Caulie or even paying as much attention to her.

Ren expected that Tiffany must have understood that the reason he acted the way he did was because he felt so much responsibility for his family, and because he wanted the absolute best for their future. But sometimes, when he looked at her going about her daily life, or watched her sleep next to him, he wondered if she truly knew his reasons. Or if it was enough that she might trust that someday the family would have more of him around. Because he knew that the version of himself he was giving at the time was a distracted, rushed figure who mostly wasn't there—and even when he was, his mind was often on his business.

One of Ren's friends said that certain entrepreneurs "could go from scatterbrained to hyper-focused and then back to scattered again," with the shifts coming when they got caught up in a project or task. That might have summed it up.

Ren really enjoyed the reverie and flow state and accomplishments of the hyper-focused times. He even thought of the obsessive concentration as a superpower—as the time when he became super effective. He did realize that the super-focus also made him impersonal and hard to approach, and he knew that this wasn't easy for those around him to deal with. But Ren saw it as a give-and-take and felt that the results the focus yielded were worth the moments his behavior turned somewhat impolite. The times when this focus became problematic were when he was faced with personal challenges: when RJ was ill, a friend needed help, or any other of the countless ways life tests you. While he tried to help when called upon, it was distressing for Ren to detach himself from the world he was in and to shift his focus to something so completely different. Often, his focus on the project worked like tunnel vision, blocking everything in his peripheral vision unless the sound became so loud he could no longer ignore it.

———

As the back-and-forth entrepreneurial journey between enthusiasm and doubt continued, Tiffany surprised Ren once again, one evening after he got home and past Caulie's welcome celebration. "Just being honest," she said, "it seems like you have been really productive lately. But it also seems like you are distant and aloof again—maybe more than ever. What does that tell you?"

It was easy to see that this sort of confrontation was still uncomfortable and difficult for Tiffany. She had never been big on such things. And Ren could see that she meant well. But he was really preoccupied and didn't have time to deal with it. He just kept going down to his office, with a shrug, a thrown-up hand, and "What do you want me to say?"

A couple of things he was working through had him reflecting on his conversations with David as much as ever. Whether he felt good or bad about his chances seemed to change weekly or even daily. And his opinion of David's wisdom seemed to correspond.

This time, David had gone too far, telling Ren that he still didn't get it. *I listen to him all the time. I take his advice and take action. How can I do anything more?*

Sure. The old guy was smart and had some great ideas. But that didn't make him perfect. And his lessons were from so long ago. David was from an old world. An out-of-date paradigm. His old-fashioned ideas about business model and leadership didn't fit this new world. David couldn't understand about valuations and what drove big capital raises and exits in this new world.

I can still use some of his ideas. But I have the best solution that everyone needs and am going to have the smartest people. And there is so much money chasing deals now. I will raise a lot of it and build a great solution and make it big! Ren could almost picture his face on the front page of the *Wall Street Journal,* with the heading "Entrepreneur Hits Home Run!" And he was going to send a framed clipping of the article to David and Tiffany.

CHAPTER 12

Heart for Success

"All you need in this life is ignorance and
confidence; then success is sure."

—Mark Twain

As much as Ren had been worried at times, success was starting to feel inexorable again at this point. He was putting together mockups and flow charts of what the initial solution might do. He even started playing with some basic code, increasingly recognizing how far he had to go—and how much he still needed to learn—to turn it into a real solution that would serve his concept.

An easier front was the business planning. Ren had invested a lot into financial planning, integrated with prospective growth and operating plans. He thought he was being thorough and got a little annoyed when David reminded him that he was naive about all of the challenges, impediments, and hurdles that he couldn't possibly account for at this point.

As Ren continued to work out where to go with his new business, to learn and meet people, and to formulate his plan, he was now committed to resolving and improving leadership issues within healthcare, starting with hospitals. The technology he was creating, he felt, could do that and so much more. He kept thinking about organizational success factors, such as psychology, culture, and leadership, that ultimately determined the success of any business. And, because he was going to build the business for healthcare, he kept thinking about Tom Strong.

Ren had always been interested in personality factors in business. When he was in college, he would sit in the library and read from the psychology journals and other related publications. Often, in reading researchers' experiments, he would read the hypothesis, review the methodology and results, and then draw his own conclusions.

At the time, learning about personality factors and excitement transfer, or what colors to wear to draw attention, essentially how to make himself more attractive, had been about picking up girls, rather than preparing for future business success. But Ren had somehow managed to learn things that later became useful in his entrepreneurship efforts, too. He became particularly fascinated with behavioral psychology, industrial psychology, functional team dynamics, communication styles, and achievement factors—and how they were relevant both in business and in life. By understanding better how different people think, listen, and process information, he could foster better communication and group dynamics.

In fact, Ren often felt like businesses and other organizations had their own personalities, cultures, and success factors. He felt like he could walk into any factory, store, or restaurant and almost immediately get a sense of whether they had the right leader. And he believed there was an essential interdependence between the traits of any organization, its leadership, and the people in it.

Among many other qualities, what Ren sought when observing businesses was trustworthiness, reliability, competence, self-discipline, and perseverance. He also felt that consideration and collegiality were important traits for anyone in a team environment. In small businesses, Ren looked for the ability to consider the "big picture"—to step back and think in terms of what makes a happy customer and then translate that into good business.

He also started to feel like for some people and organizations, success was almost inevitable—he thought of Michael Jordan, John Wooden, and his favorite sports figures that had always seemed to find a way to victory. And, unfortunately, for others there was not much chance they would win. Most of them, though, Ren felt were somewhere in between. It became his priority to build his own business around winning personality traits and success factors—essentially, to have an organization destined to succeed.

No matter what angle he approached the issue from, it seemed self-evident to him that success started with having the right leader. If he had discussed his view with others, Ren presumed many would have said his view was overly simplistic or plain arrogant, and that it neglected too many external factors. But to him, the leader epitomized the business and should ultimately own all the issues within the business. This wasn't to say the leader couldn't have bad days. But Ren thought that even if customers caught the leader during one, they would still be able to tell if the organization did things right overall and whether the bad day was just that, or the organization's way of operating and handling issues.

Ren also couldn't walk into any manufacturing facility or business of any kind without breaking it down from a functional and operational perspective. He liked going into RaceTrac, Cracker Barrel, LongHorn Steakhouse, and a handful of other chain restaurants and retailers that did a good job of institutional quality control throughout. He was even sometimes willing to pay extra for The Capital Grille, because they were just so great at doing it right. Ren felt that almost all of them were clean and consistent in quality and service. From start to finish, it seemed evident that their leadership was committed to happy customers. And, he noticed, even great businesses could go wrong if they changed to leadership that steered the ship in the wrong direction. This further enforced his idea of the importance of who the captain of the ship was.

The biggest struggle Ren had was when he tried to picture the leadership of his own business. He himself had been described by others as an innovative guy. He knew he could direct and contribute to a business in plenty of ways. On paper, he may even have had the quintessential qualities of a great leader. But he felt like that wasn't enough. Ren wanted the basic personality and character of his business to be built around someone that the industry would immediately connect with: somebody solid, hardworking, trustworthy, and dependable. To build a business that could only succeed, you had to find a winning leader. A star.

And that brought Ren back to Tom Strong. People that knew Tom trusted and liked him. And they all believed in him. That guy was always going to win—and for the right reasons. That was exactly what Ren wanted for his business. As a healthcare information technology company selling to hospitals, Tom Strong's personality and traits were a perfect match.

While Ren felt he himself had some value to offer, in terms of providing the vision and direction, a business that was like Tom was most likely to win.

Above all else, Tom was a doer. When something needed to happen, Tom just got it done and done right. For example, when his hospital wanted to implement a new staffing system, they knew they could count on Tom to get it done on time, on budget, and up to expected standards. Ren had come to understand that the kind of ability and determination to complete tasks that Tom exemplified was both rare and powerful. Ren thought of himself more as an idea guy—as someone operating well on a higher level but not as efficient at getting things done. Throughout his career, he worked on improving that aspect of himself, but eventually Ren came to appreciate the value of his own strengths and to concentrate on utilizing them for his businesses.

Looking back, Ren felt that for a long time, the world must have been full of doers—of people who worked hard through their careers and built value for their businesses. The idea people—the innovators and visionaries—were few and therefore at an advantage. But these days it seemed that finding really competent doers was increasingly difficult, and that the few doers did most of the work. This made him treasure the true doers who came across his path.

Ren knew that Tom was not a startup type or an entrepreneur in spirit. But that wasn't an issue, since Ren had plenty of that in himself. What he wanted was for Tom to be the *heart* of the company. Once the company could justify and afford it, Ren could later add a *head* of the company to take it forward.

Ren spent days on the topic, questioning his conviction and searching for weaknesses in a business with Tom at its core. But when all his quests led back to his initial sentiment, he knew he had to act.

Ren called Tom around 9:45 on a Tuesday morning. The timing was carefully calculated. By quarter to ten, Ren figured, Tom would have had a moment to get through the emergencies of the morning and to answer acute emails and calls in his busy workload, but it would still be early enough that he would not be worn out and might be amenable for higher-level consideration.

"Hey, Ren," he said, voice rising. "I thought you might call. I have been thinking about our conversations."

"Well," Ren said, "I've been thinking, too." He had wanted to broach the subject at an in-person breakfast. But he took this as a decent time to just declare his intentions: "I have been thinking about seeing if there might be some fit for you in this business."

Tom responded, "Great minds think alike! And so do we!"

Tom shared that he had already been thinking about making a change. He was bored with where he was and wanted to hit a home run for his family. He knew the need and opportunity were there, as well as anyone, for the business Ren had in mind. In two very important ways—for both Tom personally and for Ren's business—the timing was great.

However, coming to mutually agreeable terms was another matter. Tom was making good money, and the prospect of leaving for a startup while providing for his young family was a little scary to him. It quickly became obvious to Ren that Tom was negotiating with his value and his family in mind. He wanted a decent salary and a fair amount of ownership.

Ren was happy for the practice round he'd had with Sam and Trey on working through these considerations. Thanks to that experience, he felt calm and equipped to discuss the issues with Tom. Ren was almost looking forward to the talks, happy in knowing that the two would have a frank dialogue and fight any potential battles up front. He now knew the importance of objectively trying to weigh value, risk, compensation, and ownership. But it was still going to be a critical discussion. The most important thus far. And Ren knew who he needed to consult before the talks.

When introducing his old friend as his desired first employee for the technology startup, he realized that Tom probably wasn't the first one many others would have considered for the position. But after learning about Tom's skills and character, David quickly warmed to the idea.

"But just know that businesses need to be driven by business needs," David warned Ren. "These tech guys often have their technology-driven biases and perspectives and miss their mark or make bad decisions.

"I came from a sales background in our first company. People thought it was just wrong when they put me in charge of Research and Development," he said. "But I found good technology people. I leaned on them and let them do their jobs. I was able to direct our R&D investment from a customer-driven and sales-driven perspective, serving our customers' needs in a way that the tech folks couldn't have alone. Basically, I built a mutually trusting relationship with the top technophile and leaned on his functional competence—and we did it together.

"So, having this guy who understands your customers and their needs—and is good enough with the technologies and techniques you want to use—might make a lot of sense."

Ren felt relieved that David liked his off-the-wall idea. As far as compensation, David was not sure what was right. He seemed genuinely protective of

Ren's investments and ownership. But he also felt that providing more ownership and using the right vesting schedule, to determine how much time it would
take to get to the ownership, might incentivize Tom to think and act like an
owner. He also understood Tom's concerns about providing for his family.

Ren and Tom ended up negotiating for a couple of weeks. It was not much
fun for either of them. Neither one was completely happy with where they
ended up, which somehow felt like the definition of a good compromise.

Tom's base salary was below his market value. His ownership upside, over
time, seemed smaller to him than he wanted—but way more than Ren wanted
to provide at the time. It wasn't that Ren wanted the whole company for himself. If he could give up more of the company to give it a better chance to be a
bigger success, he would be good with that. He adopted a quote that he loved to
better illustrate this perspective, from his great friend Annie Heron: "I'd rather
own a smaller piece of a watermelon than a bigger piece of a grape."

Ren just worried that he was going to need substantially more equity for future
hires and investors. And there were plenty of practical considerations for how
much ownership he could give up and still be able to execute decisions quickly
enough when he eventually might own, say, less than half of the company.

What ultimately made everything come together was that Tom and Ren
trusted each other's intentions and both really wanted to make the deal happen.
So they came to a deal on base salary, equity ownership over time, benefits,
vacation, and other matters, and drew up an agreement. In a matter of days,
Tom was signed up, and a few weeks later he was ready to dedicate his days to
moving the business forward. Ren felt, for the first time, that this was no longer
a one-man show. What he had with Tom was a legit company and the seedling
of a powerful operation.

CHAPTER 13

Out of the Crowd and into the Model

"Success is simply a matter of luck. Ask any failure."

—Earl Wilson

Greatly inflated by having Tom on board and still reveling a little from the prior success of Standard Link, now well in the past, Ren was invited by his alma mater to speak to a group of students about start-ups and entrepreneurship.

He had received prior positive feedback that he was a good speaker, at least as long as he prepared and practiced. In this case, it hit him that he was embarrassingly, pathetically unprepared. He had been so busy and focused on every other issue in his business and life that he hadn't given much consideration or thought to this event. In fact, he had almost forgotten about it.

The day of the talk, his lunch with David had run long, so he brought David with him. On the ride down to campus, Ren was so preoccupied with sorting through various thoughts and ideas that had resulted from his conversation with David that he didn't have time to consider expectations for this speaking engagement. If he had, he would've probably expected no more than ten or twenty bored students in a small classroom. He was stunned when they brought him into the front of a large auditorium, teeming with hundreds of buzzing students.

He gulped as he thought, *Are all these people here to see* me? He quickly learned that he was the primary speaker, tasked with carrying the message of the day. Ren was often surprised when people in the community seemed to revere him for being a part of Standard Link's success.

However, as Ren later discovered, he was not as big a draw as his burgeoning ego had hoped. You see, he was then the third in a monthly series of five speakers brought in to address the students. Apparently, the other four were high-profile, legitimately accomplished alumni, which was why students had learned to show up for the talks. While most of them may not have heard of Ren, he had been advertised with the other, better-known speakers, so the students must have assumed that he, too, was a big-time guy. The fact that entrepreneurship had become a hot topic among college students also didn't hurt.

As Ren stepped onto the stage and was glowingly introduced, David quietly slipped away. Ren saw him settle in at the back of the audience.

Caught unprepared and off guard, Ren began by sharing what he had learned at Standard Link. He told some stories of the things he had experienced building the company and selling it, and he shared some of his current aspirations towards the new company.

What initially began as faked confidence, which Ren felt was received with mixed feelings, began to feel increasingly like true self-assuredness. He was comfortable in front of what seemed like a very engaged audience. He began to consciously use the tools he had learned about public speaking: to use one's posture and gestures to draw the audience in. Right before Ren felt like he had completely depleted his resources, he closed his mouth.

"Questions?" Ren then asked.

The first one was about ways to raise venture capital, which Ren answered with some smart-sounding ideas, largely parroted back from things he had heard from Charlie Frank and others. The second student wanted to learn ways to come up with new ideas. "Well, it helps to understand your customer's needs—the problem they are trying to solve—better even than they do," Ren replied with his best attempt at sounding confident. There was a very loud, distracting cough from the back of the room as he finished.

The third question came from a professionally dressed, studious-looking young lady seated near the middle of the front row.

"What's the secret to becoming a successful entrepreneur?" she asked.

Ren expanded his chest, extended his hand, palm down, and spoke with a deeper voice in a flawed attempt at a confident gesture, like a poorly coached politician.

"Well," he began, "you come up with a great idea in a big-opportunity space, put together a great team, work hard, and then make smart decisions."

Ren felt eager to move to the next question, but before he could continue, he was interrupted again by what was clearly an intentional sound. It was like a combination of a cough and the bark of an injured animal, and again it came from the back of the room. Ren considered it rude but was going to ignore it—until he realized the noise came from David.

With almost no pause and no intention of snark, and only genuine respect and appreciation that hopefully came across to the audience, Ren gestured toward his mentor in the back, behind the last row of students, and said, "Well, my good friend back there has built two very successful public companies. He knows better than I do. David, what do YOU think is the secret to becoming a successful entrepreneur?"

David stood up and with a clear, authoritative voice that was loud enough for the entire audience to hear, announced, "Well, it's about two things, really—timing and business model. And of those, having the right business model is more important. Because when you have it, you will find yourself in the right place, at the right time. Only then will the hard work help you make smart decisions."

The students were watching this exchange with the speaker on stage and the old guy sitting in the back, seemingly surprised and enraptured.

"It's simple cause and consequence, really. The right business model will cause you to have the best opportunity for a great idea," David continued, speaking to a quiet, attentive auditorium. "Similarly, the model will cause you to find a great team, because they will be attracted to what you do, because you are doing it right. You will work hard but it won't even seem like it as much, because you'll be working the right way, thanks to your model—you'll work for both yourself and for your customers, who are your partners. Your decisions, too, will be smarter because they'll be driven by what really solves the customers' problems and creates value for them."

Ren watched the students as David lectured. Their bodies were turned to face him, and many nodded as the man spoke.

"Beyond that," David concluded, "if you do it right, your customers will become invested in your success. They will be very loyal to you, and even become your best and most credible sales force. All because they feel like a part of your business. Which is all driven by the right customer-led business model."

It seemed like a lot to process, even to Ren—and probably went over the heads of most of the students. He didn't exactly know how to follow David's speech beyond the genuine, appreciative "Thank you" that he offered before his audience.

Mercifully, the session had gone on long enough to wrap up the gathering. Ren was able to make a couple of complementary, derivative points about what David had said about the importance of a customer-driven business model and to thank everyone.

He was surprised at the appreciation from the crowd.

The audience, perhaps appreciating Ren's sincerity, gave him a standing ovation. At least a couple of dozen students lingered in the auditorium to meet and connect with Ren and David afterwards.

Later that night, when Ren reflected back on the event, he felt like he should have known how David would answer the question posed by the bright young student. It was one of the many times he spoke of the importance of finding the right business model.

Ren had noticed that there didn't seem to be as many books, written by gurus in their field, about business models as there were about other topics regarding building a business. It wasn't something that was often highlighted, he realized, and perhaps many didn't see it as a central issue. David, on the other hand, kept going on and on about it, pestering Ren as he crafted the pieces of his endeavor, attempting to formulate a road map for the company in the form of a business model.

It would be some time before Ren fully understood the concept, but these early, repeated conversations paved the way for him to adopt a business model that would set him and his company up for success.

CHAPTER 14

Unconventional Networking

"You are one positive change, one new choice, or one unexpected chance
away from a different way of life. Hold on tight and don't let go.
Rediscover the original story that has been inside you all along."

—Christine E. Szymanski

"Always tip well—including and particularly at Waffle House!" That was one of the early gems of advice Tom Strong had shared with Ren after a night out in college, as they were feasting on greasy food and sobering up in the wee hours of the morning.

Even as cheap as he was—and even at times when he didn't have much money—Ren always wanted to get the bill for his table. For one matter, he felt guilty asking servers to break up a check. He also didn't want to have to worry about the cost of what he ordered, in the consideration of anyone else that might have to pay for it. He never wanted to feel like he owed anyone, and getting the check felt good, as if he was doing something nice for whomever he was meeting. And he could learn about the other person by how much they protested to pay for themselves. But most of all, it was because he believed in tipping well.

Ren had always been a good tipper. He was raised to appreciate that wait-staff work hard and count on their tips. He never felt comfortable being served by another person. And his parents had been adamant that if he couldn't afford to tip well, he should order less or not go out at all, rather than shortchanging a hardworking waiter or waitress.

And, to Tom's point at the time, Waffle House waitstaff worked particularly hard for what they got; those industrious servers were often stiffed by college kids who came in drunk, late at night.

Tom's wise words often echoed in Ren's mind, and from that point forward in his life, he always tipped especially well at Waffle House. He did it for its own sake, with no expectation of any karmic bonus. But sometimes good deeds do come full circle.

———

When starting a business, almost nothing goes as fast or as easily as the entrepreneur hopes. Thanks to Tom and other connections, Ren had been introduced to members of the operations team at Avery University Health System, a highly respected healthcare provider that seemed enthusiastic about Ren's idea. They had been trying to create their own solution for measuring important functions, using statistical process control, for a few years with limited success. They felt like Ren's outside perspective and concept were valuable, and he took all of Avery System's feedback as validation. The operations department seemed to be willing to provide him with their five years of experience and a couple of competent, full-time people to help drive the initial build-out.

As Ren was working with them on an initial agreement, the legal department at the hospital got involved in creating a contract. They wanted to negotiate several key points, most of which, other than the essential consideration of who owns the data, didn't seem particularly important to Ren at the time. And they seemed to be going out of their way to move slowly and to be hard to communicate with.

At their regular Waffle House meeting a few weeks into the negotiations with the legal team, Ren expressed to David his ongoing frustration that it was taking longer than expected to get the Avery relationship going.

Despite enthusiasm from the operations department team members, the agreement was moving forward at a snail's pace. Ren wondered if it was worth waiting any longer—and whether he might be better off looking for another organization to work with.

David listened carefully and nodded. "Their legal team has no incentive to move quickly. It's their job to be risk averse. In fact, if they do say 'yes,' they might get punished for it somewhere down the road. And they're not used to doing this sort of thing. They're going to be hard to work with, particularly on issues about who owns the data.

"What you need is a champion in the Avery organization to push this through. Do you know anyone with real influence to make it happen?" David asked. "Does the department head that wants to work with you have the clout to push it through?"

Ren thought about it. He didn't want to risk his new relationship with the department head by seeming rushed or even desperate, at least not yet, and couldn't come up with a workable solution.

Even after David had gone, Ren remained behind for a bit to finish his task list for the day. He was struggling and must have looked visibly frustrated, his brow furrowed as he made notes.

His favorite regular waitress, Laura, sauntered up and dropped a ticket from her yellow pad at his table.

"You know, I can hook you up with somebody at Avery, if you want."

Ren stared at Laura.

"I didn't mean to eavesdrop, but I heard y'all talk about Avery Hospital. My brother-in-law works there. Not sure what he does exactly, but he is some sort of big shot there."

Ren felt the kindness of Laura's offer, but wondered if she realized just how many people worked at Avery. She must have noted the doubt on his face when she added, "He drives a really nice car, and they live in a huge house."

Before Ren got a chance to say anything, he watched as Laura's purple-painted fingernails tapped through numbers on her phone until she found the one she was looking for. Laura tore a blank page from her yellow order pad and scrawled a name and number.

"Here ya go. Tell him I told you to call," she said.

Ren took the piece of paper, nodded, and smiled.

"That's very kind of you."

Laura winked at him. "Don't mention it."

While he appreciated the sentiment, Ren was skeptical about the usefulness of calling the number on the ticket. Absentmindedly, he put the number in his notebook and left.

———

David encouraged Ren to find a couple of other initial customers. He reasoned that, even if the Avery System deal ever worked out, if he only built the software for an elite university system, he would probably only be able to sell it to other similar customers. These elite university systems were a small universe of organizations that unfortunately would believe (erroneously, according to David) that they could build a solution themselves. It would be tough to sell to them under the best of circumstances, at least until they failed in their own efforts and finally came back, years later.

David cautioned Ren that finding the right initial customers was one of the most important and challenging things for any startup of this sort. He suggested that Ren probably needed at least nine customers that were satisfied and therefore could give references. This would give him sufficient credibility to sell more broadly.

He warned that it was critical to find the right initial customer organization—and particularly the right champions to drive the engagement within those organizations—to give Ren's new venture its best chance to succeed. He needed to find risk-takers who were secure enough to take the chance and established enough to have credibility within their own organizations to make it succeed.

For one ideal example, David introduced Ren to an accomplished and well-known CIO at Superior Health, a progressive multi-facility hospital system in New Jersey. Another friend introduced him to a strong champion who was a well-respected chief operating officer in a small, rural, for-profit hospital called Carsley Healthcare, located in Michigan. Both were willing to work with Ren to let him build the same solution he was working on for Avery. Those connections ended up being better than Ren could have hoped for. It meant he had access to experienced, competent, progressive, and credible partners in building out his initial software, which was more important than he could have articulated—and it ultimately turned out to be invaluable.

Of course, it took more hassle and time than expected for Tom Strong to move out of his old job and into his new role. And getting Tom set up and started took some administration and consideration. Ren had to very quickly set up a W-2 employee as well as address payroll, compliance, and other issues.

Ren had been working on his business plan. Depending on where the roller coaster had him each week, he spent half his time leaning heavily on David's advice and half of it frustrated with David's harping. *This is my business. Not his.*

He was designing his solution, working on initial contracts and customers, and doing what would have looked like building a company. And he was very glad for continued guidance from his mentors when Tom officially started. Ren really felt like he had a real business.

CHAPTER 15

Gathering Support

> *"Anything is possible when you have the*
> *right people there to support you."*
>
> —Misty Copeland

"Surround yourself with the right resources and service providers," Joe Chapman pontificated over a bowl of cheese grits in an early morning visit to Waffle House.

"And you can start now with the right attorney for the type of company you are starting. If you were setting up a small lifestyle business, you could possibly get away with setting up an LLC using cookie-cutter incorporation documents from some online service. Or, if you only needed a simple entity setup, you might be served best by a smaller law firm. But if you're starting an aggressive-growth business that might raise capital with multiple shareholders, or might have intellectual property issues, or might have litigation or other bigger needs down the road, you probably just need to pay more now for a big law firm. Set up the best structure now to prepare, up front, for the matters that will likely arise. You'll end up saving money and trouble if you invest a little more and prepare better now."

Joe also urged Ren to also place a priority on *fit*—the right lawyer and accountant who had the most relevant experiences with similar technology startups, perhaps even catering to the same industry. Joe wanted Ren to set the right sort of professional tone and parameters in those relationships.

"And don't use one of your buddies. If your lawyer or accountant are your neighbor or longtime friend, they're probably the wrong person," he cautioned, knowing that mixing friendships and business often creates a lack of objectivity. "You can find someone you know, but it eventually seems to go bad when people go with their personal friends for that stuff."

On Joe's advice, Ren had set up an LLC. Joe liked to point out that he wasn't an accountant. But it was easy to see that he had a lot of experience and useful guidance. As Joe pointed out, different forms of entities had different advantages, including liability protections and tax efficiency. Ren went with the LLC because he didn't foresee as much need to issue any special class of stock initially, and the tax considerations made sense.

Working through the process, he and Joe walked through many considerations, including the balance between the consequences of earnings being taxed at corporate rates or being passed to an owner's personal return. And there were a number of other factors, such as when the company might become profitable, prospective future investors' interests, and anticipated future employee ownership.

At that point, Ren had been guided to elect to be taxed as a partnership, with the ability to pass losses (that he would presumably have at first) through to his personal return. He might convert to a corporate-taxed entity later, when it made more sense to do so with earnings and possible other types of ownership for employees or investors. But the biggest thing that Ren took from all of this was to talk with the right accountant and attorney before doing anything about the entity. It seemed that tax treatment and other considerations varied at times—the best fit depended on circumstances and expectations for the business.

Wrestling with all the issues, he was glad to get a call from an old attorney friend, Gary Andersson. Gary had heard about Ren's new business venture. And he was always amusing. "Before you screw up too much," he said, "let's go play a round of golf. Maybe I can try to fix your swing and set you straight about your business at the same time."

Gary was a civil litigator, but had been around a lot of corporate contract work and other civil and criminal matters of all sorts, to a point where he had a great, broad set of experiences and perspective.

Ren hadn't even considered taking time to play golf since well before the sale of Standard Link. He had always struggled with the cost and time commitment. It seemed like when he played, there were two meters running in his head—one telling him how much time he was taking and another telling how much money it was costing—every time he lost a ball in the woods. But he looked forward to catching up with Gary and was always glad to get his advice.

While dragging him through 18 holes and a half-dozen beers on a challenging course, Gary had tried to scare him about finding the best lawyers and being as prepared as possible for when problems would arise. It worked.

"How many people do you trust? Really?" Gary had asked, rhetorically. "Let's say there are twenty-five people that you feel like would never hurt you or sue you."

He continued, "I can tell you that you are wrong about some number of them. I don't know if you are wrong about three of them or five of them. And I certainly don't know which ones you are wrong about. I just know from all of my experiences that you are.

"The moral to the story is . . . don't trust anyone. It isn't personal. Look, I love people. I really do. I just don't trust them and don't want you to."

Letting that soak in for a moment, Gary kept going, "And even if you have them right now, people change. Once you are successful, someone will try to take something from you, even if you didn't do anything to wrong them. I see it every day and have seen it a thousand times. It's a matter of time until one of your employees or customers tries to sue you."

Gary shared examples of how some of the litigants he saw may have started out with good intentions but ended up with frivolous accusations against them that would cost a lot to fight or settle—a painful, expensive process and overall headache for a busy entrepreneur. "Sometimes they have legitimate reasons, or at least think they do. But a lot of times they're just trying to get money.

"The question is not *whether* someone will try to take from you when you become successful. The question is *who* and *when*. From all of my experience in the courtroom, in many cases, it is often one of the people that you trusted. Maybe you were wrong or maybe they changed.

"I've seen it put companies out of business and ruin people's livelihoods. You owe it to your employees and customers and the other owners to protect their interests by being prepared and careful," Gary said.

"You once told me," Ren said, "that not all lawyers are created equal."

He was surprised at how Gary was emphatic on that point. With a smile, he said, "And good lawyers know all the laws. But great lawyers know all the judges!"

Gary advised Ren to build strong working relationships with all of the big firms in town. And he advocated that those big firms might have some political clout to scare off people that were fishing for an unmerited settlement in a frivolous action, thereby helping with future problems. He noted that if all the great large firms in town—which sometimes had the best relationships with the judges—would theoretically be "conflicted out" because he was working with them, it was harder for anyone to use them against him! And these bigger firms could easily pull in specialists for other issues, ranging from intellectual property to case law in other states to anything else.

Ren did prefer to use smaller-firm lawyers for many things. He often found that a smaller-firm attorney could be just as competent and might be more likely to really understand what he was trying to accomplish, as well as be more responsive. Sometimes they were running small businesses themselves and had relevant insight.

Another point was that risk-averse lawyers might kill a deal that was worth it, out of an abundance of caution. Ren was learning that from the legal team at Avery. It was their job to be protective, as anything else could also get them in trouble. But Gary felt that, for an unconventional startup, maybe the best attorneys would recognize when a matter was risky but worth facing in order to achieve the company's goals and avoid problems that could be significant later on as the company grew. In Ren's situation, that kind of lawyer would be better than one who wanted to eliminate all risk and prevent him from ever taking any steps forward.

The moral of Gary's golf-cart diatribe was this: Be cautious, be prepared for anything, and protect yourself by getting good lawyers. It was a cynical way of looking at the world but consistently paid off.

——

Ren also needed to find the right accounting firm to set up the right bookkeeping, prepare returns, and advise on all the matters that would arise.

"Of course, you want someone who's good to work with," Joe had volunteered when discussing this. "You want to look for competence and experience that is relevant to what your needs are. I suggest you interview at least three firms and try to learn from all of them. Then pick the best fit. And the good ones are valuable for their guidance and understanding of your situation, even more so than they are for their contract work and execution. Notice how much they listen and 'get' you."

Ren inquired, "How often should I meet with my accountant?"

"At first, a lot," Joe replied. "They're super important, but it's kind of like your lawyer. You have to listen to them, but there's also a risk in listening too much." Rolling his eyes, he added, "A lot of accountants and lawyers think they're great businesspeople, but they really aren't. They're smart people, but they're not necessarily experienced with your issues. You *have* to listen to them. On risky exposures, you need to go with what they say and trust their views over your own.

"But there will be some judgment calls where you know your business and understand your plans better. I'll give you an example, Ren. Let's say you expect to be profitable soon, and may want to hire employees with a special class of stock where they don't vote or dilute your ability to execute and make decisions as much—you want to get your accountant and lawyer's advice, but you will ultimately have a better idea of that than them. And that could affect whether you might want to consider being a C corporation.

"Look, there are lots of little tricks. For example, public companies, the world I came from more recently, are experts at managing their earnings. But, even for you and your software, depreciation can matter as you approach future earnings. And on some things in another business that I am involved in, the true useful life of their biggest asset is much shorter than the speed at which you could depreciate it. I don't want them—or you—to count on these accountants to advise ahead of such things. You need to think through those things yourself first, and then go to them for guidance."

As the business moved forward, Ren learned that having great lawyers, accountants, bankers, and other service providers was huge.

A lot of it was CYA, as Joe described it: "Cover your ass."

There was an ever-changing or difficult-to-navigate universe of compliance stuff, from keeping up with the terms of the Fair Labor Standards Act to how to protect against potential exposures to external civil litigation. Ren had great intentions. But there was so much to learn and keep up with. And he couldn't afford to make mistakes.

There were always going to be liability exposures that sprang from employee drama and anything else.

And while he was always careful of hiring personal friends or relatives for services, he wasn't ready to take that off the table completely, as he did selectively work with them at times and often went to them for guidance and wisdom. Doing business with friends worked out well enough in many instances.

He also wanted any deal with friends or family to be fair and make sense for both. One of Ren's buddies, who owned a truck rental business, explained it best when he said, "Look, every friend wants me to give them a free truck rental. But if I did that, I'd go out of business. Then I couldn't help them or me or anyone. No one would win. So I charge them at the low end of what is fair. And hopefully it pays back in their referrals and being better, safer customers."

Ren did find that family and friends tended to be more likely to get upset or emotional, perhaps due to expectations that were not reconciled appropriately.

He eventually decided to only work with a friend or family member when that person was a better solution than other alternatives. While he held them to that higher standard coming in, he also knew that he needed to be a little more patient, forgiving, and tolerant once they were working together. And he found that it was important to establish firm, clear boundaries, articulated and agreed upon up front, or else that person would, in many cases, take advantage and become a problem.

And Ren increasingly learned the importance of having the right accountants. They were important in compliance in paying his taxes, handling payroll issues, and tons of other considerations.

As Joe had advised, Ren conducted extensive interviews with three firms, learning from all of them. He selected the best fit and brought on an experienced employee of that firm, Brianna Jordan, as basically an outsourced bookkeeper/controller.

Brianna came in every Tuesday for at least a few hours to help with bookkeeping, bill payments, eventually accounts receivable, and much more. Having someone with her experience and objective insight paid for itself many times over.

Ren also set up his initial bank account. He knew from his prior experiences that he wanted a solid institution with a good balance sheet and a history of good lending practices. One of his biggest priorities was to find a bank that liked to cater to small businesses. He needed a banker that would understand

and look after his interests—and knew how to get things done within the organization's constraints.

Once he started a relationship with the right bank and got the appropriate accounts set up, Ren got credit cards for himself and Tom.

Joe advised him on that front to go ahead and set rules that would apply to everyone, for the purpose of consistency, precedent, and controls—and to avoid affronting anyone by making things less personal. "You have plenty of reason to trust yourself and Tom. But go ahead and come up with the rules now that you will apply for all future employees. Apply this for you and Tom now, to start with.

"As you make those policies about spending limits, utilization, reporting, accountability, and so on, you need to assume the worst and treat everyone as if you don't trust them. Don't make it personal. It's just that you owe it to anyone that depends on your business to have those policies in place." Joe's advice was consistent with Gary's.

"And even though you have reason to trust Tom, you also protect him by having these rules in place. You're protecting him from future accusations and from others around him who might try to take advantage—who might not be as trustworthy as he is. He'll also appreciate that you are treating everyone by the same standards and protecting the company from malfeasance by any future coworkers."

Ren found that American Express cards had some decent protections and benefits for small businesses. And his bank and a few other providers also seemed to cater to small businesses with low fees, decent perks, and reasonable protections.

Joe also warned Ren to be wary that employees would spend his company's money to get points. When that happened, he hoped they didn't have bad intentions and were just being shortsighted in not thinking it through—but their actions did cost the company. He learned to structure and incentivize his company's policies carefully, like those around using credit limits and to enforce across-the-board company rules about justifying expenditures, flying economy class, and more.

Ren had learned from his industrial psychology courses in college that everyone needs to be treated differently, but his career taught him that it was important to apply universal, consistent rules and protocols to everyone. Doing so kept things impersonal and protected everyone throughout the business in many ways.

Soon after Tom joined, he and Ren decided they really needed an office. They didn't need anything fancy and didn't think in terms of trying to impress any customers who might ever visit. But they did want a decent location that would be convenient. The problem was that anything in the location where they were looking was going to be too expensive.

They got lucky. Another of their good friends, Dan McGinty, also had a startup that was growing quickly. His company had grown out of its old space and found a new location, and Dan was willing to sublet their old office to Ren and Tom. Dan even threw in an old conference table and some other furnishings. The office, actually an old house, was its own story, involving a roof collapse, rodents, and squatters living in the basement, among other things. But for this new company, it made a big difference to have a place to work together.

Tom and Ren also set up a simple accounting system. Previously, Ren had used a complex system at Standard Link. It was great, and they had connected it with their Customer Relationship Management solution and used it for many purposes. But to get started in this new business, the easiest solution was QuickBooks. Then, they selected their accounting firm and eventually hired Brianna, for a relatively cheap per-hour cost.

From prior experience, Ren felt that, for the type of business that he was building, it made sense to use a PEO, a Professional Employer Organization, for employee outsourcing. A PEO was helpful for whenever a company was hiring higher-end compensated employees and wanted to provide healthcare benefits. Basically, his employees would be in a co-employment agreement with the PEO and his company, where they were compensated through the PEO, which in turn passed the costs back to his business.

The good thing about a PEO, compared to using a bare-bones payroll service and doing other things for himself, was that it helped extraordinarily with compliance and other HR practices. Pooling employees allowed them to provide much better benefits rates, and they could also provide 401(k) plans and other perks.

Ren did think that in some circumstances, and particularly if he had been going after a tighter-margin commodity type of business, he might have gone with a payroll service.

In price shopping, Ren found that when a company had up to a few dozen employees who were compensated at a relatively high level, as they tended to be in technology businesses, and who received good health and other benefits, the savings in going through the PEO worked out such that their overhead netted out decently, compared to trying to do it himself or through other channels.

After perhaps forty to sixty employees, he had learned at Standard Link that it might then start to make sense to bring more of the HR, administration, and compliance in-house or to do a hybrid model with a payroll service.

In shopping through PEOs, Ren found that none of them wanted to take on a new client with fewer than six employees. He and Tom didn't think it would be long until they hired other employees to get to that point, so they worked out cheaper payroll options for a short time until they got there.

Ren quickly learned that David's sage advice was right on target: "Setting yourself up, from the beginning, with the right service providers—lawyers and accountants and bankers and such—along with setting up the right policies and systems, will pay off in many ways."

CHAPTER 16

Karma Meets Contract

*"Always tip well. Including
and particularly at Waffle House!"*

—Tom Strong

Two weeks after his last Waffle House visit with David, Ren was rifling through his notebook. The piece of paper from the yellow Waffle House order pad fluttered down to his desk. He had forgotten that his favorite server, Laura, had given him her brother-in-law's number. After wrapping up a phone call, he turned the paper over in his hands and decided that he might as well give it a shot.

The other initial customers at Superior and Carsley were working out well so far. But the Avery deal was a huge concern by now, as it was still not moving in their legal department. Ren was beyond frustrated and wondering if it would ever work out. He had wanted Avery to be his anchor, initial development partner. But he couldn't wait on them forever. At this point, what did he have to lose?

He pulled up LinkedIn on his computer and looked up the name on the yellow ticket: Jace Moore. Could this be? Laura's brother-in-law was the hospital's chief legal counsel—the manager over all of the lawyers he'd been struggling with for weeks.

Ren wasted no time calling the number on the yellow ticket and introducing himself. He was surprised that the gentleman on the other end of the call had expected to hear from him.

"Yes, Ren. Thanks for calling. Laura told me to expect you and asked me to help you if I could. Please tell me what's up," Jace said graciously, with the faintest hint of a midwestern accent.

Ren explained his history with the operations staff and where he felt he was bogged down with the legal team. He explained where the sticking points were and why he thought they were not important issues.

Jace listened intently, asked a couple of challenging questions, and quickly identified the point on which his team might be stuck. They worked through the key issues. Ren had to give in on some matters around who "owned" the data, what information could be included when it went on his servers, and how things might be addressed in arbitration. And Avery was able to work around their concerns on compliance in individual health information management. In about ten minutes, they seemed to have worked out a deal that might work well enough for both of them.

Ren thought, *I just wasted two weeks when I could have called this guy!* He was angry at himself for not appreciating how valuable Laura's contact could be.

After breaking through with Avery University Health System and starting to work with and learn from the other organizations in New Jersey and Michigan, the Superior Hospital organization and Carsley Healthcare, Tom and Ren continued to spec out where their solution needed to go. The more it came together, the more the risk and opportunity seemed real.

Ren had been around programming and software development for most of his professional life, but he was far from a hardcore developer himself. And though Tom came with a host of valuable skills, software development wasn't his background either. So they called their developer friend, Dan McGinty, who had found significant success and carved out a solid reputation for creating the kind of enterprise solution they needed. As a friend and advisor, he set them straight on how they should look at their development needs, who they should hire, and how they should approach it.

"Developers are not a commodity," he said emphatically. "You need to hire the best. A great developer is better than ten mediocre developers in many ways.

Your solution needs to be driven by the business need, and a great architect can build out the best way to get there."

Platforms and development environments were becoming increasingly ubiquitous, but they were still not all created equal. Some would better serve their technology and development needs. The biggest takeaway for Ren was that they needed to find a real expert, and to lean on and learn from that person during the development process.

In learning their way through the technologies at Avery, Ren and Tom also reunited with Martin Neep. Martin was another old friend from college. He was a bright, good guy, and his development skills were compatible with the technologies that the Avery system used. After some consideration about whether to hire Martin as a full-fledged employee or as a consultant, Tom and Ren decided to make him an offer to be the company's second employee.

Naturally, there was negotiation around salary, benefits, and ownership, but the timing was perfect for Martin. He wasn't thrilled with his boss or prospective upside at his current company. And the credibility of having Tom on board and their initial customers was a big help. Plus, Martin really loved the idea and agreed to join up.

The team was coming together, Ren felt, almost surprisingly easily.

———

Another early step was to come up with a name for the company and solution. One of Ren's customers, Kate Quisling, the head of the quality department at Avery, kept mentioning how important a great name would be for his branding. She seemed to enjoy working with a startup and to really want Ren and Tom to succeed. Initially, coming up with the name sounded kind of trivial to Ren, but he reached out to a friend of his who was great with creative marketing, and she helped him put pen to paper with a number of options that he then took to Kate and her coworkers, as well as his other first customers at Superior and Carsley. Ren thought that, on this matter, their opinion was more valuable than his own, and he wanted them to feel like their voices were heard.

Ren was selling to people like them: healthcare administrative and operations professionals. Not to technology entrepreneurs like himself. So it made sense to go with their preference over his own. The end result was not the name

Ren would have chosen, but he went with it anyway. And that was the beginning of Dirigat.

Dirigere is Latin for "alignment" and "directed." And, *dirigat* is the plural infinitive case. Basically, Dirigat meant "we are aligning and becoming directed."

For the initial software, they moved forward with the name "HospitAlign." It didn't seem that great, but no one could come up with anything better. And it represented what they did very well.

CHAPTER 17

Fit to Be Hired

"True leadership isn't about having an idea. It's about having an idea and recruiting other people to execute on this vision."

—Leila Janah

Tom and Martin were really making things happen. And the results looked good, too—probably coming together even faster and better than Ren had hoped.

In collaboration with the initial customers, they created a really good, functional mock-up demonstration of the software. They used that to spec out and build out a decent initial product, outsourcing some of the development. It cost more to do it that way, of course. Dan McGinty had cautioned to make sure, if outsourcing development, to at least control and manage the process internally. Otherwise, they would be a less capable, less valuable business and too dependent on the contracted outside developer. But it was still the best option for now.

Hiring the early employees at Dirigat was exciting, challenging, and scary. Ren learned a lot from David, who told him that hiring for a small business presents unique challenges. A bad decision—even a seemingly innocent one by a single employee—could spell disaster. With this in mind, Ren came to think of each and every early hiring decision as mission critical for the success of his company. A larger, more established company was better prepared to weather the storm of a bad hire, whereas an unwise hiring decision in a startup like his could be devastating. Ren came to believe very strongly in the importance of hiring the right people with the ideal personality traits to make them successful, pouring what some might consider an inordinate amount of time and effort into vetting the candidates. Who they hired now would define the company's culture and direction.

"At a big company," David explained, "they traditionally wanted people to work 'in a box.' For companies that have thousands of employees, they need them to perform their job descriptions. They seem to hire people like commodities; they look for credentials, personality testing, or whatever formula they have," David explained, over another breakfast.

"They've traditionally been scared of people stepping outside their job descriptions too much—when their employees get 'cowboy,' they start having problems." David emphasized the word "cowboy" as he said it. "They need to replicate what works. Their thought process has traditionally been about 'cookie cutter.' And they see it as expensive and risky when employees move beyond their boundaries or take unprecedented actions.

"Of course, the world is changing," he went on. "Fewer people have traditional assembly-line jobs. Big companies probably don't want their employees in their job description boxes as much anymore. And they're probably learning to live with the consequences of that, as they may have to.

"And for you, as a small business, you should never hire people to work in a box of their job descriptions. Not only are you not plugging in a commodity hire in a role—the difference between the right person and an okay person can be extraordinary in a startup—you actually have to find people that work best outside of their box." David was on a roll now. And Ren was really getting caught up in this.

"As a small business, you need people that think outside that job description. And when they do, you just need to live with the risks associated with their free thinking. You may have a few role-players that don't fit that. But for the most part, you need most of your employees to wear multiple hats—and to think of the big picture, in terms of how to solve a customer's problems and make a happy customer, and how to make money for the business."

Ren weighed this in considering some risks and consequences that he was already living with from people trying new or unorthodox things.

David continued, "Most of the people you will hire—perhaps unless they have been entrepreneurs themselves or worked in one of the few environments that encourages independent or innovative thinking—will have a hard time with that, at first. It sometimes takes six months to even know if a person can do that. And you have to let them make mistakes. It can be very risky and painful. But with having the freedom to think big picture and make mistakes, they feel more ownership of their job and become better contributors.

"That's hard to do. But you need to do it. And you shouldn't mind when someone makes an honest mistake, with good reason, in an effort to do something constructive. Just know that some people will take advantage of you. And people change and circumstances change. Having so many employees thinking outside their box and doing unconventional things, even with good reason, often has costs and consequences. But it's necessary for Dirigat and other startups to take those risks. If you survive them, you typically end up better off."

Acknowledging that past performance is often the best predictor of future success, Ren still strongly believed in giving people opportunities to prove themselves and overcome their past. But for a startup with your first employees, you typically can't afford to give too many risky chances. He also knew people could change, though. And he always wanted to hold out hope that they would. Ren and Tom—and particularly David—could try to mentor and coach and encourage a person, but, in most cases, that person had to *want* to improve and be ready for it before there could be any significant movement. It was particularly unlikely that people would change basic character traits quickly. And it was unfair and unrealistic to expect them to.

Ren passionately loved the idea of finding a diamond in the rough that had been through trying circumstances and just needed the right opportunity and expectations and role models. But the early stages of a startup were not the right time or place for that scenario.

As David said, "When someone is overcoming their past issues, they do it better in the right environment. And what you are doing now is creating an environment of winners with the right success factors and positioning. Then, when you can afford it and surround them with the right people and culture, maybe you can take chances on people with potential upside but poor predictors in their past. But it would be a disaster to try that now, in a startup. Instead, you have to do everything you reasonably can to learn about people and their past.

"Beyond that, mistakes happen. You *should* get mad if someone makes the same dumb mistake, over and over again. And you should let them know that you hate mistakes that hurt customers or cost you a lot of money. But it's okay to overlook—or maybe even encourage, to a degree—mistakes of effort, at least once you can afford to do so."

Exchanges Ren had with his father years ago came to his mind in a flash. It made so much more sense now, as Ren thought back to the jobs he had, working for the family business.

In one particular case, Ren recalled that when he had complained that a job at the company could be done more functionally, Mark Hatcher had responded, "I know."

Flabbergasted at first, Ren said, "You *know*? You *own* the company, Dad! It could improve your business. You know better, and you don't do anything about it?" He was incredulous.

"I can't do everyone's job for them," Mark had told him, all those years ago. "The more I tell them what to do, the less they'll think for themselves. It will also defeat the purpose of even having these people to do these jobs, if I'm doing it for them. And of course, I could never do it for all of them. What I really need is for them to do better, of their own volition. To take ownership of the problem and come up with the best way, themselves. That's a thousand times more powerful. They will care more and feel more invested and rewarded. But the more I tell them, the less likely they are to get there."

The point had sunk in a bit with Ren before, but it only really dug in now. David drove it forward: "Particularly for high-level managers in a startup or small business, you may not have the bandwidth to invest in getting them going. You probably have a job description and budget for them, but just being straight with you, you really don't have the time or wherewithal to hold their hand. And, in my experience with my companies, I think you are sometimes better off basically just throwing them to the wolves.

"It is weird and hard for some people when they start with you—and you basically almost say, 'Go figure out your job and do it.' But, the right person for a startup like this sometimes flourishes in that environment. You may pay a price for all that down the road at some point. But those can become your best, most valuable employees. They will better identify and solve problems or find new opportunities on their own.

"Hiring the right people and empowering them and putting them in the right position is a big deal. And as a startup, you can't really afford many—or maybe any—misses. I don't mean that to put even more pressure on you. You're probably putting enough of that on yourself right now. But it helps you to think of things in that context and frame your hiring that way. Hopefully you will invest your search in the right ways."

Ren wanted the very best people, and fortunately, the combined relationships of himself, the current Dirigat team, and their advisors were huge in their relevant networks. So many of the best hires were referred from people they shared mutual connections with. Their initial team was small but proficient, with a broad range of skills. Curtis Bedford was a solid young technologist and an enthusiastic team member with bright ideas. Aric Richtor was a hardcore developer. He was a coding and development wizard, and, working alongside Curtis, he could take a vision and turn it into computational magic.

Tom described another new hire, Chip Flannery, to Ren as an "athlete," using an analogy from a football team. "Some big, fast players were going to be slotted as cornerbacks or tailbacks. Bigger, heavier players would tend to be placed at the line position that best suited their talents and body types, as would quarterbacks, receivers, and other positions. But," Tom noted, "it's also good to have some generic players that can do a lot of things. Chip Flannery is like that."

And then there was the one that brightened everything up—Cindy Day. While less technical than Chip, Cindy was also somewhat of an "athlete" in that she could take a customer's need and bring everything else together. She was effective in working with customers, often collaborating with them on design, development, and implementation, and then bringing it all back to the team to make things happen. Or, as Cindy loved to say, she was the "Queen of Get Shit Done"!

———

The months fell away as Ren and the team spent their days developing their solution and dealing with whatever the *emergency du jour* was. The Villain was always present. But the team found themselves enthusiastic and somehow having fun, at times, through all the stress.

When the weather was nice, they would picnic on a table behind the office, leading to new funny stories involving the nearby dumpster, a squirrel, or making fun of Chip—or some combination of those things—almost every time.

A lot of the bonding occurred outside the office. The team regularly had working lunches together. And occasionally someone would set up a bowling night or other activity. Some of them even invested a little time into a Habitat for Humanity build. As the team coalesced and got into a working rhythm that produced increasingly promising results, Tom continued to work hard through his relationships in the industry and from referrals from the initial customer-partners.

It wasn't easy. And it didn't go as quickly as they would have liked. But they now had paying customers, a decent initial solution that worked well, and plenty of market validation for it.

CHAPTER 18

Giant Baby Steps

"You can practice shooting eight hours a day, but if your technique is wrong, then all you become is very good at shooting the wrong way. Get the fundamentals down and the level of everything you do will rise."

—Michael Jordan

Tom had added a couple of new systems as customers and was going out to the broader market, beyond the initial development partners at Avery and Superior and Carsley. Dirigat was selling for real now. With a couple more customers paying them real money and expecting results, the team at Dirigat was learning the hard way about installation and implementation. One of the toughest challenges was getting customers to utilize the system in the best ways to improve processes and outcomes.

That led to a services component for the solution, which pleased David to no end, as it moved them toward his better model. "People want to buy a solution," he reminded Ren, "not just a tool."

The team would help a hospital to evaluate a problem and articulate the best, most functional solution—maybe around bed utilization efficiency, emergency department turnaround times, surgical supply costs, predictive staffing, or anything else important to the organization. To get there, they might offer a limited amount of consulting from best practices in other organizations, wrapped around data analysis, and sometimes tailoring custom-developed solutions—all within the HospitAlign software, as they had decided to call it. Tom and Cindy started collaborating with the early customers to work on development, implementation, and best practices. Although Tom wasn't ready to charge much for it, they were collaborating more and more with the customers to improve practices for tracking, for example, supply costs, infection rates, handwashing, and much more.

And now well over a year and a half since the original Avery deal and initial software development, there was another massive rise in the roller coaster. When the company that acquired Standard Link went public, the valuation exploded. This was a huge deal, as Ren was finally able to cash in some of his stock. Having money for the first time in his life certainly didn't suddenly solve all of his problems. It just significantly changed them.

The energy at home seemed to tick up notably after the cash-in with the public offering, too. Ren continued to be a really cheap guy, happily living as frugally as ever in his personal and family life. He wanted to be that way. But at least he was no longer apprehensive about his career prospects and being able to provide for his family. That was a huge weight off his chest and changed everything when he walked in the door each day to Caulie's happy dance. Even if he never talked to Tiffany about getting past that insecurity, she clearly appreciated his acting less distant, at least toward her, as often.

Tiffany also seemed to appreciate that they started eating dinner out a little more. She bought herself a new dress, which Ren failed to notice. On some level, the positive feelings among Ren and Tiffany seemed to go over well with RJ. Of course, Caulie was always going to be happy, in any case.

Now that he could afford to do so, Ren started investing some of his newfound capital toward hiring and technology to fuel the growth of the company.

David didn't want Ren to invest his own money into Dirigat. He kept emphatically pointing out his usual perspective that "the best businesses are built on customers' money." And, if Ren just *had* to get investments along the way, it was usually better to at least get a lot of it from value-added external investors, such as a strategic partner. "Besides," David added, "if you can't convince someone else to invest in it, it means you should at the very least take a hard look at whether you should be doing it yourself."

Ren really appreciated David's reasoning and his concern for Ren's money.

He even knew that what David said was right—for anyone else. But this was different. This was the one exception. *This time David is wrong. He keeps going on about my lack of objectivity. But the market is ready, and the timing is perfect.* What could go wrong?

Ren continued to believe that his company—his baby—was a sure thing. It was the only business ever founded that could not possibly fail. The time was now, and the iron was hot!

As he began injecting capital here and there as needed for hiring and payrolls, he initially rationalized that he was just investing ahead of receivables, which David was okay with.

And when the company brought in a new sale or big growth in a new customer organization—and needed to staff-up in advance and to add servers and resources to deliver on those sales—David even seemed okay with that, for the most part. David did become concerned, however, at those times when the company invested in a new idea before it had sold or when they tried to make a smart, strategic hire ahead of need.

Ren came to regret many of those cases when the company got poor or even negative payback on the resources and people they added in advance of their needs. And their offerings sometimes missed the market, as their anticipations of what the customers would buy were off the mark at times. For example, they built out strong capabilities around labor cost management, only to struggle with their timing, as labor was in particularly high demand at the time they rolled out the solutions and the market was bracing for other priorities at the time. Customers were not ready to embrace or understand their opportunity in that, yet.

Even when these investments paid off, he was not doing as much to make the business—at least from a replicability and sustainability perspective—a better company.

Motivated by what seemed to be a real need for Dirigat in the market, Ren felt a ton of urgency to deliver while the demand and market opportunity seemed so acute.

But, as David put it, "You go slower now so you can be a better business that can go faster later. Even though you think you have to do it now, you almost always have more time than you think. And it's often not the first to market that ultimately wins. It's more important to do it best.

"We see visionary entrepreneurs that have a product or idea and go out and raise a lot of money and build their solution and sell their company for a ton of new money. Everyone wants to be them. But at least for you with so much depending on you now, a wiser course might be for you and your company to not count on those things—but instead to position for a better chance to stand the test of time."

While it got tiresome to Ren hearing the same thing over and over again, David also kept giving his rant about the importance of business model and being a sustainable, replicable business, as opposed to just being a product and solution. He had a recurring lecture about "the Apple guy" (presumably Steve Jobs) and a few other high-profile, visionary entrepreneurs being exceptions that proved his rule—and why they could get away with it—and why Ren should not try to do that now, with his and his employees' livelihoods on the line.

"Those guys are great at product positioning. Sure, they came up with great ideas. In some cases, they turned them into great products. But most of them had prior successes and credibility and capital before they ever got good at it. And they were even good at convincing people to want what they were going to sell them—which you are not good at and is very hard for a small startup to get to."

He would continue in this recurring rant, "Don't forget that the Apple guy got fired from there his first time, and there were plenty of times where their viability could have gone another way before he found all that success.

"Even for him, timing or other factors beyond his control could have gotten in the way. There could have been a recession, a pandemic, regulatory barriers that might not have made sense but happened anyway, or any other kind of disaster."

David liked to close that lecture with words to the effect that "I don't want to take any credit from those guys. We like to notice them. And I am grateful for what they do. But, there are very few of them. And, for every one of them, there are at least hundreds—maybe thousands—of other smart people that had great ideas and raised money and shot for huge, ambitious ideas that failed spectacularly. Being a startup is risky enough as it is. And your employees and customers and your family are depending on you. Do you want to bet your livelihood and theirs without giving yourself the best chance to survive—and a much better chance to be at the right place at the right time, pulled there by your customers?

"Basically, I want you to set up as well as possible to be successful. I want you to take luck out of it as much as possible. And you don't have the money and credibility and positioning and marketing the Apple guy had before he ever got good at coming up with what people would love. I want to give you the best chance to be at the right place at the right time without luck or any of that. That is what this is about."

David put a fork in the point with "Sure, luck can play a role. But for most businesses that are not doing things right, even great luck will not matter enough to help. You should never depend on it as your strategy. Find the best model to give you the best chance to get there. And someday, when you are the successful one, with the credibility and resources and experience to do it, maybe then you can tell people what they are going to buy next."

CHAPTER 19

Of Cats and Breaks

"The only sure thing about luck is that it will change."

—Wilson Mizner

Bzzzzzzzz . . . bzzzzzzzz . . . bzzzzzzzz . . .

It took a moment for Ren to process what was happening. *Where am I? What is that?* The large red numbers on the alarm clock on the dresser told him that it was 4:38 a.m.

Bzzzzzzzz . . . bzzzzzzzz . . . bzzzzzzzz . . .

He picked up the vibrating phone and fumbled for the green button that stopped the buzzing. Pressing the phone to his ear, in a sleepy, rising tone, he inquiringly said, "Hello?"

Ren left his phone on vibrate and always answered. He was the alarm call for his home, his office, and for a few others' homes. And one never knew when there could be any sort of emergency. But he certainly didn't expect this call.

Tiffany was awake now and listening intently, with a worried look, in the faint light from their alarm clocks and the glow of the phone.

There was a frantic-sounding voice on the other side of the call. "Hey, Ren. This is Chip." At least his voice seemed wide awake.

The call was hard for Ren to process at first. "Me and Aric," Chip continued, "were working late tonight. We were doing a development session with the team from Avery . . ."

Ren pictured Aric, one of the new contract developers on the team. As he put together that this was the critical team from their initial partner, the Avery University Health System, he was starting to get even more worried. An excited call at 4:30 in the morning was rarely a good thing. And any problem with those guys would be devastating.

Chip continued quickly, ". . . and I guess we hit a wall in our work and decided to go out for a beer. Somehow, one thing led to another, and we ended up at the Cat's Meow in midtown. I think Aric thought it would be a chance to impress the Avery guys and maybe earn some points with them. But it didn't work out exactly that way . . ."

Ren didn't want to panic yet, but was ready for Chip to get to the point.

"So what are you saying?" he asked. "That's a strip club. Where is this going?"

"Well," Chip said, "everything was fun and good. At least it was good until it was time to pay our tab . . ." Chip stopped for a few seconds. "Then, I guess the Avery guys had different ideas. We'd all been drinking a lot. There had been a lot of shots. And really, it got pretty crazy. I guess the tab was pretty big by that point. And somehow people started pushing and arguing. It turns out we must have had a misunderstanding earlier when Aric had asked them if they wanted to go out. Apparently at the time, the Avery guys must have thought that meant we were covering their costs. And they didn't like it at the end of the night when they found out that hadn't been the plan.

"As you know, we don't have that kind of credit limit on our company cards or expense accounts. And I guess one of the Avery guys said he didn't want to explain any charges to his wife on his credit card. He had a lot of drinks in him and got pretty aggressive."

Chip's voice got a little less frantic and more serious. "At some point the cops were called. Things got a little ugly. And, long story short, we need to get bailed out."

Within a few hours, Ren had collected everyone's information and worked with a bonding agent to bail out Chip, Aric, and three of the Avery team. None of them seemed to want to talk about what had happened the night before. And Ren never got all the details.

There seemed to be a little blood and some bruises. They must have been in a *real* fight. But everyone just seemed relieved to be out and ready to go home at this point.

The Avery team—the project manager, Rafe, and two of his key guys— didn't have much to say. They seemed very grateful and appreciative to Ren for bailing them out. They all seemed insistent on one thing: "What happened needs to stay here. Please don't ever let anyone find out. Not our wives or anyone at work or anywhere."

Then they all disappeared on their own ways. One of the Avery guys seemed a bit curt toward Aric. But they were very friendly and good toward Ren. And Ren thought the matter was over and everyone was all good. At least for a time.

———

In many ways, the business seemed to really be taking off. The economy and investment environment seemed to be booming. And Ren started getting calls from potential investors and possible future acquirers.

Of course, the business was not at a point yet to present itself seriously to many suitors. But the team was feeling pretty confident at this point.

Ren really appreciated all of the advice and hard work from everyone. *Are we making it? Should I raise some capital now?*

Then came the visit from Tom. "We've got a problem," he said. "Avery has gone dark on us."

It had only been a few weeks since the "Catgate" incident, as Ren and Aric and Chip referred to it. They had all lived up to their agreement not to discuss the matter with anyone else. Really they mostly discussed *not* discussing it. It sort of even seemed amusing to all of them in hindsight.

Eventually both Chip and Aric had lawyered up and were able to plead "no contest" to their charges and pay relatively small fines. Presumably the Avery guys did the same. Ren never heard of any marital stress or other family or personal consequences.

Of course, Tom had figured out that something had happened with Aric and Chip. He noticed when they showed up very late to work the next day, hungover and struggling. Although Tom seemed annoyed that no one wanted to talk about it, he and everyone else had moved on.

Tom did notice that Avery became increasingly less responsive and eventually became uncooperative and wouldn't call back at all. He had no idea what was going on.

"That's messed up," Ren told him. "You know, I've been thinking of taking on some possible outside capital from investors that could help us. One of the main things everyone liked was our contract with Avery. If I have to disclose that the contract is in jeopardy, that would be devastating."

Tom looked a bit ashen. "This is an even bigger deal than that. Just calling it what it is, this could be life or death for the company. With Avery, we look like a good solution to our market. Not only are they one of the main customer organizations we're building with, but they're also our most important reference. If they like us, they can help a lot. But in the small universe of our potential customers, if they don't like us, as a small company with a short history and resulting lack of credibility, well, just being honest, that could put us out of business."

Tom looked away and Ren looked down at his hands for a short time before Tom continued. "We noticed that they started acting a little squirrely about a month ago. They got more and more distant. Now, none of them are returning anyone's calls."

Ren did some quick math in his head. The Cat's Meow night had been just over a month ago. He wasn't exactly sure, but it seemed probable that something from that incident was behind whatever was happening. *What should I tell Tom? What do we need to do?*

He bit his tongue and decided to call Rafe, who was involved that night and was the leader of the technical team at Avery. Ren left a voice message and, anxious but struggling to not seem too desperate, also sent an email asking for Rafe to get back to him.

Ren felt scared and anxious. His company, his baby that he was passionate about, was on the line. He felt like he owed Rafe to call him directly, before doing anything else.

An hour passed. The afternoon passed. Then a day passed. It seemed like a month.

Finally Ren called Kate Quisling, the department head whom he had originally met and worked with to set up the relationship with Avery. She was Rafe's boss and ultimately owned his company's relationship in that organization.

He was relieved when she answered his call on the second ring.

"Hey, Ren. How are you?" He took it as a good sign that she had his number saved in her phone and sounded almost friendly.

"Well, I think I'm good, Kate. At least, I hope so. But that is why I am checking in with you. How are we doing?"

About two seconds passed, as Ren's heart started to beat more quickly, before she responded, "I guess we should talk, Ren." She sounded more serious, pausing again before continuing, "You know I think the world of Tom and really appreciate you and what you are doing. No doubt, we need it."

By that point, Ren was already expecting the "but." And Kate didn't disappoint. "*But*, we seem to have a problem. You know I depend on Rafe and his team. And they are having trouble. They say your team has been unresponsive and is doing a poor job. He says he has been calling your guys and asking for deliverables, but that they're just not providing them. I was going to call Tom or you, anyway," she said, "but Rafe said he would handle it. I think he is worried this will reflect poorly on him. But we need to get moving. Or not."

The "or not" hit Ren like a ton of bricks. The possible implications were devastating. Kate was not a person to issue threats. But in his insecure position, Ren took it that way.

It was easy now to see what was happening. Rafe was basically sabotaging the relationship. In his role, he had the ability to kill the Avery deal, by himself, and probably put Dirigat out of business.

He really wanted to be honest with Kate, to tell her the truth that Rafe was the one that was unresponsive and not doing his part. But he knew that was an even more sure path to a serious problem. And he was not the sort to do things that way, anyway. So, he let it go.

"Thanks for the candor, Kate. There may be a lot more to the story. But the best thing I can tell you is that I will do everything I can to make sure we do right by you."

"I believe that," Kate said with an empathetic voice. "I trust you and Tom. That is what makes all of this so hard. Your word is enough for me. And we really want this to work, too. Thank you!"

The goodbyes were a lot warmer and friendlier on that call than the hello. But Ren knew his company and his employees' and their families' well-being hung in the balance.

Before doing anything else, Ren and Tom combed through the contract with Avery and reviewed all of the development project responsibilities—what each party was tasked with and what they had delivered. They charted calls and emails with the Avery team, including all the times they reached out in recent weeks with no response. They wanted to know any consequences and circumstances before doing anything else.

One of their discoveries was that the contract really didn't have great "outs" or protections for Avery to get out of the deal on short notice. And Dirigat could make a great case for having delivered everything they were supposed to, while it was clear that Avery had not done all that great in holding up their end of the deal. Even before Rafe and his team went dark. There was plenty of documentation that Avery had not provided its agreed-upon deliverables, as well as a trail of email inquiries to the Avery team over the past month, with initially only a few and eventually no responses.

One of Tom's attorney friends said he could make a great case that Avery was in clear breach of contract, with potential financial harm. But Tom and Ren were not litigious. And suing one of their customers would be devastating to their reputation. That was not a course they would pursue.

Ren still felt like he needed to speak directly to Rafe. Doing anything above his head or around him would seem out of line to Ren. Of course, since he wouldn't respond, it would be on Rafe. But it still wouldn't feel right.

Then Ren realized that to this point, he had been calling the usual number for Rafe: his office number. But he could also get his cell number! He had written it down as he needed it, in the bonding process to get him out of jail. And he still had copies of the paperwork, since he was the one that had bailed out Rafe and his team.

It was cool and drizzly as he went out and sat in his car for the call. He didn't want any distractions or any possibility that anyone in the office would hear the call, through thin walls or anything.

"Hello," said Rafe.

"Rafe, this is Ren Hatcher from Dirigat," he offered, hopefully.

It was quiet for a time before he responded, "Hello, Ren. How did you get this number?"

Ren knew better than to ask if this was a good time or to give him time to get away from speaking to him. He wanted to be careful with his words. And it would be best to be direct.

"I got it from the bonding paperwork, Rafe. I am calling to check in with you. Look, I think of you as more than a professional relationship. I have always felt like we were straight up and even friends. But there seems to be some confusion or lack of communication."

He didn't give any time for Rafe to respond or back out yet, as he kept on, "I honestly don't know or care what's going on. I just know this relationship with Avery and you and your team is a big deal to us. We need this to work. What's up?"

There was another pause before Rafe responded, "Look, Ren. I really respect and appreciate you and Tom. I really do. But I just need to get away from whatever happened that night, several weeks ago. I kind of have hard feelings about it."

Ren was trying not to interrupt, but couldn't help himself. As Rafe finished that sentence, he was already advancing, "I have only heard my guys' side of it. And I trust Chip. But I also understand that sometimes people hear different things and have different perspectives on things. Like I said, I don't really care what happened. I just care what we can do to make things work going forward."

Rafe's voice surprisingly turned much sharper. "Ren, I don't think there will be any way to go forward. I . . . really . . . just sort of feel done with all this. Nothing personal toward you."

Ren spoke as quickly as he could, "Rafe, this affects Tom's family, my family. Please just consider . . ." before he heard the click of the phone hanging up. He wondered whether his last plea had been heard at all.

Sitting in his seat feeling hollow, Ren had been mentally working through various courses of action. Could they do damage control on their reputation in the industry if they lost the Avery relationship? Probably not. Could he call the Chief Counsel who had helped him get the contract done? Sure. That might work. There wasn't much left to lose at this point. But as he thought through the consequences, that seemed like a horrible last resort. Ultimately, it could hurt the Avery system, as they wouldn't get their software. But it could devastate Dirigat and the team. Probably put them out of business.

Even if they won some sort of lawsuit or reasonable settlement, they might have to give up their dreams and their company. And it even bothered Ren to think that Rafe could end up getting fired or in trouble, when and if it eventually came out that he was the one who was dishonest and not living up to his responsibilities. This all seemed like the opposite of a win-win.

He set a meeting with Tom at their Waffle House for 5 a.m. the next morning to discuss next steps and to move toward a decision, however drastic. It seemed like a potential disaster loomed in any direction.

Then, at about 8:45 p.m., Ren's phone rang. He didn't recognize the number and thought it might be a telemarketer. But for whatever reason, he answered.

"Ren. This is Rafe."

Now was Ren's turn to hesitate, before he responded with his friendliest tone, "Hey, Rafe. I can't tell you how glad I am to hear from you. How are you?"

He responded, "Look, Ren, I'm glad you called earlier . . . I'm calling to apologize. I'm sorry."

Ren finally breathed a little, as Rafe continued, "You know, you called at exactly the right time. Any later might have been too late, from the Avery side. And before that, I was too pissed off to really hear anything. But I started thinking, after our call. I was pretty torqued up after what happened that night. But when you said that about your family and Tom's family, that got me thinking. It made me realize how important this deal with us is, for you and your company, as a new startup . . . I really feel bad and just want to apologize."

Ren was still processing the part about *"any later might have been too late, from the Avery side."* But he didn't have much time to think, as Rafe continued.

"I talked to a friend about what happened and how I have reacted," Rafe said, "and he helped me to realize, I was just really mad at myself for being irresponsible that night and for everything since. And the more I was cutting out your guys and your company, the more that feeling snowballed. You and Tom certainly didn't do anything wrong. In fact, when I think of both of you, I know I can trust you. And so I feel ashamed of treating y'all like I don't.

"I even think whatever happened with Chip and your other guy was just a dumb miscommunication," Rafe continued. "So I'm so glad you got my number and called. And I'm glad you called when you did. But I'm sorry it took that call to help me cool off. Between you and me, I think it was pretty much done between y'all and Avery. And it bothers me that it was over my mistake and my pride. You pretty much saved it by calling at just the right time."

The rest of the conversation was short but warm and friendly.

"Are we good now? We still working together?" Ren really needed to hear the words. And he held his breath until Rafe's prompt response.

"Yessir. We're good."

They agreed to keep the past in the past. As Rafe noted, "I have heard you say before that the only thing that matters about the past is what you learn from it. Well, that's my motto now. I'll take responsibility for making things right."

CHAPTER 20

Taking Responsibility

"He that is good for making excuses is seldom good for anything else."

—Benjamin Franklin

I n the early stages of building the business, every day was a new adventure. The Villain was always there, setting up barriers and challenges. And it seemed that The Villain had many faces. Some of the problems were self-created, but many of the obstacles arose from external factors. At one point, and as the economy went through some challenges, it seemed that the customers were dragging out their payments to Dirigat. And that can be devastating for a small business.

Many large public companies were increasingly pushing out their payment terms to forty-five days, then ninety days, and often even longer, essentially using their vendors as a bank. These public companies were seemingly willing to accept the eventual greater cost that would inevitably be pushed back to them over time. And for many startups, particularly some that are all about operating cash flows and have long ramp-up and delivery times, it is tough to spend a great deal of money and work and focus, deliver results, and then watch with frustration as the company's accounts receivables become bigger and bigger while the next payrolls are looming with insufficient cash to pay them.

As Dirigat was working to meet expenses, Ren didn't mind loaning his newly begotten money into the company in advance of receivables. But, with limited notice when expected payments didn't come in, it took time and expense to get his hands on cash—to settle transactions and transfer funds on short notice to cover expenses. Payrolls ran late twice, and there was one time when they had to do a partial payment to employees.

Those three occasions were a massive deal to Ren and the company. At least some of the team were living almost hand-to-mouth and had their own family considerations. Ren felt like a miserable failure when he let them down. It was personal and abject.

Feeling burned out and beat up—and very rattled after the near disaster with the Avery team that could have put the company out of business—Ren was more than glad to grab another breakfast with David.

Fortunately, the scary mess with Rafe had gone from a near disaster to being a positive. The Avery team were now going out of their way, more than ever, in working with Dirigat and ultimately providing a great technical reference in the industry. Probably only Rafe, Tom, and Ren ever realized how close Dirigat had come to a catastrophe. And Tom probably never knew it was over a misunderstanding, or how one timely phone call and a good turn of character by Rafe had saved everything.

Ren had finally worked through the cash flow problems—thanks to the cash-out from Standard Link and his guaranteeing a line of credit with the bank—but he still felt horrible for letting the company come to paying the team late.

"Good!" said David, carefully and almost gleefully watching Ren's surprised expression. "It's good because you are the kind of guy that'll take it personally and do everything you humanly can to ensure that it'll never happen again.

"For one thing, I heard some of the guys in the development room were really touched when you paid them back the reduced pay with a bonus. They seemed to understand that it happened because of the customers not paying and you not getting enough notice about that. *But,* the most important thing is that you own the problem, commit to overcoming it, and assure them that it never happens again. You're already learning how to get better at collecting your receivables. And you're taking steps to help more in the future, even at great cost and risk to yourself.

"And still, nobody will tell me whatever happened with Avery when things went bad there. But it shows how vulnerable your company still is. You need to evolve to a point where they depend on you. Where they can't afford to break off with you. But whatever happened, I do know you took responsibility and took action and somehow fixed it.

"What I need to know—what you need to know, and what the team and customers pick up on and feed off of—is that you feel personal responsibility," said David. "It's like with your new puppy."

"Caulie," said Ren, looking at David. He might have wondered where this was going, except he had been through enough of David's rants that he no longer speculated on what he was talking about. He was used to it now and had learned to trust that the point would eventually come together and demonstrate something useful and important.

"Sure." David didn't seem that interested in Caulie's name. "When you brought that new puppy into your family, you told me that your son growing up with a dog was a good way for him to learn about responsibility. You're right about that. And to get where you need to go, taking responsibility is where you get started.

"To this point, it has looked to you like your business was getting better. The path so far has felt like fun and games. And maybe there were some good things that happened. I know you have a great idea that people want now. But it sure has seemed to me like you were still just doing the same things as everybody else. And maybe with good timing and being smart, it would have worked out okay, like it did in your last company.

"But for me, sitting back and watching you seeming all cocky about it half the time and scared the other half, the way a lot of startup entrepreneurs are, I don't know if I saw you really getting it. I can't see you doing what you need to do, and becoming who you need to be, to really give your business its best opportunity.

"And Dirigat being at a point where a single customer getting mad at you or not paying their bills fast enough could put you out of business looks like proof to me that the company is still really flimsy. What you really want to become is the kind of company and solution that they can't fire. Where they need you a lot more than you need them.

"You thought you were getting better, Ren. But for me, in some ways, it has sort of felt like you were on a downward path. Because you were not really becoming the leader that you could be and you were not finding the right wisdom—about business model and everything else—to give yourself the best opportunity.

"You could take this as a chance to really turn that around, though. This can be the turning point, if you make it so. If this is going to be when you shift to the right path for your business and yourself as a leader, it needs to start with taking personal responsibility.

"Look, Ren," he continued, "if you took the problem with Avery or the customer's late payments as an excuse, you might *allow* them as an excuse. If you blamed the hospitals that are not paying or the team for not giving you more notice to come up with cash, that would be one thing. But the way you took it so personally and brutally is a great start toward the answer. The greatest winners don't accept excuses. And *anything* that gets in their way, to them—whether legitimate or not—is just an excuse."

Eyes wide and mouth open a bit, Ren looked shaken. "But things happen! You saying that I can never accept anything getting in the way is like saying there will never be any impossible disaster or extenuating circumstance. I've even heard you say that CEOs, head sports coaches, and some other leaders often get too much credit and too much blame.

"Don't get me wrong, David," said Ren, "I think I may see where you are coming from. But isn't that insulting to everyone that has ever had anything go really wrong and not made it?"

David was ready to answer before he even finished: "No. I don't have any interest in insulting them. I don't know everyone's circumstances and have no wish to condemn anyone for any of the health problems, legal disputes, family issues, or anything else that stopped them, along their way, without knowing their travails.

"I told you earlier that all that stuff is the bad guy in your story. It is. In fact, sometimes The Villain even *is* a real person. I can't tell you how many times I have seen companies die because a key employee was stealing or did something irresponsible or unethical. So yes, bad stuff happens. A lot. Every day. Many problems are very real and significant. The only questions are when it will happen, how bad it will be, what you can learn from it, and how you can best protect yourself—before and after," he said with emphasis.

"Saying 'no excuses' in ownership—the way I mean it—is almost like saying 'there's no use in crying over spilt milk.' Girding yourself in that attitude should hopefully make you at least a little more immune to those things or more likely to overcome them in some cases. Does that make sense?" David asked, searching Ren's expression.

Not seeing as much agreement as he wanted, David pressed on, bringing up a recent, unrelated matter that was fresh on his and Ren's minds. "Take Curtis, for example. He's a great guy. He has most of the big things you look for: character, smarts, credentials, sense of humor. So, why is he struggling so much?"

Curtis Bedford was an important part of the development team. In his mid-twenties, he was one of the youngest people at Dirigat. Ren and David liked him—as did most of the team—and were a little surprised that he didn't interact well with a couple of his coworkers at times. Ren could see he was acting insecure and was trying to impress the others.

At one point, Curtis voluntarily opened up to Ren and David at lunch. It turned out that Curtis struggled at times with anxiety. He shared that he had come from a demanding family environment and lacked social confidence, particularly in being around girls. And he was beating himself up about it and wondering what was wrong.

Of course, it was a personal matter. Ren had been reticent to weigh in when Curtis shared about it. David was another story. Seeing that he was looking for help, David spoke with a shocking warmth and empathy. He delivered a tough message with such genuine affection that it only came across as love.

"Look, Curtis," he began, "you have a lot going for you. You say people don't like you. But I think they do generally like you just fine. It's more that they don't respect you. And that may go back to you needing to respect yourself. Respect for yourself, respect for others, and others' respect for you all go hand in hand.

"You could spend less time wondering why you are struggling and acting insecure," David had continued, "and more time doing things that might help you in the direction of where you want to be. Maybe try doing what confident people do until you get there.

"Just sitting around playing video games—as you've told us you do—letting go of your appearance and hygiene, acting all insecure around girls, and then wondering why they don't like you just doesn't make any sense," David said, with obvious affection and empathy.

"Starting at this moment, you could be moving in the right direction. Take responsibility. And take action. You can get up, go work out, eat healthy, take more care in personal hygiene, and model confident behavior until you even fool yourself into being confident! Or at least stop yourself from actions that take away from it."

David proceeded purposely through the conversation, and Ren felt like he was observing an amazing delivery—incredibly different from the tough way he often delivered hard messages to Ren and others. It worked powerfully, as Curtis seemed to drink it in with all of the love that it came with.

David continued. "By blaming your parents and others, you put the focus on punishing them for what you see as their transgressions. Their intentions may be different than you think. But, even if they deserve the blame—who cares? The only thing that matters from that is how you choose to take it. Don't accept any excuse for what others may have done to you. And the only thing that matters going forward is *who* is taking the wrong, or right, actions *now*. You could still make everything better with a few decisions and actions. And maybe living well would be a better revenge anyway."

Since that time, Ren had noticed a difference in Curtis. Curtis seemed to take David's speech incredibly well and already seemed to be taking action in his life. Ren believed it would only be a matter of time until others would notice, too, and Curtis's life would improve.

David had brought back that conversation to illustrate his point, as he proceeded. "Look, Ren," he said, "before we go any further, it's the same thing for you. Curtis had to move past his excuses and take responsibility and action. The same thing with every leader of every organization. We need to start with you taking complete responsibility. I think you need to believe that your business and your life are going to be what you make them. I want you to take responsibility—one thousand percent—for your business and your life and everything else.

"Some believe in fate, or luck, or science—or God, as I do. But you have to agree with me that you're at least better off tackling your issues with complete ownership, so that you will at least best address everything that you *can* control and affect."

David stated, flatly, "There's no way to stop all the circumstances that can get in your way. If God or fate has a plan, I am not fighting that battle. I am just talking about controlling everything you possibly can, armed with an attitude that sets you up to get past all challenges as well as possible. For all of the hurdles that arise, the people who overcome them the most are the ones who accept them the least."

Ren nodded and felt better. Sometimes the roller coaster took him up and down in a single conversation. The lecture was hitting him pretty hard. But it was something he at least could understand.

He had been a wrestler through high school and in college. And his old coach had wanted him to evolve this mentality to make it about what he could control, and not what he couldn't. Injuries. Bad officials. Not having the right practice partner. Going against the toughest opponent on less rest time. Or anything else that would come up each match. Coach wanted him to take full responsibility and not succumb to any of those variables.

Coach had not been saying that those things weren't happening. He had been saying that you address them when you have to. And, as he had said, "I believe the greatest in this sport hardly ever noticed or cared about any of that."

Ren thought back to when he was younger. *If I had accepted any of those*, he thought, *I might have allowed them as a cop-out. It was only by refusing to do so that I could give myself the best chance. And ignoring them by taking responsibility for everything was critical before moving forward.*

"Think about it," David said. "There are a lot of examples of people who overcame every kind of adversity and challenge and rough background and barriers. We all love the stories of Helen Keller and Stephen Hawking and so many others. If they can do it, why would you allow yourself any excuses?

"Again, I'm not saying there aren't factors outside your control. Maybe one will come along that is somehow truly insurmountable. I'm just focused on you having the best chance to overcome everything else until then.

"What I'm saying is, as Harry Truman and Tony Robbins and so many others have suggested, it is your life and your responsibility. So, take complete ownership of it. The only thing that matters about the past is what you learn from it. And the measure of your success may come down to how much you don't succumb to any impediment!

"All of this then comes back to my going on so much about business model. Whatever may happen beyond your control, I'm setting you up now for the structure to give you the greatest chance at success."

CHAPTER 21

It Is THAT Important

"Luck is not a business model."

—Anthony Bourdain

D avid had been coming into the Dirigat office regularly for several months now, almost always wearing his signature preppy attire as though he was heading out for a game of golf or tennis. That's just who David was. Tom and Ren had even set up an office for him to use, which he seemed to appreciate. It was a place to work, away from his home, and everyone at the company was glad to have him around, for both his advice and his personality. The patterns of his office visits, however, were a little mysterious to Tom, Ren, and the team.

David's office was near the back of their workplace. He was conspicuous when he came in, greeting everyone and sometimes making funny or sarcastic comments as he made his way to his space. He was also normally plenty obvious when he left for the evening, too, wishing the team a good evening and inquiring about their post-work plans.

But the guys would sometimes see him, usually in the afternoon around 1:30 or 2:00, quietly slip out the back door and disappear for a few hours at a time. Then, rather than making a production of coming back, David would furtively return through the back door and inconspicuously—or so he thought!—slide back into his office again.

David wasn't an employee and could come or go anytime he wanted: so, why the sneaking? And where could he be going for a few hours at a time, a few times a week, on what seemed to be a regular schedule? What could this credible older guy be hiding? He didn't seem the type to have a mistress or a gambling habit. Everyone at the office seemed to be having fun with their speculation.

The level of curiosity was building among the team, but Ren felt that David's business was David's business, and he decided to honor his privacy.

Now that David was in the office so regularly, he and Ren would go out for breakfast or lunch even more often. In fact, they were becoming regulars at a few local restaurants. So it wasn't surprising when David tapped on the frame of Ren's open office door around 11:20 one morning and asked if he was hungry. Since his lunch plans had just been canceled, Ren eagerly obliged.

On that fine Tuesday, Ren and David spent most of the ride from the office to the restaurant in a detailed conversation about hamburgers, condiments, and pickles before arriving at a restaurant that wasn't in their usual rotation.

As their conversation went from ketchup to Ren's still-evolving business model, a constant topic that David incessantly came back to, Ren surprised himself by blurting, "David, I really appreciate you. You have been talking about business models for months now. I honestly appreciate that, and I know that the business model is a very big deal. *I get it*," he said, with a hint of frustration he hadn't seen in himself until it infused his voice. "But you could be giving me *so much other* important advice about product positioning, development, hiring, strategy, and so much more. We have a bigger team and so much more on our plate now that you could help with. What's the deal?"

David looked directly at Ren.

"Look, even I get really tired of talking about finding the right business model. And I *know* you are tired of hearing about it.

"I realize that you *think* you get it. But if you did, you'd be doing things differently. And we wouldn't still be having this conversation," he continued, letting his magnetized reading glasses fall on the attached string around his neck.

Ren felt himself get aggravated.

"Listen, Ren. I know you're not intentionally misunderstanding the concept, but I also know that a fuller understanding of this will serve as the foundation for everything else.

"If I told you that I could really help you give this business an opportunity for great success, would you want me to?"

Ren nodded his skeptical agreement, wondering where this was going.

David then inquired, "And if I told you that finding the right model was essential to give Dirigat its best chance to become a truly great company—and help your customers and employees, and the whole world—would it be worth it to you to sit through the same rant, over and over and over again, in exchange for that?

"The thing is," David continued with a little more emphasis, "if you get the right model, it addresses and drives those other things: the product positioning and development, hiring, and everything else. And until you get it right, those other things don't mean as much."

Ren shook his head, as if trying to shake loose cobwebs. Why did David just keep on and on about this, saying the same thing over and over? Other people seemed to think Ren was a smart guy and an accomplished businessman who was good at this kind of stuff. Dirigat was now producing great results and making progress. Why couldn't David just let go, when there were other important things to be considering?

"You can read from any of your business gurus and do any kind of internet search for success factors," David said, as if reading Ren's mind. "They will tell you it's about your team, your timing, how big the opportunity is, and other considerations. No doubt they are right. Those things are all a big deal. I think persistence and understanding your customers and other essential factors are incredibly important, too," David said, taking a sip of water.

"But if you have the right customer-driven model, you will almost be forced to do all of those things well. If you don't have the right model, you will probably eventually miss on a lot of those. At the very least, it'll be hard to stay ahead of bigger companies that can spend more—or other innovators who are also smart and maybe lucky in their turn."

Ren hadn't come to this lunch expecting to hear this same lengthy, passionate soliloquy. He took a deep breath. "David, when you first started going on so much to me about business model, I looked it up. I just wanted to make sure I understood what you were talking about. My favorite business guru, Peter Drucker, says it's 'assumptions about what a company gets paid for.'"

David nodded. "That's not bad," he said. "I would just say it is how you are set up to do what you do—in your case, as a for-profit business—to get paid for creating value for your customer.

"Some people will talk about Business-to-Business, or Software as a Service (SaaS), and other catchy positioning or delivery considerations. And I guess you could say those are models. But that's not where I'm coming from."

David gestured around at their surroundings in the deli-style restaurant. "This can apply to every kind of business. Some people would think if you have a sandwich shop, you have a ready-made model: the way everyone else does sandwich shops," David said. "If it were me, I would still be looking for a better model that would force me to build a better sandwich and to better involve and engage my customers as partners in driving my business.

"I can try to guide someone to what I believe is the right model for them and why they exist. But that wouldn't be the best version for the business, because any entrepreneur will always execute it better if they examine their own sandwich shop or other venture and then come up with their *own* model.

"If you do it right, your customers will be more loyal and that will be your best—and maybe your only—chance to assure that you always stay ahead of bigger companies and all of the new innovators that could pop up for a time.

"In your case, software is increasingly becoming a commodity. Someone can always do it faster and cheaper than you. And bigger companies can afford to play that one-upmanship game to stay ahead, although, ultimately, they have some existential model considerations too.

"As you well know, advanced technologies, tools, and development environments are becoming increasingly ubiquitous. Intellectual property is becoming less valuable. So the barriers to competition are falling away bit by bit every day. This is making everything more of an execution play—and you should always try to execute better and provide better value than your competitors. But you need to know that it is harder to consistently build a business for sustainable success *unless* you can create advantages with a better model. For you, as a small business, the *only* way you can feel *assured* to compete and give yourself the best chance to stay ahead is by being driven by a better model."

Dirigat looked to outsiders like an enterprise software company in the business intelligence and performance improvement space. But what David really wanted was for Ren and the rest of the company to see themselves internally as a funded-development and solutions-driven enterprise-software business in that space. Most of their revenue was from selling the software, and that is what would excite investors and others. But what really guided the company were their funded development component and their consulting and solutions practice, in which they had both expertise and deep relationships. While the revenues in those lines were much smaller, the company would evolve to derive essentially all new development and efforts from those areas, forcing them to be more customer-driven and better positioned in their market.

"That's all I'm going to say about the model for now," David said. "Not because there isn't plenty more to say, but because there's no use before you let this sink in."

Ren nodded, feeling relieved the rant was over. For now.

CHAPTER 22

Epiphany!

"Having the ability to be brutally honest with yourself is the greatest challenge you face when creating a business model. Too often we oversell ourselves on the quality of the idea, service, or product. We don't provide an honest assessment of how we fit in the market, why customers will buy from us, and at what price."

—Mark Cuban

Ren still tried to eat lunch alone at least once a month. There were so many people in his life. So many business-related breakfast and lunch meetings—one or even sometimes two of each, every day of the week. There were even plenty of business meals on weekends, as that was often when Tom, Martin, and others could also make time. Having dinner with his family every day was an important priority for Ren. Any open spots were filled with family commitments, neighborhood gatherings that Tiffany pulled him into, and other social interactions. Even though he had fun with them at times, they were essentially foisted on him at a point in his life when he had so many other priorities and so little time.

It seemed that when Ren was in his office, there was a constant line of people behind the door, asking for approvals, wanting his opinion on ideas, or his help in making decisions. There was never a dull moment. At some point, Ren realized, the CEO's job ends up being about putting out fires. He'd done his best to get the right people and empower them to solve their own problems. But he clearly hadn't figured out the trick yet.

With all of the distractions, Ren largely gave up on getting real work done during regular business hours. Sure, he could meet people—and direct and learn and teach. But if there was actual development, production, or delivery involved, he pretty much only attempted that early in the morning, late at night, or whenever he could find time on weekends.

And Ren really did enjoy many of the social interactions. He liked people. He just needed a break at times. He recognized that he needed to energize alone. So taking monthly opportunities for "alone lunches" was useful for clearing his head and even sometimes gave birth to his best ideas and observations. On a muggy Atlanta Thursday in July, without giving it much thought, he ended up back at his favorite alone lunch destination, a Carrabba's restaurant by the highway.

Upon entering, Ren was greeted by a friendly host and escorted to a booth that was tucked away in the back of the restaurant. Ren always liked to sit facing the dining room, positioned so he could see the door. This was a security reflex that seemed hardwired into him. When entering restaurants where he was recognized, without his even asking, the greeter would take him to a booth in a back area that suited this need and also accommodated his interest in avoiding people for a short time through his meal.

His favorite server, Carmen, showed up almost immediately with two glasses of sweet tea. They knew him well and took good care of him here. The sweet tea was to Ren what coffee was for many others: It kept him going through his long days. He also knew that throughout his meal, Carmen would stay ahead of him in producing ten to twelve glasses of the brownish, sugary, caffeine-filled energy.

Carmen didn't presume the rest of Ren's order but looked a little surprised when he ordered less, and a little healthier, than usual: the Chicken Bryan with sauteed spinach and a Caesar salad with anchovies.

In a thoughtful mood, Ren paid more attention than usual to Carmen's competence and demeanor. She was somehow professional and welcoming and friendly, all at the same time. It called to mind something David had spoken adamantly about over time, including in a conversation the week before. In one of David's patented rants about business model, he'd also gone on about understanding what customers were *really* buying—and having the model serve that.

He hadn't been intentional about this restaurant that day. It was just where he often ended up for these "alone lunches." But, for the first time in a while, the service and atmosphere and meal got Ren's conscious attention. He'd been at this Carrabba's enough that he didn't do his usual math on the restaurant's layout, efficiency, and planning and control systems.

Prompted by the great service and thinking back to David's line of questioning last week, he thought, *Why do I really come here for this alone-time lunch? To this Carrabba's? There are so many good restaurants around here. And I have an option to not go to a sit-down restaurant at all: I could pack my lunch or get carryout and hide in my office with the door locked. So what really drives this decision? And how do I translate it back to my business?*

A lot of Ren's coming here for lunch was a commodity decision. The location was convenient. The food was good. The prices were fair for what he got. And it was easy: It was easy to get in and out of the parking lot, and parking spaces were abundant and easy enough to park in. It was rarely crowded; if he got there before the lunch rush, at least by 11:40 a.m., he could almost always be seated immediately and served quickly.

This Carrabba's was the sort of chain restaurant, by the highway, that locals just didn't come to very much. That was one reason this place was so good for his alone-time meals: He could avoid the distraction of seeing anyone he knew for this short time.

Beyond those reasons, *what else brought me here today?* Ren had always thought and studied a lot about conscious and subconscious influence factors. He recalled David's rant from the previous week, which had referenced a Japanese technique where you ask "*why?*" five times, in the quest for deeper understanding.

David wanted him to use the technique to work toward the real underlying answers, which might be security, comfort, trust, fulfillment, and so on. He added, "And, I think maybe one of the big things is validating identity. Think about it, Ren, you are both a Waffle House and a Capital Grille guy. Maybe a decent number of others are that way, too. But most people are one or the other."

Ren loved The Capital Grille. He was as cheap as ever and enjoyed a meal at a Waffle House as much as anywhere. But he loved to go into any manufacturing facility, distribution center, retail store, and especially any restaurant that really did things right. And when it came to food, service, and attention to details, nobody seemed to do it right, and to do it right more consistently, than The

Capital Grille. It was worth spending a little more sometimes to patronize, and to learn from, them.

"Who goes to Waffle House and who goes to Capital Grille?" David had asked Ren.

"Picture a typical Waffle House customer." As Ren was just starting to visualize, David interrupted by providing an answer to his own question: "You're seeing a middle-aged guy, maybe heavyset, dressed in jeans and flannel, with facial hair, pulling up at the Waffle House in an older-model Ford and ordering hash browns and bacon and coffee."

As that picture came together in Ren's mind, David pressed on, "Now picture a typical Capital Grille customer. You see a middle-aged, upscale professional. Someone who comes across as groomed and image-conscious, pulling up in their Mercedes and ordering a Stoli Doli and a stylish meal."

One of Ren's friends always recommended the Capital Grille's vodka drink, the Stoli Doli, which was basically vodka and pineapple, aged together deliciously in-house and served in a light martini glass.

"Of course," David had said, "these stereotypes are not perfect at all. But if you go into those places regularly, as I know you do, you know they are fairly accurate. And some places, like a beauty shop or a bowling alley or an art gallery, are even more consistently representative of their own stereotypes.

"Every great marketing and product-positioning person knows this and thinks about their audience a lot. And with this being so accurate, what does that tell you?"

After a great deal of consideration, over the years, regarding how people get really invested in showing and validating their identities, Ren also thought now about how people were using the internet to demonstrate how they lived and who they hung out with, as they always had, but in different ways, pre–social media. And he thought of David's observation that when Capital Grille kind of people were there with the kind of friends that reinforced their identity, they wanted to take a selfie and share it with the world. Perhaps, when Waffle House people were at Waffle House, some of them did the same. That could bring those people to those restaurants as customers. And they might be the most credible advertisement to their friends.

That doesn't just apply to the kinds of restaurants people dine in, Ren thought, but the sort of places they go to get their hair cut. To where they buy their computers and cell phones. To what sort of fishing equipment they use.

The list seemed endless. Even in business-to-business sales it was, at the end of the day, most often a person making the decisions. And those decisions were often driven by other consumers. Ultimately, such validation ended up driving every business, Ren gathered, and the customer—whether consumers or other businesses, which were driven by people and their own eventual consumers— was the ultimate boss in every case.

Feeling a little rush, like he was on the verge of better understanding something he had suspected all along, Ren recognized that good quality, convenient location, price, and convenience mattered. But with "no decision" as an option and a number of other good restaurant options nearby, it took more to succeed.

He thought about how the staff at this Carrabba's knew him and made him feel trust and comfort, of how the hostess greeted him with a smile, and of how Carmen remembered his preferences and took such good care of him. Maybe, Ren thought, it was because he tipped well. But it struck him that he didn't care so much why they took care of him as he did about how that affected his decision to keep coming back.

There were also subconscious factors that went into creating an appealing atmosphere, branding, and product positioning. Maybe in some cases, the relationship factors were a big deal. For Ren, it came down to trusting that he could get a good experience and enjoy the product, all in an easy and convenient way.

For Standard Link and now Dirigat, he had learned to buy from a commercial line of laptops for his employees. The cheaper brands always had more problems and cost more over time. To Ren, as a self-confessed IE nerd, what mattered was "mean time between failures" and "long-term cost of ownership." It was really about quality, consistency, knowing what he was getting. It was about trust. Dirigat was committed to bringing that sort of reliability to hospitals and healthcare, helping them to provide better, more affordable, and more consistent care and thus having their patients trust them even more.

There was also a sort of Maslow's hierarchy, from most critical needs and rising to higher-level wants, behind their decisions. Once a customer met their essential needs—starting in many cases with necessity and trust, in price or quality or other important determinants—then other matters such as convenience and status and loyalty increasingly became more important to them.

Ren knew that the cost of acquiring a new customer was usually much greater than keeping an existing one, even in commodity products. In Dirigat's business, with a long sales cycle, a huge price point, and a relatively small universe of potential customers that all seemingly knew and interacted regularly together, reputation and customer retention were a big deal.

Thinking about how supply and demand affected what customers might really want, Ren knew it made a difference whether there were a few competitors competing for a lot of customers or a lot of customers clamoring for a few solutions.

The purchasing dynamic changed yet again when "no decision" was an option—like choosing to eat out at a restaurant or not, or like buying a new shirt for aesthetic reasons or sticking to the old, worn-out one. In Dirigat's case, the prospective customer organization had often decided to do something, or maybe they were required to, and then someone down the line had to figure out which vendor to hire for the solution.

Ren thought about how his manufacturing customers from his previous job had to buy a solution. It got more complex when it came to restaurants.

While everyone was buying for some of the same underlying reasons, in terms of trusting consistent quality, relationships, and such, some of the issues changed when going to consumer products. Direct consumers often had the option to choose between a number of consistent, quality options, as well as often having the option to not buy at all, which made the decision factors harder.

With so many seemingly ubiquitous, good options, and with all of the trust and commodity factors well addressed, Ren figured, maybe the differentiators then became more about status and validation.

There was also an important consideration of whether you were an incumbent choice. It was different if you were trying to persuade someone away from their current option than to accept it as the current option. Ren had learned that in many cases, you might better persuade people to remain with their current option through incentives and positive reinforcement, but that you might be more likely to get people to change with fear or negative reinforcement regarding other options.

Ren knew that momentum matters in decision-making. Getting people to change their restaurant choice—or software-enabled performance management solutions—takes interruption and incentive. But what could Dirigat and other businesses do to apply these known behavioral patterns and tendencies and translate them to successful business?

Ren remembered from college courses that people notice negative experiences more than positive ones. And that they assign more weight to them, convincing themselves that the negative happens more frequently, even when it doesn't. He knew that one bad experience will kill several good ones. Moral of the story? Never be bad.

But on a positive note, Ren knew from psychology courses that occasional reinforcement typically beat consistent reinforcement too. Maybe he could build something around that, along with the validation aspect?

More questions gradually formed:

Let's say I am doing everything else right in the hierarchy of what people are buying: I produce great quality, create high value for customers, price fairly, make my product easy to buy, get people to trust in me and the product, and get them to like it. How do I grow more and do better from there?

How can I tweak what I am already doing to get people into loyalty clubs, speaking well of us on their social media, and so on? How can I use occasional extra positive reinforcement to encourage more loyalty and growth and sales?

Maybe, Ren thought, *I could build something around that, along with the validation aspect.*

For consumer businesses, it might involve social media. When people had a meal with good-looking friends at Capital Grille, they put up a selfie. Could there be, in what Dirigat does, a way to offer a customized product or solution that allows people to show off their identities?

It seemed that the same considerations should apply to Dirigat, as well as to any other industry. Although the products and solutions may be hugely different, wouldn't it still be the same thought processes and considerations at work when considering making the purchase?

How much does the relationship between the decision maker and the salesperson matter in, say, a manufactured commodity business? The obvious answer is "a lot." But, Ren pondered, what could be added to the equation to make the connection even stronger?

Ren's mind drifted back to his Chicken Bryan: *What if I were running this Carrabba's?* He thought about why no locals came. Could they engender the same loyalty with other locals besides him? Part of him selfishly didn't want them to—due to potentially harming his occasional alone time. But he was mostly pulling for the restaurant and wanted them to do as well as possible.

Airlines understand that some of their customers are buying a commodity:

the cheapest way to get where they need to go when they need to be there. For other passengers, including some corporate customers who were the most regular travelers—spending their company's money, rather than their own—rewards and status might have played a role in their purchase decisions. And there was also a social media or other identity-validating-and-demonstrating component for some decision makers.

Ren preferred to fly with Delta Airlines. There were a number of reasons, including that they seemed to do the best job of getting his bags on his flight. But maybe part of it was more than the commodity components and the trust they had earned. What was his status there worth to him—and what were the additional non-obvious reasons behind it?

He also thought about how he spoke well of Delta. Word-of-mouth credibility from existing customers was worth a great deal.

It started to feel like the big-picture questions were becoming clearer. Ren needed to figure out how Dirigat could make customers into his best sales force. Help them to be more devoted—or even make them feel like part-owners—and to make them feel more known and appreciated. He needed to learn how to bring this all back to the actual people, working in the hospitals, buying Dirigat's solutions. And for all that to happen, Ren needed to understand what business Dirigat really was in.

First, he had to win on merit by creating more value for his customers than what they were paying him. Beyond that, from David's prior lessons about the construction company, he knew that his customers wanted to keep their jobs, to look good in their company, to meet their schedule and budget, and to have easier, better lives.

And, Ren found himself coming back to how, at the end of the day, the customers will buy from the vendor they like the most. And the customers—most of them humans, rather than some program or process that only looks at empirical numbers and ratings—lend greater credence to the vendor that makes them feel attractive, comfortable, secure, cared about, and basically just good about themselves.

At a recent conference Ren had attended, the larger group had been divided into breakout groups. As Ren sat in one of them, he noticed the subset of people there who seemed to want to speak out and demonstrate to the group how smart they were.

He could see that, in some cases, it was about status and validation. And in many instances, the people who spoke up actually were really smart and had real value to share. In those occurrences, everybody wins.

Maybe Dirigat could tap into those customers. Maybe, Ren thought, they could even create some sort of a curated model to allow opportunities for those individuals: for the ones who want to get up in front of others and talk about what they are doing. That group of people gets the validation and deserved credit they are looking for and, along the way, makes the solutions and products they use look better. They also feel a strong sense of loyalty and investment toward the company, which was all great for sales and often instructive in how to make the solution even better.

Great people worked in hospitals. Some of them, including many of his customers, were really competent in a stodgy, bland, bureaucratic hospital environment. Maybe some of them were also creative and wanted to indulge and even demonstrate that. Some of them might really love to speak and publish—and show off for peers and bosses—what they were doing, working with an interesting, if frenetic, startup. Perhaps that would be fun and validating for them.

And so it was that, sitting in a back booth in that Carrabba's, Ren had an epiphany about understanding, at a deeper level, what customers are really buying, where that meets any business model, and, he reluctantly admitted to himself, how David's seemingly endless rants had been right on point.

Ren stopped by his home before going back to the office. After her enthusiastic greeting, he gave Caulie a treat. He gave RJ an especially big hug. And he surprised Tiffany by suggesting they go out for dinner tonight. They could go to RJ's favorite restaurant. And Ren thought a lot about why it was RJ's favorite choice.

CHAPTER 23

WAYAWAYG

"If you don't know where you are going,
you might wind up someplace else."

—Yogi Berra

David and Ren continued to carve out time for one-on-one meals together. For the next meeting, just a week after Ren's epiphany about business model and understanding what a customer was really buying, they went to their regular Ruby Tuesday restaurant near the office.

The restaurant was convenient, and David really liked the salad bar. Ren thought the service was pretty good and appreciated the broad menu. The pair ate there regularly, often arriving by 11:30 to beat the lunch rush.

That particular day, the host seated them near a window. After exchanging a few niceties, David reached into the satchel at his side. Ren hadn't noticed the satchel as they'd walked in, and was a little surprised as David pulled out a stack of papers and a pen and tossed it across the table in front of him.

The pages remained relatively well stacked as they landed over Ren's unused fork and beside a sweating glass of iced tea. Ren looked down at perhaps a couple dozen pages of paper and a blue ink pen—the free kind that probably said the name of an orthodontic practice or some law firm on its side.

He didn't have time to process much before David began to explain. "A while back, you mentioned covering more than just my thoughts on business model. Here's something a friend had me do a long time ago. This is a *very* big deal. It is the one thing that really should have come before the business model and what-your-customer-is-really-buying conversations.

"I want you to write down what your life will be like in fifteen years in as much detail as you possibly can," David explained, gesturing at the papers. "Describe where you live. Draw pictures of your house then. Write down what car you drive, what boards you're serving on, what charities you volunteer for, how much money you make each year and how much you have in the bank, what you look like, and anything else you can think of.

"Put down any details about your relationships with your family and friends," David continued. "If you really want to do it well, write a 'day in the life' story, representing a typical or particular day in your life, fifteen years from now. Again, visualize and write this down with as much detail as you can. Not only that, don't do this on your computer: I want you to hand-write all of it."

Ren felt smart, maybe even gloated a little. "I've actually already done this, or at least something like it. I think Tony Robbins and a lot of the self-help guys have you do basically the same thing," he said. "In fact, I think a lot of those personal improvement gurus also get you to do a vision board.

"And," Ren continued, "I've heard that at least some of the self-help guys make the point that having a clear vision of your life helps put your subconscious mind to work to get you there. Having this articulated expectation and visualization will make you more likely to get to your fifteen-year plan."

"I guess all of that is right," David answered. Ren registered a note of impatience in his voice. "The power of the subconscious mind is real—and putting it to work for you is a big deal. But what I want you to do is well beyond those exercises. Here's how. When you are done writing about your life in fifteen years, I want you to do it again, except this time you describe how you envision yourself in *ten* years."

He continued, "And then I want you to do the exact same thing for five years from now, with all of the details. Same as you did for fifteen and ten years from now.

"After that, I want you to do the exact same thing again, with all of the same detail and visualization, for three years from now. And then for one year from now."

That *was* different from anything else Ren had encountered. He was starting to see just how powerful that could possibly be in forcing himself to work out where he needed to be at each point, to arrive at the later destinations.

David continued, "I hope you will put some effort into this. And that's not all—when you've finished all of that, I want you to do a detailed written evaluation of your life now. Articulate any relevant detail that you can think of that drives or impacts the decisions you make and what you're going to do. That may include things like spending a lot of time with your family, your faith and causes, how far you live from work, financial considerations that weigh on you, such as how much money you're making and how much you need to cover your bills, and anything else that you can think of that matters.

"You should also write down what you hate to do, what you love to do, and other things that affect you. Include things that you feel you need to get better at or develop in, too."

David continued, "I realize you probably already have a bunch of this in your head. But it's more powerful when you put it in writing. And, making it more specific and really visualizing yourself living it is worth a lot.

"Not only that," said David, emphatically, "but there is a power in having a sense of inevitability. One of my old psychology professors told us that, if we had to summarize *all* of psychology—from every different perspective—in one sentence, it would be that *we find what we are looking for*. That means a lot of things. And one of them is that if you envision success, you are more likely to find it. We define our reality with our expectations.

"Feel free to customize this exercise. This is really about understanding your life now and where it will be at these points of time in the future. Anything that helps you get there and visualize and understand is good."

While other people may have found David's style hard to follow, Ren was getting really good at it. He appreciated the heck out of David, at least most of the time, and what he was learning from him. And this exercise made a lot of sense to Ren.

David kept going: "You could spend a great deal of time doing it, but I want you to finish it in four weeks. It doesn't have to be perfect—but it needs to be done well enough by then. As you know, you could take whatever time you have, but if you gave yourself six months, it would get complicated. You can always come back and add more later.

"I have done this exercise with many people, including a number of successful business leaders and entrepreneurs," David said, "and, with only one exception, my sister, who said she didn't want to decide the direction of her life, just about everyone seemed to love it and consider it powerful and a life changer. But the one big, recurring challenge that comes up sometimes is just forcing yourself to get it done. I have learned to overcome that with a definitive completion date.

"Go ahead and pull out your calendar and let's schedule a meeting for four weeks from now. Use me for accountability. I want you to bring it when you meet me again that day. You don't need to show it to me, but do have it with you when we meet here again," David said, emphasizing the importance of having the exercise *finished by then* rather than having it be perfect.

Over the next four weeks, Ren really got into the exercise. While he maintained a packed schedule, it was somehow easy to find time to do this exercise that let his imagination and dreams about the future take over. He felt like he was building out his life, making it exactly what he wanted. He found himself eager to share the documents with David.

Per David's guidance, Ren customized the exercise. For example, when he was working through his "life now" section, he ended up doing a modified SWOT analysis, systematically evaluating his strengths, weaknesses, opportunities, and threats.

In learning about SWOT analyses in college, Ren liked the way they forced him to address those four areas. However, he always liked to end things on a positive note, so he swapped "threats" and "opportunities" to be his own sort of "SWTO" analysis.

———

In an effort to get a better handle on his weaknesses, Ren reached out to his old advisor, Joe Chapman, and was thrilled to find out he could meet up for breakfast the next day.

He drove to that meeting with a little trepidation, thinking of how best to get Joe to tell him the painful truth. But Joe was straightforward, and Ren was overthinking. And after a few catch-up niceties and ordering, Ren told Joe what he was looking for and just asked, "What's a weakness or dangerous trait about me that I need to know about?"

Joe's answer came almost before he had finished asking.

"You're a pleaser," he said.

Wow, that *hurt*!

With aspirations of himself as a resolute leader who wasn't going to get pushed around by anyone, Ren wasn't the type that wanted that label. At all. Building a business and leading people was less about trying to please everyone and more about doing what is right. But as the brutal sting sunk in, he felt grateful to Joe.

Ren tried to live by a rule: If someone he respected and cared about ever told him something that hurt his feelings, he worked on the assumption that it was true. And he usually looked back later and found that it *had* been true.

Ren admired Joe as much as David or just about anyone. And damned if that hard comment from his respected mentor didn't really wound him to hear.

Of course, Joe took some off the edge off by explaining more. "Being a pleaser has been a good thing for you, so far," he explained. "It's why you've developed these traits that lead people to like and respect you. Your empathy and warmth are a great strength that has come from it. To your credit, you had the good character to be genuine and honest, and that worked along with being a pleaser to help you become a guy that people trust. Even prior to that, I think there is a likelihood that it helped drive you to go to a good college and get your degree. To be honest, you were probably trying to please your parents in doing that.

"But now, you need to be aware of it in order to become a stronger leader." Joe explained that Ren needed to train himself to make firm decisions, regardless of the problem and no matter if the solution was popular—or pleasing—to those around him.

Moving forward, he thought a lot about Joe's words. And while Ren didn't change his nature, he learned to own it and work around it to be a better manager and leader. That pivot helped him draw firm lines, have tough conversations, sometimes even with customers, and to fire people when he needed to. Ren continued to be considerate to others' feelings, but it was liberating to also be aware of his own pleaser tendencies and to compensate for and overcome them when necessary.

———

About a week into the four-week period of working through this exercise, Ren found himself across from David over breakfast at Waffle House, sharing his enthusiasm for his mentor's assignment.

David seemed pleased with Ren's eagerness, but he interrupted. "There's another important part of this exercise that I could have done with you first," he said, "but I have my reasons for wanting you to do it out of order. If you really want to do this right, I want you to take another blank sheet of paper and write down as many words as you can that articulate values and priorities—anything that might possibly be important to you. You might use words like faith, family, character, helping other people, or anything else.

"Once you have all of those words that are important to you written down on a piece of paper, you can cut them out into separate pieces. So, you should probably have up to a few dozen little pieces of paper with words on them that are important to you. Or, instead of cutting them out, I guess you could just rewrite them all in an organized manner, according to their importance to you, on another piece of paper.

"In either case, I want you to organize those words according to importance, flow, and what they mean to you. You could have a hierarchy or a circle or whatever works to represent them best to you." David was really going now.

Ren was trying to picture this and how it might lay out for him—and how he might order those things.

"I'll pick an example," David said. "From getting to know you, I believe freedom is important to you. So 'freedom' should be one of your words. But it's important for you to understand that freedom can't exist without responsibility."

David gestured forward with his right hand and nodded agreement with his own assertion, as he added, "If someone breaks the law, they go to jail and lose that freedom. If someone breaks the rules within their family, they will lose their freedom associated with their relationship. And if someone doesn't take responsibility financially and otherwise to enable freedom, they will also struggle in reaching it.

"I won't tell you where to put freedom and responsibility on your page, but I will tell you that as you organize your words and write their importance, those two should probably go together somewhere."

Ren left the meal interested in the new assignment—but also aware that he'd just been given even more introspective work to do. It seemed like a lot to pile onto his already full plate. However, he'd come to trust David's advice tremendously; if he said an exercise was important, Ren intended to take his word for it and throw himself into it.

As Ren started to write down, contemplate, evaluate, and organize his words, he reflected on what was most important to him. Faith? Family? Integrity and character? His business?

He also caught himself in some deeper fundamental questions: *How do I define success? What is my reason for doing any of this? I know I want to serve my purpose in this world. What drives me to push so hard and makes me so passionate about all of this?*

———

The remaining three weeks until the accountability meeting for David's exercise flew by. When the time finally came, the pair went to one of their favorite new spots, the OK Cafe. After they sat and ordered, David asked Ren to produce his work.

He looked impressed when Ren brought forth a big stack of paper with a lot of writing and pictures all over. But that expression didn't last long, as David said, "Take the pages you've written about your life in fifteen years, ten years, five years, three years, and one year—and put them down in front of your right hand. Then, I want you to take the pages describing your life now and put them in front of your left hand."

Before David could continue speaking, another long-ago lesson came rushing powerfully back into Ren's mind, like a thunderbolt. One of his earliest mentors had often said, "If nothing else, at least know who you are and where you are going—and at least always go in that direction."

As Ren looked at his left hand and then his right, he felt the weight of both of these great mentors' wisdom being passed along.

David explained that if Ren could keep his priorities, circumstances, and direction in mind, all of his decisions going forward would get easier and clearer. He could always ask himself an easy question: *If I make this decision, will it take me in the right direction, closer to my goal?* If the answer was yes, then it was the right way to go. But if the decision took him further away from his desired destination, then it was the wrong one. Seems obvious and powerful!

With the help of his documented goals, Ren began to evaluate different aspects of his life. He recognized, for example, that he hated sitting in traffic for his daily commute. He discovered that he expected to live in a different location within five years, in one that better suited his goals and constraints. So, he decided that his family should move sooner rather than later to improve their lives.

Ren recognized that he hated a number of other time-consuming tasks, like waiting in line at the post office. He could find someone that didn't mind it as much, had a better temperament for it, and would be glad to do it for him, with a mutually beneficial deal for both. And it paid for itself tremendously, as he could get a much better payback on his time when applied to where he best created value. He sought administrative help the next day.

David also suggested that Ren should do these same exercises for his business, at Dirigat, plotting out five years, three years, and one year, since ten and fifteen years would be too far out for a business in a world that changes so quickly.

David noted to Ren that, if he was seeking to be an *intra*preneur, working for another organization, or if he had partners in this vision, the exercise would be about comparing and matching his vision and values and life expectations with the other company or partners, or fostering a venture where all of their items overlapped. David often spoke about being an intrapreneur—that is, as David explained, someone being entrepreneurial within a bigger company or any existing organization—and making sure all of this lined up for the intrapreneur within the organization.

But since Ren was the entrepreneur and creating his own business, the business should exist to serve his examination of his values, of who he was, and where he was going: whether it was to make the world a better place, make a bunch of money, save the environment, empower his employees, or some combination of priorities. Ren followed David's advice in doing this exercise for Dirigat as well, and found it to be very powerful to find such clarity and certainty in so many of his decisions.

David had also spoken a lot about the values and priorities exercise. "That is very important, underlying everything. You might think I would want you to come up with your values first. But I actually like for you to evaluate who you are and where you think you are going before that. So I had you do it out of order on purpose.

"I think there is some value," he pointed at Ren as he spoke, "in comparing where you are and what you think you want and then measuring and changing, if necessary, to match those priorities."

Doing David's exercise became a north star in Ren's life. Everything from the location of his new home, to strategic decisions in Dirigat, to better positioning expectations in business relationships, seemed to make his life better as he consistently made decisions that moved him in the right direction.

Ren loved the exercise so much that he got David's permission to use and evolve it, eventually creating a document for it. Since it is used to answer the question "Who are you and where are you going?" Ren took the acronym "WAYAWAYG" and used it with a number of friends and groups, including many very successful CEOs and leaders of all kinds. Maybe he could put it in a book someday, he thought.

———

The weeks following David's exercise ended up being pivotal for Ren and Dirigat.

Having the clarity that comes with a defined vision gave Ren an empowering sense of purpose and motivation for himself and for his business.

It changed everything.

Others around him seemed to pick up on the newfound assuredness and confidence that came from it, as it found its way into his posture, gestures, and manner of speaking.

Ren realized that decisions are much easier when you have certainty. Problems usually come from being conflicted, indecisive, and languishing in indecision. And he no longer suffered as much from wasting time and focus on looking back and second-guessing those choices.

Having this clear articulation to measure all decisions against suddenly made most of them simpler: *Does this take us where we are going? Or does it take us away from that?*

The one- and three-year goals served an immediate purpose. Ren realized that if he was going to be where he expected to be in fifteen years, he needed to first reach the five- and ten-year marks—and getting to them required urgent action. *I have to start now*, he thought.

Ren recognized that he loved to learn, to build and repair things, and to teach. He had cultivated an incredible group of mentors and felt passionate about sharing with others what he had learned from them.

From then on, whenever anyone came to Ren with an interest in potentially selling their business, hiring a new CEO, going through a divorce, or making any other big life decisions, he took them through this exercise.

Doing the current SWOT analysis was also useful for Dirigat, perhaps most importantly in assessing what the team needed to do in order to get their leadership team right. And for his personal role in the business, the exercise helped Ren to recognize and address responsibilities that he needed to get better at—and some things that he didn't want to do anymore. It was impactful for him to think about what he hated to do and what he loved. Administrative and repetitive tasks were not the best or most efficient use of his time. He could work around those things, if he wanted to, or could find someone who was a better fit. But there were many bigger considerations as well.

With encouragement from David, Ren also created a five-year version for Dirigat. As David said, "Five years is plenty for your business. It's hard to forecast beyond that for a business in this fast-moving world. The world always changes. The only thing different now is that it changes faster and faster. Those who can't keep up will fall behind faster than ever."

As Ren worked through his five-year WAYAWAYG exercise for Dirigat, he enjoyed updating the priorities for his business. He started with the statements from his original business plan, solicited input from Tom Strong and others, and came up with a list of things that he believed in, including integrity, honesty, diversity, appreciating customers and employees, creating long-term value, and much more. With agreement and buy-in from Tom and others in the business, those values and priorities became foundational for the company and its business plan.

As Tom noted, "A plan is not a plan until it is in writing."

CHAPTER 24

Cultivating Culture

"Culture eats strategy for breakfast."

—Peter Drucker

I t's not quite right to say that the months fell away. They flew by at warp speed, with Ren and the team spending each day intentionally, if a little frenzied. However the time passed, it was gone and Dirigat was moving forward.

With the advancement of the business and solution, it was time to hire more. Ren and the team felt like this was an essential opportunity to establish the right culture and hopefully attract the best people to get there. They expected that the next vital step in setting up the team for success was establishing the right culture with the right people.

As anyone who does much hiring discovers, sometimes finding the right person for the right role is simple, but at other times it can be a real struggle. Everybody wants to hire the best people and the best people will always be in high demand.

One thing that helped in finding good people at Dirigat was that they had significant credibility and exposure from the involvement of respected leaders like David, Tom, and their advisors. And, after Dirigat became successful, the leadership team expected that people would line up to get to work for them.

Success begat success in finding and hiring top-notch candidates. But that kind of success, including a positive company culture that people would love, took time to build.

Particularly in the early hires, at a time when the economy was booming, there was a great demand for developers and other key positions.

One of the decisions the company had to make was whether or not to use headhunters and recruiters, and if so, how much. Ren saw the value in utilizing them. Sometimes they found candidates he might have never encountered when mining his network. He also liked the personality and aptitude tests that many of the best recruiters used to screen candidates. Myers-Briggs, DiSC, and other assessment tools could uncover helpful insight into people's communication styles and how well they'd succeed and contribute to the company culture he was trying to build. And the technology assessments were not great but were effective at screening out most of the least-qualified applicants.

Tom and Ren ultimately decided that, since they were looking for highly specialized people for a few of their important positions, they would leverage search firms to tap the small universe of candidates. Ren found that it would cost a lot less to pay the "extortion," as he only half-jokingly called it, of the high fees to a good headhunter than it would cost to make a mistake in not finding the right candidate—or of hiring the wrong one. And using contract placements allowed them to utilize and evaluate candidates before making a longer-term commitment.

Ren always negotiated on the fees and payback periods, particularly as he felt that recruiters' compensation periods were usually not long-term enough to sufficiently align their incentives with his. It often took a long time to know just how good a new hire was and how well they would fit. He found that the best headhunters were willing to compromise their terms with Dirigat in hopes of a mutually beneficial, longer-term relationship. Ren always appreciated the people who looked to the future instead of trying to make all their money on one placement or deal. He reciprocated by using the good headhunters or staffing providers over and over and sending referrals their way.

Once the right pool of qualified candidates was found and screened, the next issue was identifying who would be the best fit to build the kind of environment he wanted for Dirigat. Ren had done some hiring before, but bringing together a team for Dirigat felt much more personal. And he knew he had to get it right the first time around.

He knew it would be much harder to change company culture further down the road. But, Ren thought, if he started with the right people and got them to work in the right way, his vision for Dirigat would almost become self-fulfilling.

From the beginning, the company was committed to an ethos of values, empowerment, opportunity, and success. It was all built around Dirigat's mission, vision, and values statements. And they added a culture statement and used it for each new hire.

COMPANY CULTURE

We care more than our customers about creating value for them and solving their problems.

We have a culture of service and a culture of sales, where we build a great business that makes the world a better place by creating value and solving problems and turning that into success.

We have a culture of empowerment, where people are not afraid to make decisions. And with that,

We have a culture of accountability. We hold ourselves accountable at a high level. And because we are empowered to do our jobs, we want to be held accountable for our results.

We have a culture of inclusion and diversity. We place a genuine priority on this and know that it makes us a better business.

We have a culture of hard work and strong, constructive motivation and results.

We are frugal, fast, and fun, along the way. We value competence and communication and teamwork and mutual respect and consideration.

And most importantly, we have a culture of integrity and honesty and good character.

———

In addition to looking for the right competence and fit, Ren and the Dirigat team continued their emphasis on big-picture thinkers. They continued to find that, particularly for higher-level and manager-type positions, just telling them what the problem or the goal was and then letting them address it on their own, in their own way, changed everything. It felt freeing—and almost inconceivable at first—to Ren that he could just leave somebody with a problem or give them complete responsibility over something, exit the situation, and that the person would often increasingly come up with a better solution than he ever would have come up with himself.

Some of the best hires that Dirigat made were people who had at some point attempted to build their own businesses. In many cases, they best understood both what needed to happen for the customer, as well as for the business, and how to get there.

———

Even with their best efforts and purposefully working toward setting up for success, employee drama remained the biggest challenge for Ren and Tom and the team. Perhaps this was partly because there weren't any clear rules for how to operate. Instead, many were judgment calls that had to be made on a case-by-case basis. Many situations were bewildering. How do you best handle it when two employees that need to work together on the same team get in a personal conflict and refuse to speak with each other? You're not their parents, but you need to find a solution.

There were lots of questions from Dirigat's leadership about when to "over-parent" and when to "under-parent" the team. Every situation was different. And for Ren, sometimes it depended on the person and their level of responsibility—coder versus manager, salary and hours, and so on.

No matter how much Ren tried to set his team up for success, he often had to address when managers were afraid to hire people who were smarter and more capable than themselves. He strived for a culture where leaders didn't fear being bested, but would embrace the opportunity to get smart, creative individuals to solve problems with them.

———

David's ostensible sneaking out of—and back into—the office continued. By now, the team was taking bets on where he was going.

Cindy was surprisingly considered to have the best odds, with her speculation that he was moonlighting in a barbershop quartet, a supposition that came as David was observed singing to himself in his car as he pulled out for one of his excursions. This was advanced when someone thought they saw a vest and one of those straw-looking hats that the quartet members sometimes wear in his backseat.

But there was also good money on his visiting a pool hall for some sort of weekday afternoon league, or maybe a recurring poker game. And of course, speculation about a possible mistress just wouldn't go away, although Ren felt he knew David better than to suspect that. Whatever the reason for David's disappearances, finding it out had become a big deal to everyone.

Chip and Curtis worked out a plan where the team would take turns trying to follow David for advancing segments of his journey as he left the office so there'd be less chance they'd get caught tracking him.

It started with Chip taking the first turn, one Tuesday, following David in driving away for a time, until David turned onto a side street. The next Thursday, Curtis waited around in his own vehicle to pick up David at that same side street for the next segment as he came through there, and so on.

Everyone seemed to have fun with the speculation and planning their sleuthing activities. Traffic, miscommunication, and a couple of amusing side adventures that included a fender bender prevented the detective team from finding out where David was going, until they finally gave up on the effort.

And so the mystery continued to deepen.

CHAPTER 25

Aligning Incentives

"Show me the incentive and I will show you the outcome."

—Charlie Munger

Figuring out how to pay folks was always a big deal. As Dirigat continued to move forward, Ren believed that when they had the right opportunity and model, the next important step was getting everyone in the right roles. After that, it became about aligning incentives.

With salespeople, this was easy. They got a commission—an incremental cost that was directly built into the pricing. You just needed to make sure they didn't sell a bad deal for the company.

Wanting the sales guys to be hungry, Ren liked to pay them a lower base salary, offset by bigger, preferably uncapped, commissions. But he struggled at times when, with a shortsighted interest in just getting paid quickly and generously, they tried to sell things that maybe sounded good to a customer but just didn't make sense for Dirigat or in some cases couldn't be delivered.

One of the biggest considerations was *how much* they could sell of what they couldn't-quite-deliver-yet but figured they would be able to in the near future. Obviously, the company *had* to deliver whatever was sold. Not doing so was never a consideration. But it was healthy to drive Dirigat by pushing to sell ahead of where they were at the time. The trick was in the balance, though. The goal was to sell a little too much in the present and then somehow find a way to deliver what had just been sold, with great results.

Sometimes a customer would be willing to pay well for, say, a new data interface or added capability for the software. The salesperson would sell it to them while the development team was either still working on developing it, or already overwhelmed with delivering what had been sold before. In many cases, the developers found that they didn't have the time or wherewithal, or even the ability, to get the customer what they needed.

This led to Ren trying to keep his sales team focused on longer-term compensation and in selling future bigger deals they could confidently assure to happier customers.

For positions other than sales, the compensation structure depended a lot on the role and responsibility. But Ren knew that, unfortunately, people often looked at what others were making. There were already enough employee issues without inconsistent compensation standards, so he tried to create an empirical, consistent system—even as the company, its circumstances, and what it could afford changed.

Ren couldn't keep people from telling others what they were making. He knew of times when someone at the company apparently lied about their salary, telling their peers they were getting paid more than they were. This caused its own set of problems.

While Ren tried to at least discourage others from talking about their salaries, he realized it was risky for him to even bring the topic up. But whenever the opportunity presented itself, he liked to remind people that "Nothing good ever comes of it for anyone. Always best to keep it to yourself."

Financial transparency and open-book management was another issue that came up at Dirigat. Besides being tied to compensation and to how people, sometimes mistakenly, would view the company's momentum, there were plenty of other perception issues that could arise.

Perhaps, Ren thought, there wasn't a discrete right or wrong in terms of how much information was wise to openly share, but that these decisions were about "picking your poison."

While he liked the idea of alignment and empowerment and of people knowing what they needed to do to get compensated, he had learned the hard way with his previous company that transparency, where employees had full access to the company's financials, could come at a great price.

Some people would argue against him, but to Ren, open-book management was usually a net negative, over time. It seemed like a great concept when things were going well, but he felt that any positive feelings seemed to wear off quickly. And whenever the economy got bad, or there was a disruption of any kind, for example when the customers went too long without paying their bills, there could be significant harm. After the cash-in from Standard Link, Ren knew what he could do to keep making payroll. But nothing good came from employees fretting and gossiping about it, on pure speculation without knowing themselves what could be done.

The biggest thing that Ren didn't like about transparent management and financials was when people only got part of the story. The problem was the same as with eavesdropping. Ren would be fine if someone heard *all* of anything he said and understood the context behind it. But problems invariably arose when people only heard *parts* of what he said and didn't have the full perspective of everything that might be relevant.

It was a problem, too, when the listener didn't quite understand the topic discussed. Perhaps they didn't understand financial reporting or even the difference between cash-basis and accrual-basis accounting. An employee could get either worried or overly optimistic without understanding how circumstances were in the bigger scheme of things.

There were, for example, a couple of times when the company had worked out a quicker payment schedule with a reliable customer, but needed to hold off for certain milestones before they could book and invoice. This meant that the receivables were actually better than they looked on the balance sheet, but to anyone looking at the balance sheet without knowing what had been done, the numbers might have been concerning.

With those and many other hard-learned lessons in his pocket, Ren avoided open books and transparency on things like compensation, ownership, and the company's balance sheet.

———

With Dirigat's growth, Ren was all about getting the best people who were the right fit, and then empowering them to succeed in their jobs. Having and keeping good people was so important—and replacing them so painful, risky, and costly—that it was worth it to overcompensate and overindulge the team with freedom and opportunity. Ren's goal was for Dirigat to be such a great place to work that it would ruin the employees from ever being able to work anywhere else.

Not that they were ever easy, but usually, the base salary and benefits were not the biggest challenge. For an idealistic startup like Dirigat, the base salary the team wanted was simply enough money to pay their bills. It seemed that everyone greatly appreciated the company's commitment to providing the employees with good benefits.

Of course, healthcare coverage and other matters affected people's families and well-being. Even if the business had been an assembly-line factory, paying market-competitive wages to employees who only served a simple repetitive function, Ren would still have offered the best benefits that he could afford. And, to any extent it might be affordable, he also would have continued to pay at least above-market rates. Paying more often ended up saving money over time in reduced turnover and exposures.

With expensive, higher-end hires, it was an even bigger deal.

Sometimes compensation was more about appreciation than dollars, particularly when someone was already making plenty to pay their bills. Some studies showed that compensation was perhaps seventh in a list of factors in priorities for employees, behind factors such as leadership, good working relationships, and respect. Environment, culture, and learning and development opportunities were a big deal as well.

Ren also shared David's affinity for aligning incentives.

He thought of it, as many have characterized, as essentially a "carrot-and-stick" model. Experience had shown Ren that sometimes he really needed the stick. But the carrot was always his preferred option. Affirmation, positive reinforcement, and the resulting confidence were powerful. And making sure everyone's incentives aligned well with the company's seemed to have a remarkable correlation with success.

A lot of it was obvious. In bonuses, for instance, Ren felt that the additional compensation should be partly based on the performance and success of the individual position—depending on the person's responsibilities and where they resided in the company—and partly based on the results for the company, as you wanted the employee to want success in both. The percentage of division between the two depended on weighing the value of what the person did against the overall results for the company. And it seemed that putting more weight on the company's performance helped with bigger-picture perspective and goals.

In theory, the best way to align incentives in the long run, at least for key employees, was to have some ownership in the company. But it was never that simple.

And each employee seemed to take their ownership differently. It seemed that some people could have two-tenths of a percent of the company and feel and act like an owner, while others might own eight percent and still not have as much sense of ownership.

Ren thought sometimes it might not even be a bad thing to have someone who would never be satisfied. Sometimes you wanted a company leader or sales-person to have a big ego and to never be content. But what made them good for their job made them a constant battle in regards to their compensation—and this always made for a challenge. Each situation called for different circum-stances, weighing company needs, when the person came in, at what level, and longer-term expectations, with a best effort at consistent protocols.

If he could make the business more successful by the employees owning more, Ren would go that route. At least he thought he would until he started weighing it against future dilution concerns. There would be potential needs for hiring more team members or capital raises down the road, execution if he ever got below a controlling interest, and other factors such as hassle and compliance that arose with more shareholders over time.

A few of Ren's advisors wanted him to use some kind of phantom stock, stock appreciation rights, or other ways for employees to share in the upside. Employee stock option plans, where team members have a right to some por-tion of ownership at a fixed price, had some advantages for the company, but at times, the employees didn't seem to appreciate them as much. Maybe, Ren thought, it was because the ownership seemed more remote or esoteric to them. And, he figured, if it didn't serve the purpose it was intended for—to get employ-ees to feel like owners and to appreciate their upside and align incentives—why even do it that way?

On the advice of some friends and attorneys, given tax considerations and other factors, Dirigat ended up going with individual stock options to key employees. Since the employees got the options based on the current value of the company when they started, there was not a taxable event at the time. There was no gain to start, just a right to get stock in the future at its current value. Ren used a two-year cliff, where the employee could get their first vest-ing, or the right to purchase stock and potentially sell it, after they remained for a couple of years. Then they were incented toward company success; and the growth in the company was valuable to them with not having a taxable event until it was cashed in.

For a longer-term alignment, Ren used a longer-than-average vesting sched-ule of five years, where it took that amount of time before they could have full rights to all of their potential options. Of course, there would be accelerated vesting on certain exit or change of control events, to ensure the employees' greater ownership if the company sold.

But there were also challenges around strike price, execution terms, cost and time constraints in getting valuations done, tax effects, and other factors that most people don't think about. And there were times when an employee was let go or left under murky terms and ended up with ownership that didn't serve well.

The biggest problem was when employees' expectations were unrealis-tic. Many people wanted near-market salaries but were joining a technology startup to hit it big with their ownership. If the employee anchored their hopes, coming in, to impossible expectations, it seemed like the problem never went away.

When Dirigat was trying to hire a prospective new employee, that person wanted to feel that they were joining a startup that was going to be the next great multibillion-dollar unicorn. And each of them—and their family and friends—saw themselves owning at least ten percent of that company. While that did a great job at getting the prospective employees interested, the math could never work for the company and its future needs. There were only so many shares to go around. And with impossible expectations, even if someone came in with a chance to own a half-percent of the company, they never were going to be happy until they got to the ten percent that they all believed they deserved. Too bad, Ren thought, there was no way to get to a million percent!

CHAPTER 26

Positioning for Success

*"Positioning in pursuit of your purpose is
critical to your success in life."*

—Oscar Bimpong

D avid liked to say that once you have the right employees in the right
spots in the right model with the right compensation, the next priority is to set them up with the best chance to succeed.

With the team growing at Dirigat, Ren learned that that is when you really
go to work for your team. It reminded him of a lesson that his father and grand-
father had taught him so long ago: The company pyramid is upside down.

As David put it, "Your *customers* are, in fact, the *ultimate boss*. Your
employees work for your customers and define your relationships with them
and therefore your success. So, if you have the right team of people doing the
right things, then your job as the entrepreneur or CEO becomes arming them
for success.

"Make no mistake," David said. "Your *employees* are *your boss*."

He let that sink in before continuing, "Maybe you don't want them to realize that most of the time. You do still have the power to fire them or impact their

compensation and the rules they have to live by at work. But a great part of your job is about helping them do their job."

Ren still thought of it as *I work* with *the team. We work together and* for *one another*. And he wanted to make sure he addressed his half of that equation and worked for the team at least as much as they worked for him by focusing on setting them up for success.

He had already considered the culture and success factors he wanted to establish and build from. But he knew that just having the right people and the right culture was not enough. He also needed to provide the team with the information and understanding that would empower them and produce results. He wanted to make sure those results were in alignment with Dirigat's business model and the product that the customers were buying, that created value for them. After all, that was what Dirigat helped hospitals to do with its HospitAlign software and solutions.

Ren thought about how the HospitAlign software could integrate with his internal Customer Relationship Management solution and his accounting software. The goal would be that everyone could empirically see and understand where they stood, how they were doing, and where they were going. If done correctly, this sort of system would even help with the company's evolution.

As David had said, "No matter how well you communicate, the most important part is not what you say but what people perceive: what they see and hear. And if it impacts their job, compensation, or livelihood, it seems like they almost always receive and remember it differently than how the speaker had intended."

David liked to explain that people didn't listen or recall well about any subject that was emotional to them. They often seemed to edit history, over time, to suit the way they *wanted* to remember things. And he liked to point out how people were resistant to change.

"But," he added, "alignment and understanding can even help overcome their resistance to change.

"Uncertainty and emotion, particularly about topics that could affect your employees' jobs or compensation, can cause distress," David noted. "But if those same people can see empirically, in your everyday actions, that you are trying to work toward a common goal, that helps tremendously. This kind of objective, clearly delineated, and consistent system could help offset some of the problem. If they have a green, yellow, or red indicator, they know what is going to happen.

"Clarity breeds confidence. Employees can understand where they are going more clearly if you can help them see the big picture and then identify where the smaller individual issues are in relation to it. Even if someone is not a visual learner, being able to see the indicators makes it easier to buy into them."

Ren thought that he and his team could build a great tool—his own HospitAlign software, used within Dirigat as it was with his customers—to serve a culture that could change and evolve when it needed to. He saw how a lot of this tied together: the culture, the processes, the systems, the alignment, and the empowerment.

In working for his employees, Ren's most obvious task was to provide them with the resources and direction they needed to do their jobs as well as possible. In some cases, it was providing them with a laptop, an expense account for travel, office space, or some other simple thing. Sometimes administrative support helped. Or it could be connecting them with a coding expert, systems engineer, or a hospital quality manager. The key takeaway for Ren was that in order to do his job well, he needed to know what resources his team needed so that he could procure them. And that was best achieved through open communication and dialogue.

For a few of the deployed employees who were working remotely at customer sites, the company came up with regular reporting protocols, so that Tom and Ren and the team could see what everyone was doing. From that, they could at least predict what people might need. Some liked to communicate regularly and reached out whenever they needed any help or resources. Others needed prompting.

Ren focused on building relationships, asking targeted questions, and creating a system for regular interaction and feedback. That was not a great long-term solution, but it worked well enough for a small business with only a few deployed employees. He also interacted regularly with everyone in the office and felt there was useful feedback and information traveling in both directions.

Dirigat's company rules and protocols also tied into its systems and processes. Ren never wanted burdensome paperwork or procedures, but knew that some of it was increasingly necessary as the company grew. He also wanted to create sustainable, replicable processes to support the company procedures: "Here is what you do to get a new credit card, and here is what your credit limit will be," or "Here is how to communicate and get support for that," or "Here is the process for a reimbursement check or report form."

The company would eventually get to the next phase in evolution where those protocols became requisite on a greater scale, to assure priorities like consistency and even liability protection. But, for now, Ren just learned to reasonably standardize such things as they went along. David had some exercises for such matters that helped Ren in achieving this.

CHAPTER 27

Fostering Sales and Solutions

"Luck has nothing to do with it, because I have spent many, many hours, countless hours, on the court working for my one moment in time, not knowing when it would come."

—Serena Williams

As he continued meeting people and trying to learn more about building his business and about the industry that he was entering, Ren never failed to be encouraged by hearing about successful entrepreneurs who had "made it."

Perhaps the most inspiring in the bunch was Sid Richardson.

By the time Ren got together with Richardson, Dirigat's HospitAlign solution had been built out solidly and was impactful for their customers, and they were ready to sell it on a broader scale. But sales weren't materializing the way they had hoped. As David so matter-of-factly put it, "Wishful thinking is not a sales strategy."

It was at this frustrating point that Ren crossed paths with Richardson, who was, among many other things, considered a pro at selling tech solutions to hospitals.

The timing couldn't have been better. He had become friends with Richardson's son, Chase, years earlier and discovered that he and Richardson had a number of mutual friends—including David, the man everyone seemed to know. The more Ren learned about Richardson's impressive history, the more interested— and almost intimidated—he was to meet the man. Not because of Richardson's resounding business success, but because of how much he had overcome to get there and how well thought of he was by people whom Ren respected.

Richardson had a remarkable story. He had grown up in the state's foster care system and emerged from his challenging background to build a truly great company, providing to hospitals solutions that included software, technology consulting, and more. From what Ren could learn, Richardson's own company had been another typical entrepreneurial roller coaster in its early days—with the highest of highs and lowest of lows—until he found a formula that worked and could be replicated. And it certainly was working now.

Richardson HealthTech Solutions, or RHS, was a shining example of what a great business could be: Their customers loved them, their employees loved working for them, their innovations and solutions helped to enable better healthcare, and they contributed significantly from their substantial earnings and wise guidance to important causes.

Ren was mystified that this guy and his company could be out there doing such great things so modestly. When he attempted to do his usual pre-meeting "stalking," it was challenging to find much about Richardson through the internet. He mostly had to get his information from mutual friends. Ren began to think maybe that was a good thing.

It was with eager admiration and a little trepidation that one sunny Wednesday morning Ren arrived at RHS at 8:35 for a nine o'clock meeting. It took longer than expected to get through the RHS campus, park, and find Richardson's office. Ren had learned to build in extra time and show up for meetings early. In this case, that habit paid off as he walked in at 8:59.

Richardson must have been incredibly busy, running this successful business and doing plenty of good for the world. But Ren found that the man was gracious with his time.

After a few niceties, Ren shared about his new venture and what he wanted to do. His story and explanation must have wandered and rambled because Richardson, in the kindest way, interrupted, "You need to be able to articulate what you are doing very clearly and concisely. I saw a one-page business plan on the internet recently. What I liked most about it was that it forced you to be able to explain yourself clearly and concisely. You can look it up, if you would like to try it."

Ren felt a little embarrassed that he had not been clear and succinct enough.

"I think I have a sense of what you are trying to do," Richardson continued, "and I think the need for it is real. But I also think you don't have a great understanding of this industry yet and may have a hard time selling broadly here."

The only other person who had ever spoken so frankly to Ren on their first meeting was David.

Richardson said, "Some people might say that I know this industry. A lot of what I have to share is specific to selling a solution at a comparable level to yours into hospitals and healthcare. But there are also many universal truths to sales. Buried in some of this there may be concepts that would be relevant to other industries and other types of solutions.

"To begin with, you need to really understand your customers and your market. Particularly at first, you need to understand what they can buy—and then make it easy for them to buy it from you. And, you absolutely need your customers to trust you. The best way to get there is always just to merit their faith and create real value for them. People often buy from the vendor they trust and like."

Ren shared that that guidance was consistent with what David had been preaching.

Richardson nodded. "David's a smart guy. I think, if I'm understanding what it is you want to do and you do it right, you're providing something your customers really need. In that case, I really hope you find your way.

"I think David likes for you to lead with a consultative sale. There are some good reasons for that. But, as he will tell you, consultants like to have software solutions to build their practice around. That provides essential ongoing value to customers that they really need. It also makes the consultants 'sticky' for ongoing business, where they can keep engaged in the organization and keep selling more—and more effectively—over time.

"And," Richardson added, "you then get your customers to increasingly use and depend on your solution, until you are helping them so much and creating so much value that they are locked in with you. The first thing you need to do is to really understand what your customer is buying, and serve that."

While Richardson shared much of the same perspective as David about selling into healthcare, he added some tactical guidance on how to position the solution. Richardson also highlighted that, in his experience with software-solution businesses, customers "buy simple. They buy what they understand. And they buy more power and then they don't use it."

Richardson stressed the importance of knowing what to sell. "Always keep in mind that most of your customers want to buy a solution, rather than just a product. There may be a few big-budget organizations that have departments that want a tool they can customize and use—or even think they can build themselves, until they find out the hard way that they can't. Most of those will ultimately do better with something more turnkey, too. They just don't realize it.

"I think you should also give thought to your product positioning—probably before you even prioritize sales. You should think about what it will cost, how it will be implemented, and how they can buy it." Richardson put his head back and paused for a moment.

Ren's wheels were turning as he recalled David delivering essentially the same message. He sometimes grasped new concepts more fully when he heard them multiple times from different angles, and hearing this same idea from two people he so appreciated underlined its huge value. He may as well have been reading a business fiction book that kept repeating certain points, in hopes that the lessons might soak in better each time. It may have been worth the tough reading in order to consider and receive the insights more effectively.

"At this point," Richardson said, "deriving how you position your product in your market would be a bigger deal than focusing on how you sell it.

"There are a small number of huge successes out there that were based less on great business models and more on genius product positioning and marketing," he said. "I don't know how they can replicate their successes forever. But basically, they started out creating cool solutions that they knew people would want, and then did an amazing job of persuading and convincing people to buy these products.

"Those consumer product geniuses started from positions of success and credibility. Would they have been able to do what they did without that?" Richardson asked, rhetorically. "They had fortuitous timing, in most cases, and leveraged a lot of positioning and resources and hype into what they accomplished. You shouldn't count on being able to pull that off now. And yours is not a consumer product. But I want you to think about what you *can* learn about positioning your solution.

"For instance, with the type of enterprise solution you're providing, the price point could end up in the hundreds of thousands of dollars, and eventually well into the millions. That level will probably be necessary for your business to survive in the universe you are going after.

"At that price point," Richardson continued, "you need to be working with the CEO or some other high-level champion in each customer organization. But if that person is your entry point, you'll have a hard time getting organizational buy-in from the people that are key in actually using and implementing your solution. The problem is this: No one in operations wants something pushed down on them. If the CEO or COO tells those folks to buy your solution, they will do it because they have to, but they'll then tend to be resistant. That's not a formula for organizational buy-in and ultimate success."

Ren sat there processing. While he had heard some version of this from David, there was something about Richardson's rendition that drew him into deeper consideration.

"I know David wants you to have a consultative sales model. And I like that. For one thing, you may find that it's hard for your best initial target customer in hospitals to buy software. At the least, their IT guys and their legal department might be a hassle.

"But on the other hand, you may find that your target—maybe a chief quality officer, nursing manager, or management engineer—can approve a purchase of up to, say, five thousand dollars a month, without having to get much in the way of higher approval." The entire time he talked, Richardson had a friendly look on his face, which Ren really appreciated.

"You may find that customers know how to buy consulting easily enough, since they are used to doing it, and don't have to jump through as many hoops to make that purchase as they would for an enterprise software solution. For them, it's ideal that they don't have to overcome those hurdles and take the time and extra work to be able to buy your solution.

"A big fundamental shift in your thinking should be this: Instead of trying to force them to buy what you think you need to sell, find a way to be adaptive. Understand the current market and what your customers know how to buy and what makes it easy for them. Build out from there to what best serves them.

"So," Richardson continued, "maybe you sell them up to five thousand dollars a month in consulting to get in the door, if that is the amount they can purchase without higher approval. Maybe you even throw in your software, on a small scale. Instead of an enterprise solution that needs to get through legal and IT, maybe you start with a desktop-served application that solves a critical problem at hand. That helps them meet whatever 'the letter of the law' is for their requirements. From there, you can build out within the organization. In essence, they will buy your more expensive software solution gradually over time, without as many of the hurdles and impediments that you would otherwise face.

"And, you can still build up to the CEO, with better buy-in, when you come up through the hierarchy from the right people in the organization. The organization will get better value and hopefully the CEO will like it better, too, in the long run.

"Beyond that," Richardson continued, "and just being honest, Ren, I really don't think you should even go on sales calls."

Why was he saying that? Ren was a little concerned, but he had sufficient reason to trust Richardson's judgment and didn't interrupt.

"For one thing, you come from such a different world in technology and manufacturing. In the businesses that you were in before, you would budget for a need and then requisition for it. But in healthcare, there is so much less method to the madness. In some cases, a hospital will be deciding between whether to spend a million dollars on your software or two million dollars on a new medical device or imaging system. And sometimes they will just decide to buy both and charge more.

"Of course, that's just one example of the issues," Richardson advanced. "Hospitals are all so different. It's like that with companies that sell to disparate consumers. People from outside the industry may tend to lump provider organizations together. But that's wrong. When you've seen one hospital, you've only seen one—each healthcare provider organization is vastly different from the next.

"Comparing a rural, for-profit, hundred-bed hospital to a big, urban, not-for-profit health center is not like comparing, say, McDonald's to a different kind of restaurant chain, like Steak and Ale. It's more like comparing McDonald's to Lockheed Martin. These different hospitals are in different businesses."

Richardson continued, and Ren tried to keep up. "Some hospitals are run by operators and businesspeople. And others are run by doctors with clinical backgrounds. Most of the hospitals' decision-making will probably never make sense to you.

"That's not necessarily a bad thing. Sometimes you are okay if they're just focused on clinical quality, even over efficiency—at least when you or someone you care deeply about is the patient. When you're lying on the operating table, you don't always want everybody asking, 'What's the cheapest way to change out that hip?' And, there's a case to be made that over time, better care is cheaper for all of us. But sometimes insurance payors and healthcare providers can lose sight of that.

"There are some things that are unique to healthcare. But whatever your business is, you need to get a handle on the forces that drive your industry and how it works. The one thing that everyone will agree on about the healthcare industry is that it's driven by reimbursement—and reimbursement changes regularly, sometimes in ways that are hard to understand.

"When selling these solutions to hospitals, you ultimately get paid according to the force that drives the industry. You really need to understand about reimbursement and compliance and how hospitals respond—or at least try to respond—to that.

"Also, be forewarned," Richardson advised, "you'll always have a hard time hiring the right salespeople."

"Why?" asked Ren, even more concerned about what might be wrong with himself.

"Well," Richardson answered, "for one thing, they're sales guys. So, they'll be good at selling you on hiring them. But that doesn't mean they will be a good fit for your product and market."

Richardson saw the distressed look on Ren's face. "In case it makes you feel any better, I've been doing this for a long time and don't think I'm good at it, either. I'm not sure who is. But there are some universal truths that tend to work in all selling. I am talking about what you learn from Dale Carnegie and Tom Hopkins: building relationships and trust, truly understanding customer needs, and having genuine interest in solving their problems."

Carnegie and Hopkins were two of Ren's favorite authors and hearing their names helped him to dial back a little to Richardson's dissertation that was so similar to those from David.

"You also can tell a little about how sales candidates will deal with customers by how they sell themselves to you for the potential hire.

"When I am making a key hire, I try to really get to know someone. Sometimes my wife and I will invite them and their spouse to dinner. I also learned the hard way to do a thorough background check. We made some mistakes before where we didn't do that and suffered from things we could have learned easily enough.

"Even if you check all of the boxes," Richardson added, "sometimes you hire someone who was great with selling something else in the past, but whose experience doesn't quite translate into what you are selling and who you are selling it to now. Sometimes it's a 'fit' issue. With the long sales cycle that comes with a solution like yours, it can take a long time to find out if you have the right person."

Ren readily agreed with Richardson's advice about keeping salespeople hungry with low base salaries and big commissions.

"They will do their best job when they are almost desperate. And the great ones seem to tend to feel desperate, even when they are not," Richardson said, smiling. "Of course, for you as a startup, you may need to offer more base salary—or at least a draw ahead of sales—in order to get the best salespeople started. The best people can be selective because they are very in-demand. They may want more from a startup, at least until it seems credible and safe to them.

"Here's another trick: To any extent you can, you also want to put your sales guys in charge of your accounts receivable. And don't pay out commissions to them until your business gets paid. As a small business, you will live and die on your operating cash flows while you wait on your receivables. The cost of building your business is brutal. Since your salesperson has the relationships that can push on the customers' accounts payable, having your sales team on that is the best way to get paid fast."

Ren never got really close to Richardson, but he considered him to be one of the best, most important, and most inspirational relationships in the roller coaster ride of building the business.

CHAPTER 28

A Bad Day

"You have to dream big and go for it. Surround yourself with people who believe in you and ignore those who try to bring you down. Never give up, no matter what—overcoming obstacles makes you stronger!"

—Shannon MacMillan

It seemed like The Villain did his greatest harm when he could sneak up on you.

Sometimes Ren felt like he could almost visualize the sinister, hooded-and-cloaked Villain, lurking just over the next peak in the roller coaster, maybe holding a cartoonish bundle of dynamite, ready to bring about the next fall or blow everything up altogether. Only, this wasn't a cartoon. His family, and increasingly others' families, were depending on him to find the way through it all.

The Villain liked surprises. Just when Dirigat seemed ready to turn a big corner, he chose to deliver. And The Villain seemed to find a way to get people to help him with his work.

"Are you sitting down?" asked Chip, on the other end of the phone.

Ren made the answer clear with "I'm on speaker in my car." He was parked in front of Waffle House, for another visit with Joe Chapman.

Chip asked, "Anyone else there?"

"Just me. But I don't have much time until I need to go into a lunch meeting. What's up?" Ren was apprehensive and almost afraid to ask.

"We just found a big problem in the HospitAlign solution," Chip said. "Basically, we got a really concerning call from the Superior guys . . ."

This was starting to feel like the Cat's Meow call all over again. Superior was another crucial customer. Of course, Avery was still the most important customer as a development partner and reference. But Superior, another original partner and well respected in the industry, was surely the next most essential. And they were always great to work with. *What could it be now?*

"They found some problems in the software. Somebody there was comparing what our software indicated in their staffing plan to what their actual numbers were. And our output was way off," said Chip. "Basically, our software is giving wrong answers."

Ren responded, "I appreciate you letting me know, Chip. But I don't know what to tell you other than 'Fix it.'"

"Well, that's why I'm calling you," Chip responded. "They actually called us a couple days ago. We have been scrubbing our code, checking their inputs, and testing out everything. But we can't figure out what's wrong."

"So, if this has been going on for a couple of days, why are you just telling me now?" Ren was starting to lose patience. He had never yelled at Chip, but could hear his volume go up with each word.

"Sorry. I just think things are getting a little frayed in the office now. We've tried everything and can't find the problem. And we decided it was time to let you know. We didn't want you to hear about it from Superior."

That was not the answer Ren wanted to hear. It must be really bad, if they were worried about him getting a direct call from the system.

"Look, Chip, I'm going to go into this meeting. And when I get back to the office afterward, I hope you have it figured out. And, if you don't," Ren could hear his words becoming more forceful, "we can see where to go from there."

Chip's response surprised him. "You do that." And then Ren heard the click.

For the first time ever, the lunch visit with Joe was a little weird. Usually, they started out with friendly greetings. But this time, Ren, in his rattled state from the call with Chip, started right in by asking Joe questions about dealing with people. And he didn't listen very well to the answers, probably missing out on some wisdom from his great advisor.

At some point, Joe just looked at him for a while. "What's going on?"

He seemed disappointed in the curt tone of Ren's answer. "Software developers."

Ren wasn't ready to get into it right now. He wasn't proud of being short with Chip, and was still stunned by how the normally affable Chip had spoken before hanging up on him. After squirming in his chair for a few minutes, unable to concentrate on what he said or what he was being told, Ren realized he was so concerned that he just couldn't sit there any longer.

"Joe, I can't tell you how much I appreciate you. But," he said, "I really, really need to go. I'm so sorry." Ren dropped a twenty on the table and got up and left, missing the troubled look on his mentor's face. He walked to the car fearing he may have upset or offended a dear, invaluable mentor, but feeling like he had no other option but to get to the office as fast as he could.

———

By the time Ren got back to the Dirigat office, he had cooled off a bit. He realized that Chip and the team must have been under a lot of pressure and had probably not gotten much rest over the past couple of days. Ren also acknowledged that he hadn't been sleeping much lately himself, either.

He walked into the development room, expecting to see the team hard at work, diligently making their way through printed pages of code or tackling algorithms and formulations on the whiteboard.

Instead, the room was quiet and only two people were there. *Where was everyone?*

Aric seemed to be working at something behind his desk. Curtis looked surprised to see him walk in and quickly reached under the lower right hand of the monitor in front of him. The monitor immediately went dark, but not fast enough for Ren not to notice that Curtis had been playing an online game.

Frustrated, Ren turned around and walked out. He went into his office and started writing out some thoughts about the development team and protocols for work. Sometimes it just helped to put pen to paper. But he could feel himself getting more and more worked up, as he kept going. *How can they blow this off?* Ren was equal parts puzzled and angry. *We're going to have some new rules around here!*

About fifteen minutes later, Ren heard, passing through the hallway behind his closed door, the team finally come in. They had obviously gone to lunch together, leaving only Aric and Curtis behind for their gaming and whatever. The team was pretty noisy as they came in from the rainy day outside, and Ren could make out some loud comments from Cindy about playing softball this upcoming weekend.

It sure doesn't sound like they are very concerned about Superior or the problem.

Ren gave them a minute to settle in and saved the changes to the memo he had been writing. He needed to discuss it with Tom and Martin before doing anything, anyway. *This is supposed to be their job. Where are they? Why aren't they in the office?*

He could feel himself getting more irritated as he walked out of his office and down the short hallway, back into the development room, where everyone was settling in, now talking about college football, rather than working on the software problem.

He walked into the middle of the room and just stood there, quiet.

When Cindy said, "Hey, Ren!" and looked like she might continue, he just stood there and looked at her.

The room got silent. This was new.

Ren looked at Chip and said, "So what's the deal with Superior and the software?"

"I already told you," Chip said.

Again, this was not like Chip. But now Ren was less worried about hurting Chip's feelings. He just wanted to know what was going on. *Why are they not treating this more seriously and urgently?*

As everyone in the room now sat quietly, eyes wide, Aric stepped in. "We don't know, Ren. We have been working for two days, some of us with hardly any sleep. We just took a break for a bit to grab some lunch before we get back at it."

After a short pause, Ren's face, in a dark expression that he had surely never shown to anyone in the room before, looked at Curtis and barked, "Well, turn off the video games and figure it out!" Then he kicked the trash can next to the doorway fairly hard, spreading trash to the corner of the room, and stormed out.

Ren couldn't remember really showing his anger to anyone in quite some time. *Where had that come from?* He walked right past his office, got into his car, and went home.

When Ren arrived at his house, in the middle of a workday afternoon, all was quiet. Caulie was out, probably crapping all over the backyard, he crabbily thought. He didn't have to fight his way through her welcome dance and excitement.

As he entered, he could hear Tiffany finishing a call and walking his way.

"I've got to go," she said. "Ren just came in. He never comes home this early. Something must be up. Gotta go. Bye."

She was in the living room before he could get down to his office.

"What's up? Everything okay?"

"No! If I want the development team to do any work, I have to push them myself. 'Cause nobody else will." He was almost shouting.

Ren's loud voice must have awakened RJ from a nap. He could hear him from his room down the hall. "Daddy?"

Ren pushed past Tiffany, ignoring RJ and leaving her to deal with him.

Downstairs in his office, he pulled the door shut and immediately set to work again on the memo, as well as a long email to Tom and Martin.

At some point, before he could get much done, Caulie started barking in the backyard. Must have been a squirrel. He opened the window to the backyard and yelled, "Shut up!" It got quiet.

After what must have been a few hours, Ren heard a knock at his door. He looked up past the window and realized that it was pretty dark outside.

"Do you want some dinner?" Tiffany asked, with obvious caution in her voice.

"I'm busy," he responded, but then followed quickly, "Okay. Thanks. I'll be up and get something in a bit."

He got back into what had by now turned into a very long and quite unfriendly email and memo. Why weren't Tom and Martin in the office solving the problem when all this stuff was going on? Ren realized it might be a good idea for him to cool off a bit before sending the email, when he had to go back through to change some inappropriate words to "dysfunctional," "counterproductive," and "nonsensical."

He also noticed an email that Chip must have sent, just before that first call before his lunch meeting, with more details about the software errors. Ren, in his frustration, had missed it earlier. *What is going on? This doesn't make sense.*

It was probably another couple of hours before he looked up again. Now late, he finally went up and found where Tiffany had put his dinner away. He thought the hockey puck was just as good cold anyway, and ate it while standing at the kitchen counter. He drank his milk directly from the carton, all the while looking around suspiciously, hoping Tiffany wouldn't catch him in the act.

As he came back through the living room on his way down to his office, he noticed Tiffany sitting in the dark, on the couch. She had been watching him the whole time he was scarfing down his leftover dinner.

Instead of busting him for drinking from the milk carton or giving him grief for being so abrupt earlier, she walked over to him. "Ren, I can see things are not right. Can I do anything to help you? Do you want me to rub your shoulders to help with the stress?"

Sometime later, after the shoulder rub turned into some way-way-past-due quality time together, Ren realized that he felt much less stressed and ten years younger.

"How long has it been?" he asked.

"Way too long," responded Tiffany, as they lay in the dark, in bed. "You have been so busy and preoccupied lately. And you come to bed so late, after I've been asleep."

"Well, I must have really needed that," said Ren. He could feel the tension continuing to fall away. "Look, I'm sorry for how I acted earlier. I just had a really weird day."

"I can tell" was all she said. But her tone invited him to continue.

"I was probably rude to Joe Chapman. I yelled at Chip, of all people. And Curtis. I don't know what's going on."

He couldn't see Tiffany's face in the dark. But he could picture her patient, inquiring expression, just a couple of feet away.

"It's weird. We had a problem come up today. Or at least I just found out about it today. But I think it's more than that . . . " After a thoughtful pause, he pressed on, feeling like maybe he was getting somewhere. "I think it is a combination of a lot of things. Maybe I feel out of control. Maybe all the pressure from the last couple of years has just hit that point.

"And—just being honest—I probably need more sleep. And," Ren smiled in the dark, "I feel like I've been a time bomb in so many ways, for so long. I'm sorry for bringing it home."

Tiffany waited to let him finish. "Look, you've been distant again. You even yelled at poor Caulie today. And you were a jerk to me again. You're always saying that you notice people's insecurities. Well, I guess I've got to a point where I know, when I see you acting like that, that you're insecure about something."

If Tiffany had meant to encourage Ren to explore the thought she expressed, she had succeeded.

"I wonder if in the end, it all still comes back to the way David challenged me as a leader, a long time ago when I first met him. It feels like the business is getting away from me. Like I don't have control of things anymore. On the surface, I can see all this stuff about taking responsibility, finding purpose, becoming a leader, and all this supposed wisdom about business model and knowing what my customers are really buying and stuff. But there are times when it's like I'm lost, and everything is passing me by."

Tiffany offered, "I can see how running a business that's still finding its way can be extremely challenging. But sometimes it takes time for people to recognize growth. Maybe most of all in yourself. Based on everything I've seen and heard, you are doing a really great job. From what I can tell, everyone at the company seems to respect you more than ever. I expect you're doing great as the captain of the ship,"

Ren nodded, thankful for the feedback. "I guess David must be proud. And it does seem like people at the company are responding really well. Well, at least they *were* before this latest episode. But Tiffany, it really is a roller coaster. I mean, it's like three steps forward and two steps back, all the time. Maybe there are even times when it feels like we took ten steps back. And I really feel bad about whatever got into me today and whatever harm I might have caused."

Tiffany fell asleep, but Ren's thoughts kept him awake for a long time. It felt as if something he had never dared to even contemplate was slowly rising near the surface of his consciousness and, with some more coaxing, might present itself soon.

———

Awakening ten minutes before his alarm went off at 5:40 a.m., Ren felt refreshed. That was the best night of real sleep he'd had for some time.

Then he recalled the events of the day before. *I wonder how much damage a flawed entrepreneur can cause with one bad day? What if I burned a bridge with Joe Chapman? And the software and Superior problems are still out there! And, crap, I sure hope I didn't send that email and memo to Tom and Martin.*

By the time he got dressed and ready and got down to the kitchen, he was pretty worked up again. The only relief was when he realized that he hadn't sent the email and memo.

It all felt better, though, when he found a couple of plates of Tiffany's cookies sitting out on the counter—her delicious chocolate chip cookies, with lots of pecans. While Tiffany still made the hockey puck at times, presumably as she must still think he liked it, she was otherwise becoming a good cook. And her homemade cookies were incredible. They were covered nicely with plastic wrap, still warm. Tiffany must have been up baking them at dark-thirty this morning. There was even a note with a smiley face: "Take these to the Dirigat team and Joe and anyone else that might need them."

She was good!

———

When Ren got into the office, a little earlier than usual, it was already buzzing. He had expected to be among the first there and to hide in his office, to catch the team and share the cookies—and a sincere apology—after they all came in.

But that plan didn't work out.

When Cindy and Tom were already waiting and followed him into his office, Ren tried to prepare himself for the bad news. *Did Chip or Curtis quit? Did we lose the Superior deal? How bad was it?*

He had no one else to blame for this but himself. *I can blame The Villain for the software and Superior. But I took it from there. The worst of it wasn't The Villain this time. I helped him and advanced the cause for him. The worst of the problem was me.*

Tom pulled the door closed as they came in behind him. And Ren finally turned from behind his desk to look at the pair as they stood in front of him.

"We solved it!" said Cindy, with a chipper look on her face.

Not expecting that, all Ren could say was "What? You did what? I mean, how?"

"Superior," Cindy said. "While you were busy kicking trash cans yesterday, Tom and Martin were up at the site, working with Superior. And Curtis and Chip spent the whole night working through everything.

"Thanks to a big effort from everyone," she continued happily, "it never even turned into too much of a problem. We were all pretty busted up here. But Tom says the folks up at Superior never got too bothered about it. Most of their users didn't even notice the problem and it is working great now."

Tom finally chipped in, "Agreed. They're all good now. Like Cindy said, things never really were that bad. Other than the group that noticed the problem and called us, I think the development team at Superior was a little worried at first. But after we flew up immediately and made the response such a big deal, I think we are as good as ever with them. Especially now they can see that some of the problem was on their end."

Cindy nodded, listening to Tom. "It started with a data feed problem from their end. Well, really with the way the data was formatted and called into the application, coupled with some things our HospitAlign was doing unconventionally. But our guys came through. Curtis and Chip and Aric pulled another all-nighter and got everything working great now.

"To tell the truth," she said, "I think your acting so weird yesterday really got their attention. They were really stressed and burned out. But when you yelled at 'em, I guess they had never seen anything like that out of you. And it kind of shocked and scared everybody when you raised your voice and kicked the trash can. It was so unlike you.

"What you didn't know is that they were already pretty stressed. Chip and Aric had been going at it like crazy the past few days. I had to *make* everybody take a lunch break yesterday, just before you came in. And I *made* them take some time to do something else—*anything* else—for a little bit before working on it with fresh eyes. But after you kicked the can, they got back to work. I mean, like, they went at it."

Ren listened to Cindy and felt the heat rise on his cheeks.

"Anyway, I'm about to send Chip and Aric and Curtis home now because those three need to get some sleep.

"And," Cindy continued, "it turns out there was half a cup of coffee in the trash. Now there's a stain in the carpet that looks like a fat guy. Maybe a little like Tom here." She drew a little relieved grin from the guys. "So, I guess everything worked out okay. We just wanted you to know."

The trusted friends walked out, leaving Ren feeling guilty. Before he could even get up to take Tiffany's cookies out to the team and apologize, Cindy stuck her head back in the door.

"I told you everything worked out. But don't do anything like that again!" And he saw her stern smile start to fade as she backed out of the doorway and walked away, back toward the development room.

Cindy had scolded everyone around the office. She wasn't everyone's boss there. Just a member of the team. But she may as well have been their boss, the way she pushed everyone around and made things happen. Ren assumed she must have scolded her parents a lot throughout her childhood. That was just Cindy.

And it was later that afternoon that Tom came to visit again.

"You have no idea how much you should appreciate Cindy right now," he said. "Of course, I heard what happened yesterday with the yelling and the trash can. What you don't know is how important it was that she was there to make everything cool."

Ren could picture Cindy, taking charge as he stormed away, turning his actions from bad to good with her magic, and everyone's concern or freakoutery into constructive action. He thought about Tiffany getting him back from the ledge, and Tom and Martin jumping on the grenade and making things right at Superior.

And when he took the cookies to Joe Chapman's office, he was relieved to see that his mentor wasn't the least bit angry, but just concerned about Ren's well-being. However much he had tried to help The Villain with his work this time, disaster had been averted!

It was worth a lot to be on the roller coaster with such a great group, Ren thought, recognizing how fortunate he was to have his team. But with the company growing, it was time to see if he could stay lucky and add more great people like them to Dirigat.

CHAPTER 29

White Knuckle Interview

"Roadhog!"

—Mr. Magoo

rap! Ren thought.

His alarm was going off and Tiffany was shaking him. It took a moment to even realize where he was—and that he had overslept and was going to be late to an important interview.

As good as Tom and Hank and Cindy and the team were, Dirigat had reached the point where they needed a real director of R&D to drive the software forward, and today's interview was with a strong candidate for the position.

Startled and struggling toward consciousness, Ren quickly rose from a terrible night of maybe an hour and a half of sleep. He had only intended to crash for a half hour or so.

He *hated* being late. Being on time was one of those things, like always returning phone calls and doing what you agreed to do, that was critical not only to business but also to common courtesy. He was not living up to those essential obligations right now.

Even before he got dressed and brushed his teeth, Ren called Tom at the office and asked him to meet the candidate, to show him around, and to start getting to know him until he arrived. Normally, Ren would have gone first and then done more of the introductions. But with the shameful oversleeping, that was the best solution. He was almost twenty minutes late when he rushed in to meet the candidate who, fortunately, hadn't even seemed to notice.

Carl Joseph had an amazing résumé. He was a big-time guy looking for a second career, having retired relatively young from running the research and development organization of a billion-dollar company in the healthcare information technology space. He had come with good recommendation letters from people whom Ren respected, so Ren didn't delve deeper into why he had retired so young.

Ren liked Carl right away. He seemed like a big changeup from the startup's culture. That could potentially be a good thing, Ren thought. Now that Dirigat was growing, the organization needed to get a little more process-driven and professional. Carl would bring additional credibility and relationships to the organization. A comment in one of his recommendations was that developers would flock to him, which could be a great benefit to Dirigat.

After years of studying about reading people, breaking down barriers, and using good interview techniques, Ren felt like he owed it to his team as well as Dirigat's customers to get a strong understanding of the people he was hiring— especially now, when each and every hire was so impactful.

He typically went to great lengths to research candidates, knowing that résumés and reference letters rarely told the full story. Ren knew that the better connected he was, the easier it was for him to find out about candidates. Though it wasn't an exact science, an abundance of clues, taken collectively, tended to paint a fairly accurate picture of the kind of person he might be interviewing.

Ren found that personal connections from his network were advantageous for useful, honest feedback. When someone applied or was being recruited for a position at Dirigat, he would go on LinkedIn or through their résumé and find someone who knew them or who could at least find out the truth about them. Time and work invested in hiring just the right candidate had a great payback.

However, between what Ren had learned so far about Carl and with Dirigat's urgency to fill the position—Tom had actually used the words "like, yesterday!"—Ren didn't spend his usual network capital to do in-depth research about Carl before the interview.

One of Ren's mentors had suggested that if a reasonable opportunity to do so presented itself, he should ride in the car with potential hires. Sometimes, Ren would invite a candidate into the office to meet the team and see the space, before taking them to an informal interview lunch with Tom. When it was time to head out for lunch, Ren would typically have Tom drive separately, leaving himself to ride with the candidate. The candidate could then leave straight from the restaurant, and Ren could ride back with Tom, giving them a chance to discuss the potential hire while everything was fresh on their minds.

As they got through the initial visit and walked through the office, introducing more of the team to Carl, lunchtime was approaching. Per his formula, Ren asked Carl for a ride—which Carl was happy to oblige—and then asked Tom to meet them at their favorite Taco Mac restaurant, a few miles away from the office.

Seeing someone's car, particularly when they weren't expecting it to be seen, could offer valuable insight. Ren didn't care in the least if the car was nice. In fact, he usually thought better of people who drove practical vehicle brands, such as Hondas and Toyotas, and ones that suited their circumstances, like a minivan or SUV for a parent. But while the status of the car didn't impress Ren, how well it was kept always got his attention. If the car was messy or in bad shape, that could be a red flag for some jobs. If he needed an organized personality for project management, could that person fit? If they didn't take care of their car, was it reasonable to expect them to take care of Dirigat's servers or office equipment?

Carl's car, a Ford Taurus, didn't reveal anything especially concerning. It was neat and orderly enough and demonstrated a practical sensibility for someone who had been so successful.

Ren also felt like he learned a great deal by observing how someone drove. Of course, candidates would drive differently with him in the car, since, in most cases, they were trying to impress him to get the job. But as they made their way through traffic while having an in-depth conversation, they would almost always reveal a lot about their personality. If the candidate drove carefully and followed the rules, Ren considered this to potentially be terrific for someone applying for a position in the company where they needed to do the same, such as in accounting. For a sales job, he might want someone who was a little more aggressive. For some other positions, Ren might look for someone who was more considerate toward other drivers.

In Carl's case, his driving would have been concerning for any position imaginable. Carl was a horrible driver. Actually, he drove like a madman! He weaved in and out of his lane, swerved to avoid hitting a stop sign, and, in essence, was just dangerous behind the wheel. Yet during the entire scary ride, Carl kept speaking calmly to Ren, as if his driving was completely normal. This may as well have been a typical, everyday commute to him.

Placated a little by Carl's calmness and rationalizing that maybe Carl had just been too caught up in the conversation, Ren was trying to be cool. But in an effort to see if Carl would volunteer a history of traffic violations, he asked, "So, if you joined us here, what would your commute be like to work, with Atlanta's terrible traffic and the accidents that always pop up?"

With a completely straight face and tone, Carl said, "I don't know. Commuting is never a problem for me at all. All of the wrecks always seem to happen behind me."

Somehow, Ren managed to hold back an explosion of laughter from the implications of that. He put it aside, for now, as they were pulling up at the Taco Mac.

The lunch conversation had a few odd points, but, overall, there were no huge red flags for Ren or Tom.

When Ren got in Tom's Jeep to head back to the office, he finally released his laughter. He told Tom about his scary ride to lunch. They both laughed the whole way back, picturing Carl causing wrecks behind himself and not even realizing it, like the old cartoon character, Mr. Magoo. And they discussed how Mr. Magoo would fit with the team.

Ren would learn the hard way that he could not afford to bring in anyone on the initial team who didn't already have the traits he wanted to build the company around. Once Dirigat already had a team with the character and success factors it needed, then they could selectively add someone here and there who could evolve toward their potential. But it would have been difficult to bring in a bunch of people with traits that were different from what you wanted, mix them together, and then have any reasonable expectation that they would gel into what you hoped for. And the team was probably not going to spontaneously evolve better traits than their leadership demonstrated.

Ren also liked self-disqualifying interviews, where he encouraged people to join the team if they fit—and to save themselves and the company time and challenge if they didn't. In doing so in the interviews, he kept coming back to the mission and vision and values that he had written for the first business plan. Tom and others had helped him to refine the list and suit it to their business as it came together. And, that was what they tried to hire for.

Ren always preferred objective consideration over subjective, but recognized that many people leaned on their intuition or gut instinct in hiring, as well as in many other aspects of the business. David had advised Ren not to lean too much on gut feelings at first. He felt that these feelings derived from our subconscious, as we take the other person's tone, posture, gestures, attire, and any number of factors into account. David did suggest that they could become more valuable over time, with experience, and as their inner sense proved itself more reliable.

As Ren's intuition developed and improved with experiences, challenges, and successes, he started paying greater attention to it. After sufficient experience and learning, he felt sure enough to say that "When you meet people, *you kind of know.*"

Ren certainly never rode anywhere with Carl again. Still, he and Tom wanted Carl to work out to such a degree that they looked past the driving—and probably overlooked some other warning signs, too—and hired him promptly. They felt they got a relatively good deal, compared to what they feared he might demand in terms of salary and compensation.

Eventually, Ren learned to keep in mind the great advice that he got from Sid Richardson to "hire for trust, competence, and culture." And he found that early hiring was an essential opportunity to define the organization's culture and competence.

CHAPTER 30

Taking It Up a Notch

*"Treat your salesperson like you would treat your
most important customer—because he is!"*

—Colleen Stanley

After several months of intensive work, the software continued to come together and look increasingly promising for the broader market. Tom decided that it was ready to be taken to a trade show for showing off and for marketing it to more customers. It was time to sell more.

The Healthcare Information and Management Systems Society was the leading American association for healthcare information technology. The organization's annual trade show, now just referred to by industry folks as "HIMSS," was ground zero for anything big or new in healthcare-centered IT. Thousands of people gathered for the event every year, even though attending it was expensive and appearing as an exhibitor even more so, which meant there was ongoing debate about whether it was a worthwhile investment. But year in and year out, top companies and startups showed up and showed off for existing and prospective customers—and for each other.

"It is going to be great exposure for Dirigat," Tom told Ren, "and exactly what we need right now. We are ready."

Tom worked out a budget for the trade show, he got a booth, and he even got some swag made up. He ordered customized pens, notepads, postcards, and even chocolate and butterscotch candy, wrapped in plastic and adorned with the Dirigat logo.

Curiously, it irked Ren that the swag made him so happy and proud. As far as he could figure, it bothered him because it seemed cheesy, smarmy, impractical, and not cost effective. At the same time, he loved it because it was his company from his idea—his baby—proudly displayed on those pens and pads and candy.

Tom also got some banners and promotional materials made and put together an engaging demonstration of what the technology could do. He, Ren, and a couple of the guys flew to the trade show, which was hosted in New Orleans that year.

Even though the objective was technically all about work, the city, with its delicious food and dynamic culture, made for a fun trip. The HIMSS attendees seemed intrigued by Dirigat's young team and their new idea and approach. Although they made plenty of connections that at the time felt promising, only one strong, direct, actionable lead panned out in the year following the trade show. That lead came from a guy in their home region: a quality manager at a large local municipal-authority hospital with a level-one trauma center.

Even though the quality manager seemed genuinely interested in Dirigat's HospitAlign solution, his organization, Grover Health System, was notorious at the time for not paying their bills. For a startup that needed cash flow, Grover didn't seem like a good investment of time and resources.

Yet interestingly, the quality manager just kept calling and asking for a proposal. He seemed to love Dirigat's idea and to really appreciate Tom.

Tom respected the quality manager and felt that he owed him a response, so eventually, he came to them with a deal that would justify the risk to Dirigat. Tom was sure Grover would decline, as the deal asked them to pay more than Dirigat might normally charge, with about 80 percent of the amount up front. To Tom, that was the only way Dirigat could afford to have them as a customer.

It was nothing short of a shock to everyone at Dirigat when Grover accepted the offer. And Grover ended up being one of the best, most progressive, and loyal paying customers that the company had. The lesson both Tom and Ren felt they learned from the experience was that it was risky to prejudge how a lead will turn out.

Other opportunities also started to trickle in, slowly at first, but more rapidly as time went on and the word about Dirigat got out. Some of the new acquaintances came from relationships with the initial customers or contacts that Tom and his team developed, but most of the best deals came from word-of-mouth referrals.

It didn't happen as quickly as Ren and Tom had hoped it would, but the transition from just thinking it would sell, to seeing it *actually* sell broadly, was exciting.

In hindsight, much of the early success of the company came because the customers trusted Tom. This was because he genuinely *was* trustworthy in all of his dealings with them. People knew Tom was going to do his very best to do right by them and to solve their problems. He cared even more than the customers did about creating value for them and solving their problems.

Tom was the opposite of your image of a smarmy sales guy. All he did was keep presenting the solution and customer testimonials and working leads. He understood most of the customer organizations very well, and while he wasn't a sales-closer guy, he did a great job of high-level business development and relationship-building.

———

As the company grew, the team needed again to hire more people. Ren always wanted to minimize expenditures and hire behind the need, but the needs were becoming considerable. And the cash flows were starting to increase, with more sales to justify the hiring costs.

Tom, with help and advice from their old friend Dan McGinty and others, really showed a talent for finding and hiring good developers and team members.

They brought in a small number of really strong developers and technologists who fit right in with the existing team of Aric, Chip, Cindy, Curtis, and the rest. They had to outsource some of their development once again, but, on the advice of David and Dan, Dirigat continued to manage and control the development internally.

Tom had hired some specialist developers, but he also brought in a couple more "athletes," as he still called them: people who had a broader skill set than many hardcore, skill-specific developers and who had worked in, and understood, hospitals. This was very useful in bridging the gap between the customer and the solution.

One of the best things happened when a couple of young, talented people who had worked in provider organizations came to Tom and Ren with an interest in working with them. In the mold of Cindy and Chip, they came from a hospital environment, married an understanding of customer needs with technical expertise, and had an ability to bring it all together. Rick and Leela both had some technical proficiency in utilizing statistics for quality and consistency, as well as solid competence in healthcare, data management, and software development.

Neither of them was a consultant or at all "salesy," but both of them functioned very well in hospitals. This was great for delivery and installation, implementation, and particularly customer relationships that turned into ongoing business development.

However much Ren now "got it" and wanted to get better at it, Dirigat still had not really fit the model that David wanted. But these new additions, along with Tom and Cindy, were driving what could be described as paid consulting and development. That sort of work forced them to create more market-validated solutions and made their customers into valuable partners. And it was working!

But, as might be expected, the more enthusiastic and happy everyone else seemed, the more Ren worried. He had already observed that entrepreneurs and CEOs very often tend to become contrarians. Ren saw this as a defense mechanism that evolves and works to their advantage. When things are good and everyone is celebrating and happy, the leader gets worried, notes all of the hazards looming, and is looking for when and where The Villain is going to next appear. But when things are not going as well and everyone else gets worried, the same leader gets positive and constructive, looking for opportunities, recognizing that tough times are the best times to improve the business and take any advantage over their competitors.

Ren wasn't surprised that others thought he was a devout optimist, rather than this sort of contrarian. It made sense. When things were good and everyone was celebrating and Ren was worried, he kept his mouth shut, not wanting to rain on their parade. On the other hand, when things were not good and everyone else was distressed, he would cheerlead and share his enthusiasm with everyone.

Now, as things seemed good and positive, Ren was alone in getting increasingly troubled. One of his main concerns was that, even with the new hospitals slowly coming in, Dirigat never got good at closing new customer sales. Closing a deal took way too long and never went well enough. Another big worry for him was the fact that even as Dirigat was ramping up and delivering solutions, the business was struggling with cash flows.

At least initially, Ren felt that he was the only one to realize how deficient the company was in selling.

He was not a sales guy. But like Jane Goodall with her gorillas, Ren had lived among a hardcore sales culture and had learned from it. Dirigat did not have that kind of culture.

Ren's friends, with whom he had started Standard Link, were hardcore sales guys. They had created the ultimate culture of sales. Sure, the company had some great expertise and carried great products, but it was all about selling, in a way that people outside of that environment probably wouldn't understand. They had grown Standard Link from nothing to thirty million dollars in very-high-margin sales, with a great customer list, in just a few years—primarily by being great at selling.

The culture of sales had been pervasive throughout Standard Link. When Ren had started the support desk at that company, their mission was to first solve the problem, and right after that, to figure out how to turn it into another sale. Per Sid Richardson's advice, Dirigat was now trying to hire and build a culture for sales.

With any business and in any organization, people largely follow what the leadership emphasizes and demonstrates. At Standard Link, that had been sales—not just in terms of business development and building credibility, which Dirigat was probably okay at now—but also about closing deals, and everything before and after.

Standard Link used to have a company-wide call every Monday morning at eight. And even if the call took half the day, it went on until every single person in the company, including the receptionist, explained where they were in all of their sales-funnel efforts.

There was a lot Ren learned about sales success from his Standard Link founder friends, but the one thing that stood out most was the extreme emphasis on selling, which, Ren understood, was essential. The sales-centered culture was pervasive, infectious.

Ren and Tom always prioritized a culture of service and excellence, but with the kind of competent, high-integrity people they were hiring, that was not going to be a problem. It felt like Tom and his team would go to great lengths to deliver great results. It was worth a lot to not have to worry about that imperative consideration.

When Tom started with Dirigat, Ren had taken him to meet with a good friend who had quickly built a $350 million business, primarily on being great with sales. Ren wanted Tom to see what the friend's mentality was like. That friend had told them that his sales mindset was about "selling as much as you possibly could—and then somehow finding a way to deliver." Tom would never be able to think like that, and it wasn't what Ren wanted from him, either. He liked the idea of Tom being the one who was charged to deliver, with his commitment to excellence. But Dirigat now needed to get better at the "selling as much as they possibly could" part to really make it all work.

———

Ren always thought of people as either being more "form" or more "substance." Basically, substance people were all about merit and value and delivering what they said they would do. Form people were about looking good and convincing people to buy what they were selling. He thought the form people could be at least as important to success as the substance people, but he wanted them in lesser ratios. Dirigat felt to Ren to be full of substance people, so he knew he needed to balance it out by hiring more form people for sales.

Although he worked hardest through his life to be better at the form, Ren always thought of himself as very much a substance guy. Form felt more elusive to him, yet it was something he knew could be valuable.

He saw that a lot of substance people didn't succeed, even with merited and valuable solutions. And he sometimes saw people that seemed "almost all form," as he thought of them, go out and raise money and sell a lot—and then hire or buy substance to eventually create a platform that could become substantive and successful.

So, while Ren had felt that it was important to start the company around the ultimate substance guy, Tom Strong, he had seen more huge, fast successes that were started by form people: leaders that built a currency and market positioning with hype and then hired substance guys, got out of their way, and found great results.

David understood and embraced Ren's form and substance thinking, but noted that there would always be a healthy friction between the two types.

———

In the meantime, the mystery of David's Daily Disappearances—or the "3D Mystery," as the team in the office now called it—only deepened! *Where* was the dude going and *why* was he sneaking around?

At some point, Ren got elected to jump on the grenade and ask him. He was a little reluctant to do so, but eventually, over a delicious burger at the local LongHorn, he asked David what was going on.

David, perhaps surprised that his excursions had been noticed, dodged the question and changed the subject. But Ren called him on that and asked again. David's cheeks betrayed a tiny blush, from which he quickly recovered. Then he said, "That's my business. I actually wouldn't mind telling you, but if everyone's enjoying the mystery and speculation, I'll keep on letting y'all have your fun!"

The biggest thing that seemed to initially come out of that conversation was that David came into the office less frequently—and no one saw him sneak out again.

It was only a few weeks later that Ren figured out what had been going on.

CHAPTER 31

Pennies Take Care

"Money's a horrid thing to follow, but a charming thing to meet."

—Henry James

O f all the terrific things that David Olden did for Ren Hatcher and his business, one of the best was the connection to Jon Weiser.

Ren had heard the name a number of times, always said with reverence. When people said his name, they seemed to look up, inspired, and emphasizing the last name, "Weiser," as if stating some secret code word. The legend of Jon Weiser preceded the man himself. Before meeting him in person, Ren had imagined him as at least ten feet tall and made of titanium, with glowing eyes of diamonds.

Weiser had been CFO for a handful of successful public companies and had served as an advisor to a number of others. The word on Weiser was that he didn't sleep. He may have been an artificially intelligent robot of some sort.

One story came from a friend who had fired off an email to Weiser, inquiring about a complicated subject, just after midnight. He was shocked to receive, just an hour later, a perfectly succinct four-page response that solved everything.

Another mutual friend asserted that Jon Weiser did more work in a day than anyone else did in a month. Ren had assumed that was hyperbole—until he actually worked with Weiser and found it to be true.

While it seemed to embarrass and bother him, Weiser was credited with holding the record for the most billable hours in the audit practice at the largest global accounting firm. This milestone was from the early years of his career, and was allegedly never surpassed in the decades after he set it.

Ren, of course, "scored" people according to how they would deliver. In aggregate, on a scale of 1 to 10, how they would perform in always getting things done well, on time, and as promised, including in cost. Tom Strong's score was exemplary, ranking in Ren's estimation as an 8 or 9. Most good people were in the 7 to 8 range. Weiser would go on to be Ren's only 10. As impossible as it seemed, he always came through ideally, in every way.

So when Ren first met Weiser, expecting a superhuman character, he was surprised to meet an average-looking, fifty-something, balding gentleman, with a warm, friendly expression. He looked a bit like Captain Picard from *Star Trek: The Next Generation*, a fictional character that Ren really appreciated and learned from. Yes! Ren believed you could actually learn from fiction! And, while he was not a giant in stature, Ren continued to always think of Weiser as such.

As Ren introduced himself and explained Dirigat, he expected the usual sequence of order-your-meal, chitchat, and then eventually get to the matter at hand. Yet, while as nice as anyone, Weiser didn't seem to want to waste time with the personal stuff. He just wanted to know more about Dirigat and what Ren was doing.

Weiser was a great listener. Ren learned that he picked everything up quickly and asked very smart questions. He cut to the chase, in every case where it was appropriate. And he shared great wisdom from many angles.

Weiser sagely told Ren, "With public companies, I live in a world where we are all about accrual basis. Depreciation and managing earnings and such matter to us. But for you and virtually all early stage companies, it's all about operating cash flows. As a startup, you live and die on your success in this. Of course, you need to keep accrued earnings and expenses at the top of your mind. But you evolve to think in cash basis first—making payroll and so forth—with accrual basis underlying some of your considerations as well.

"As you grow and capitalize more into R&D, we can work through that and get a better handle on your payback and return on invested capital. But, for now, let's talk about operating cash flows and focus on your financial model."

And they did. Ren had thought himself good at the financial side of things, but Weiser took it to a whole other level.

During that first conversation with Weiser, Ren walked through what he thought were both his profit and his loss centers in Dirigat and where the dollars were coming from and going to. Ren couldn't help but brag a little as he shared how little the company was spending on general and administrative, or G&A, costs.

Weiser seemed to really appreciate Ren's emphasis on that frugality and to strongly approve of it. He underlined the importance of what came with it: the fastidiousness and discipline—and even the measurement itself—that made you better. "In taking care of the pennies, you *will* better take care of the dollars."

But he seemed to choke on what Ren was spending on his development team for research and development, R&D, to build out the software in advance of selling it to the market.

By this point, Ren completely agreed, as Weiser was endorsing David's advice that a more incremental model, with direct costs that were built into pricing in each sale, would force him to have a better solution. But Weiser was also making a practical point about covering the ongoing costs in a better way. He seemed to feel, like David, that it would be much better to get the customers to fund that more directly. Weiser was just coming at it from a different angle, adding a new perspective to David's essential rant.

"And," said Weiser, "I would at least want a relatively quick cash flow payback on anything you capitalize into R&D. I can't tell you with certainty, at all, that your R&D investment to try to be ahead of the market is a bad bet for now, but I tend to always prefer an incremental model.

"David has probably talked to you plenty about a funded development model," he continued, as Ren thought, *Man, has he ever!* "There are a number of reasons for that model, and one of them is because software R&D works like a lot of other rapidly depreciating assets in that you can often replace or surpass it, cheaper and better, at any point. When he was running research and development, David might have spent ten million dollars and three years to build a new software solution, only to find that, by the time he was done, he could build the same thing for half the money in half the time. That is, and will continue to be, the case in technology and for many solutions. And if your solution is great, someone will basically steal it and may do it better."

"I get it," said Ren. "I know you and David want me to build a better, more market-driven solution by doing it for our customers. But it's not always easy. We started with our own innovative concept that the market obviously adopted.

We have some innovative ideas, the opportunity is really hot now, and sometimes it's still hard to follow David's advice and go slower now, to be a better company later."

"Don't get me wrong," Weiser responded. "Funding your own development in advance of your market may be necessary in some rare occasions. You should speak to our mutual friend, Sid Richardson, about what he calls 'morphability.' But you still seem to me like an exception that proves the rule. From my own more financially oriented perspective, I agree with David that it will always be better when it's paid for by your customers."

Weiser transitioned, "And, I particularly hate *obligated* overhead—those operating costs that are ongoing expenditure commitments and unavoidable. Like expensive office space and some of your internal general and administrative. And I also think there is business value in thinking about all of your cost structure, for pricing and for making better decisions."

"I couldn't agree more," said Ren. "And thanks for bringing it back to a tactical, financial consideration."

Weiser nodded, as he continued, "If I need to, I will live with some *discretionary* overhead. Particularly when I can allocate and directly apportion it as a cost of acquiring new customers and new business. For instance, when you run an externally sourced marketing campaign—as opposed to hiring internal marketing staff for that purpose—you can choose to continue that expenditure in the future but are not obligated to do so, if you don't find the results you were looking for. You can more easily build it into your pricing and almost think of it as an incremental cost where you pay it as you go along, over the next 'however many' customers that come of it, to assure payback.

"That's not an accounting thing. That's a business-justification and spending discipline thing, and a model consideration."

Having so many employees on payroll had largely been viewed as an obligated overhead to Ren. Although, with this in mind—and as he finally really understood the model—he got better at allocating and placing employees directly with customers. And the discipline of doing that was making Dirigat a better business in many ways.

As Weiser advocated for a better system to tie everything together in alignment, Ren took much more from this great new mentor who had both a financial *and* a business perspective. One such nugget was about value-added analysis.

"You can do your own value-added analysis for every employee and every other asset and function in the business," Weiser said during one get-together. "Are you familiar with that?"

Ren nodded in a sort of wobbly way that he hoped would demonstrate to Weiser that he had been exposed to it but wanted to understand more.

"You should be able to trace and account for every dollar somewhere—every penny of revenue and every penny you spend. You can even weigh risk, over time, and allocate that where appropriate.

"If you really want to understand your business and financial model, take every single dollar and allocate it to an end point. Force all revenue that comes in to go somewhere and force everything that is spent to come from somewhere. You should do this with every business, not just software. But since you're in software, your obvious cost of goods sold is going to be low and your contribution margins should be high," said Weiser.

"But none of it may be what you think," he added. "Some of the power comes from seeing it more objectively and empirically, measured against where you create value.

"You can look at whether—and, if so, how well—each asset is paying for itself. You are forced to justify, say, your general and administrative expenditures and where your incremental expenses and real earnings flow, and the place where your investments should and shouldn't go. Where does the money for your power bill, your receptionist, and your insurance come from, allocated on perhaps a percentage basis to each sale, as you utilize them? Where is the payback on each of them? By seeing the justification of every element of your company, you can get a better sense of what your *real* profit centers and your *real* loss centers are."

Ren was enraptured. Whenever he got advice from Weiser, he found it exceptionally specific and useful.

"For example," Weiser continued, "let's consider the travel involved when delivering a new implementation. When you tabulate all of the costs of deploying the team that does the installation, including their travel and risk and other hidden costs associated with having them out of the office, as well as other direct costs in technology and any other incremental expenditures that you can come up with, you might find that it represents, say, about ten percent of each dollar of revenue from a new installation.

"And then when you start breaking down all of the contribution to overhead, you should also be able to direct every penny of the other ninety percent.

Of course, some of that will ultimately go toward shareholder value, in terms of retained earnings that are invested going forward, or dividends, or otherwise. But you should also be able to allocate each portion of your obligated overhead, including G&A. So, if you have a receptionist who answers the phone, you should be able to apportion their costs and where all of the pennies and dollars flow to and from. And I like to justify how that pays back in direct and indirect value to the business, whether now or longer term. Same thing with your insurance, rent, and every other cost, including that research and development in your software."

Weiser let that sink in for a moment before moving forward. "You also need to think about the opportunity cost of any dollar you are spending, measured against its potential highest and best use. Try to do your best 'guesstimate' of incorporating risk in that consideration. If something is not essential, could those dollars or resources be deployed elsewhere, with a better payback?

"And if you can allocate the value applied to the receptionist or all of the cost of the R&D and everything else, you need to understand whether the payback on that expenditure is worth it."

Weiser added, "Complicating that, you also sometimes need to step back from just looking at how the numbers flow today and also weigh intangible values, prospective future paybacks, and other strategic considerations.

"Like, you might find that hiring a consultant doesn't pay for itself in the immediate term but is important for future growth. In that case, you would allocate the portion of this loss center that is an investment and apply the same discipline in examining where that payback will come from and how, hopefully over an easily measured metric to determine how well the investment worked."

Caught up in this, Ren had lost track of time before realizing that he needed to get to his next meeting. He chugged the rest of his sweet tea while waiting to get the check and credit card back—he had hardly noticed eating his food. And he was ready to go, when Weiser got him with one last statement, regarding something that Ren had really been wrestling with.

"You also need to find a way to build risk and other costs into your decision-making and model . . ." Ren turned his head sharply at the mention of pricing risk.

CHAPTER 32

Weiser Fiscal Counsel

*"Financial fitness is not a pipe dream or a state of mind.
It's a reality if you are willing to pursue it and embrace it."*

—Will Robinson

On arriving at home in the evening, after meeting Jon Weiser earlier in the day, Ren was still caught up in their conversation.

He pushed past Caulie's dance and enthusiasm, and found Tiffany and RJ waiting for him as he passed through the kitchen and into the family room. Caulie followed him into the room, still a bit excited from his arrival for the evening.

"Don't get mad," said Tiffany.

No good news ever starts that way. "What's up?" Ren asked, head sideways and the left side of his mouth raised.

"Well, since the Standard Link cash-in and where you are in your business, I was thinking we need a vacation. Through all you put into Standard Link and now Dirigat, you haven't had a vacation . . . actually *we* haven't had a vacation in years."

That wasn't what Ren expected. "I mean . . . I guess I could use a break. But I just don't see it happening right now."

"Well, I booked a cruise," said Tiffany, after a little pause. "And I was a little worried. But the good news is that I booked it for six months from now. It is only four days, in the Caribbean. And you have six months to get ready for it."

Then Tiffany put her head down, eyes looking up at him. "I booked it non-refundable, so you won't back out. I know you won't waste the money."

Appreciating her intentions and processing it all, Ren was somehow a little annoyed and relieved at the same time. *At least I'm in a little better place to do it now and we can afford it. We probably need it. And who knows, maybe it will be fun!*

RJ was really excited when he found that Ren's mother, Carol—his Nonna—was going to be staying with him and Caulie when Mommy and Daddy were gone on the cruise. His Nonna spoiled him!

And Ren had so much on his mind, he just let it go.

He didn't speak much through dinner. It didn't occur to him that Tiffany might take his silence and distraction as being unhappy about the nonrefundable cruise. Ren actually only had mild mixed feelings about it, if anything. At this point, he was still caught up in his conversation with Weiser from earlier in the day. The older new friend had left him with a subject that had been on his mind a lot lately.

Ren emailed him later that evening, asking to connect again at the earliest opportunity. Knowing that Weiser was a very early riser, he offered to meet him at a convenient Waffle House the next morning, as early as he would like.

As soon as Ren hit send, he worried that wanting to meet again so soon may have been too pushy. But he was only slightly surprised when Weiser responded, almost immediately, "Great. See you there at 5 a.m."

———

When Ren arrived at the always-open Waffle House at 4:45 the next morning, Weiser was already there, sipping from his cup of coffee. By the time Ren sat down and ordered his big, greasy breakfast of bacon and hash browns, scattered with cheese, jalapeños and chili, and eggs scrambled with cheese, Weiser was past any small talk and ready to continue their conversation from the prior day.

Weiser cleared his throat. "If you haven't already discovered it, one of the hardest things to build in for a small business is the cost of risk. Great businesses make a science of understanding it. And for most big companies, most of those costs just automatically get built in to pricing and overall cost structure, over time.

"Take a huge national consumer retailer, like Target or Walmart, for example," he said. "Over a many-year average, they might have experienced that for, say, every 10,000 customers that come through the door, they will lose some expected amount from shoplifting, from breakage, and from purchase returns and allowances. And as one potential example of risk, they probably find that some number of employees, vendors, and customers that come through the door will try to sue them for some reason, all of which cost something to address and respond to. Some percentage of those lawsuits would justify settling, at a significant cost, and a tiny percentage of those might have enough merit to actually cost a lot of money."

Ren pictured the somber and shrouded Villain working his way through a Target, disrupting the store's efforts at every opportunity, as Weiser continued.

"All of that, over time, ends up necessarily built into their pricing that they pass along to you, the consumer. To get where they are, they had to. Or they would have gone out of business.

"Of course, every company carries great risk at a great number of points every day," he said. "But small, inexperienced companies like Dirigat don't have a handle on that yet. Often, they don't even have the data points they need to be able to see it all, on a sufficient scale, to integrate. Frankly, if you did price all your risk, you might find it daunting to build your business."

"I've heard that from David before," Ren acknowledged. "But it helps to come at it this way. Please continue."

"Small businesses don't consider pricing in a lot of less obvious costs," said Weiser. "For instance, you have the IRS allowable mileage for company vehicles, which should hopefully cover your expenses for fuel, as well as wear and tear on tires, brakes, engines, and so forth, for a sensible vehicle. In theory, it should also cover things we don't consider as much, like depreciation of the vehicle, for whenever you want to trade it in for the next one, and allocating insurance.

"But it won't come close to covering the additional costs, to you, of an employee getting in a fender bender. And one thing you can count on is that if you have enough employees out driving around for sales calls, implementations, and offsite development meetings, fender benders are going to happen. The question is not if, but when and how often and how bad.

"Hopefully no one gets hurt, but there is still the lost work time, cost and time handling the insurance claim and repair, or even addressing any lawsuits, however frivolous," he said, rolling his eyes to demonstrate his earned cynicism about such things.

"Bigger companies, as with the other risks we mentioned with the department stores, have built that into their cost model," Weiser added. "They evolved to it, as it happened to them, each time. For you . . . well, you just have to anticipate as well as possible. And you need to have sufficient gross margins to justify whatever you do. And of course, all businesses, big and small, pay insurance to mitigate that risk—that you could allocate to each vehicle, employee, and other asset.

"Bringing it back to your services and consulting solutions at Dirigat," said Weiser, "and even the deployment costs for your software installations and such, it makes me think of an analysis that we did on our consultants at one of my companies. In addition to what we paid them, we were paying them for additional vacation time. We supplied them with considerable benefits. We also provided our consultants with a computer and phone that we depreciated as rapidly as Generally Accepted Accounting Principles would allow, with good reason, as those items had a short useful life for us. And there were many other costs that we found that were not as obvious.

"We also spent a lot of money on downtime when they were under the weather, or not working for any other reason," Weiser continued. "And we found that over a large number of consultants, there was considerable risk in having them on board, along the lines of what I already brought up. That could include employees that had an illness, family issues, became less productive for whatever reason, or perhaps even stole from the company or tried to sue the company for whatever, usually frivolous, reason."

It was easy to see from his expression and tone that Weiser had encountered plenty of consternation and frustration from such litigation or threats of it. Ren had seen this in plenty of other instances as well, and his lawyer friend, Gary, had warned about it. Such things seemed to inevitably create huge unnecessary pain and expense for most businesses.

"Then we weighed the dollars that we invested in deploying these consultants versus the opportunity cost of investing those dollars benignly in relatively low-risk opportunities."

There was so much power behind Weiser's soft-spoken, thoughtful process through all of this, as he kept going: "And what we found is that, for new consultants, we needed to generate at least two and a half times what we were paying them to justify even having them.

"In your case, your cost in paid-services people and any consultants that you add might be a bit lower because they are contributing additional value toward your software development, as well as future earnings that could ulti-mately come from that. So in your case, you may find that you just need to have the consultants bringing in maybe one and a half times more than their direct costs to be viable."

There were some very good things that came from those first couple of meetings with Weiser, on consecutive days. He became increasingly involved in helping Dirigat. And going forward regularly for years, he provided valuable new perspectives on financial discipline. Even more importantly, Weiser pro-vided great guidance and consideration on financial decisions and how those tied together almost inextricably with being a good business.

———

Weiser started coming into Dirigat's office—not consistently like David, but fairly regularly. Ren appreciated the times when he helped him to focus and clarify; when Ren would give a long, overcomplicated explanation, Weiser would follow it all with a simple translation, maybe one sentence that explained every-thing that really needed to be said. He constantly kept Ren and the team in line.

Weiser worked with Ren and the team to create a clear system to track every dollar. Ren's goal had been to integrate the company's accounting sys-tem, Customer Relationship Management (CRM) solution, and Dirigat's own HospitAlign software that tied everything, clearly, to the company's goals. While that never worked as well as Ren had hoped, just thinking that way helped him spectacularly. And of course, the discipline and process to get there was healthy, in and of itself. Ren came to a much better understanding and consideration of his real cost and profit centers—and did a much better job with his expenses, revenues, and eventually earnings, too. It was powerful to have a better handle on knowing, for example, who was paying for themselves and how. And that all enabled better decisions on whether and where to invest any resources.

And Weiser was also good for the culture in the office. Just his presence there set a tone of competence, professionalism, and productivity because of the respect that everyone felt for him.

One of the more compelling things about Weiser was that everyone trusted him and his objectivity. So, when there were frictions or disagreements, he was a perfect mediator. Whatever he said was enough. Everyone just said "okay" and moved on.

Weiser also helped with some of the important things that they don't teach you in college. For example, the cost of carrying receivables—and the resultant cash flow planning and using financing or better forecasting to overcome cash flow challenges. He had seen a number of small businesses seemingly "grow themselves out of business." On this topic, he gave Ren a little lecture.

"One of the lessons you're learning in your business already," said Weiser, "is when you have millions of dollars in receivables, but you don't have enough money to make payroll. Some people are on the other side—they're rich with cash because of an equity investment or debt, but they don't have the cash flow to justify those things. That can set up future problems. But the issue at hand for you right now, in this moment when you are growing and your customers are paying so far behind your expenditures for them, is meeting payroll."

With the exasperation of his experiences weighing on him, Ren said, "Yes, we keep learning lessons around receivables!"

Increasingly, it seemed like customers were dragging out their payables 90 to 120 days, basically using their vendors as a bank and indifferent to the fact that the cost would ultimately have to be passed back to them.

And of course, there were always extenuating factors that equated to payment risk. Dirigat was better off than many small businesses in some ways. They knew that they were going to eventually get paid by almost all of their customers, and so they didn't have to completely write off as much. But for cash-flowing their bigger deals in advance just to be able to deliver, Dirigat was in a worse position. Sometimes the company had to invest up to hundreds of thousands of dollars up front to develop, staff, and deliver a solution. Then they had to wait for several months before getting paid for most of it. This was expensive and painful, including the opportunity cost of having those funds and obligations tied up, rather than available to deploy behind other growth opportunities.

Ren shared this with Weiser in another conversation. "We have a customer who got hit with some big financial woes and now says they won't pay any of their vendors for the next six months. We need to continue delivering our service to them because they're a hospital, essential in saving lives, and they depend on us. And we also can't afford to have them, as a result of us pulling back, speaking ill of Dirigat in the market. Even if the decision came down to our survival, they still might hurt our reputation, which would also be a killer. But the cost of delivering to them over the next six months, without getting paid, is going to be horrible to us on cash flows.

"Another example is what happened with our biggest new contract," Ren added. "They required us to staff up and to be ready to go the minute they signed the contract. So we did. Thankfully, they signed. And thankfully, they pay their bills more timely than most. But from the time we started hiring and spending until the checks started to arrive, we had a brutal cash flow problem.

"And we aren't always lucky. Take, for example, that big new system in South Florida. They required us to ramp up ahead of their purchase and implementation, but, just before they signed, the CFO who was going to buy our HealthAlign solution and a lot of services around it left the organization. After the CFO left, it took us a year to get the CEO to a place where he was ready to sign. Meanwhile, we carried a good part of the overhead, just waiting for the signature. It wasn't a complete loss, as we were able to use some of those resources elsewhere. But it would have broken us if we hadn't had a source of capital. And then the CEO left—again, just before signature!"

To address that sort of concern, Weiser helped Ren in thinking through where his financial model met his business model. Starting with creating value by serving the customer's needs—and then driving to get there with the right business model—he increasingly dwelt on the financial dynamic serving that.

Ren got better at more directly considering every factor in his cost structure and pricing. And he did a better job of weighing and allocating all expenditures, including less tangible ones such as expected risk over time, as either obligated overhead, discretionary overhead, or incremental. Connecting them with each dollar and making decisions accordingly made the company a much better business.

Armed with Jon Weiser's wisdom, Dirigat learned to make more objective decisions—driven more by data and results and less colored by subjective consideration. Follow the numbers!

CHAPTER 33

Passing the Baton

"Growth is never by mere chance; it is the
result of forces working together."

—James Cash Penney

The numbers were getting a little better for Dirigat, as they now had a few dozen customer organizations representing more than a hundred hospitals. The revenues were growing considerably, and the company had close to forty employees. The business seemed to be coming together. But with that the problems didn't go away—their nature just changed.

While it certainly hadn't been easy, the product development seemed to now be doing a great job, staying largely on schedule and only slightly over budget. The team seemed to be in good shape, with the right people. And the HealthAlign solution was looking good.

But like most entrepreneurs, Ren was always going to be concerned. He would have said that it was often with good reason. For one, everyone at Dirigat was so busy that there didn't seem to be enough method to the company's madness. They were bringing in new customers without the right sort of planning for delivery.

It increasingly struck Ren that the constant rush forced Dirigat to mostly respond to problems and just react, rather than to be proactive. He also worried about burnout on the team. At Standard Link, he recalled that everyone had worked way too many hours a week. Almost everyone there was either single or divorced, and the business was their life. For a time, Ren, too, had bought into that and thought it was great. But he eventually recognized that it wasn't sustainable. He cared about Dirigat's employees and their families, and he knew it wasn't healthy for anyone to go like that over longer periods of time, without at least a break or an end in sight.

Ren wanted a business where everyone would work nights and weekends when they needed to. But even though he was living those entrepreneur hours himself and had come from that driven culture, he didn't want the team to always have to do that. He wanted them to go home to their families and to not get too burned out; to be able to keep up their pace over a marathon rather than just a sprint.

He also worried about putting the right systems, methods, and processes in place to serve the growth. He knew the product and solution needed to evolve, along with how they were getting there. The most painful part of it all was that Ren felt overmatched in the spectacular number of things he needed to do to get the company to advance, culturally and structurally, to what it needed to become.

———

During this time of evolution at Dirigat, Ren's family was growing, too. Tiffany gave birth to their second child, Christopher, on a Tuesday in early September. RJ was at a fun age. Caulie had somehow remained as excitable as ever. And now, with Christopher, the family seemed complete. But the birth also reinforced the greater need for time management and planning with Tiffany, and led to the return of the sleepless nights that had, for a while, become less common.

Ren had always admired busy entrepreneurs and business leaders who found a way to make their families and occasionally even their personal lives a priority. The birth of Christopher brought a realization that, as much as was going on at Dirigat now, at least he was in a better place in his career to spend more time with his family than he was when RJ was born.

It was nice that RJ was old enough to help out a little following the birth. Instead of needing his own diapers, he could go get one and bring it to his mom or dad when the baby needed a change. But still, Tiffany had too much to deal with. And Ren realized that for his family's sake and for his own, he needed to find more time for this essential priority.

As he was rocking Christopher to sleep in the evenings, with time to reflect, he realized that he was now as worried about Dirigat as ever. And the worst part was that Ren wasn't even sure what, exactly, he was most bothered about.

———

As the business continued to have its good and bad days, Ren's appreciation of David's wisdom seemed to move in the opposite direction. He was still crossing paths with David pretty regularly. And somehow the better Ren felt about his own leadership, the easier it was to accept what David had to teach him. But whether or not he wanted to embrace what David had to say, Ren realized he was always glad to sit with his mentor.

At their next meeting, over a hearty breakfast, in their usual booth at the regular Waffle House by the office, Ren brought up some of his pressing concerns to David.

David nodded slowly. "I can see you're still on that roller coaster, where it feels like you've arrived sometimes and then not so much at other times. Right now it feels to you like The Villain is closing in. I know because I've been there before.

"There was a time when you thought Dirigat was getting better, but I thought the business was not doing the right things and seemed pretty flimsy. Now, it is kind of the opposite to me. I actually see that the company is becoming more of a real business, in some ways. And I see you growing up and doing some of the right things, or at least moving in that direction.

"But, I really think maybe you should take a hard look in the mirror. I guess the problem may be you." He watched carefully as Ren's eyes got bigger.

"It looks to me like the company needs to continue to evolve. And for that to happen," David said, carefully observing Ren's face, "you probably need to find someone else—maybe a new president—to run it."

That struck Ren like a slap in the face.

"Just hear me out," David said. "So many times, I see a company that seems to hit a wall of one kind or another. There are always symptoms. In a lot of cases, their revenues get flat. That's dangerous. In a growth business like what you are building, when your revenues are flat for any successive years, you very likely have a problem. And in many cases, you are the last one to be able to see it."

Ren was about to respond that the company's revenues had actually continued to climb, rather than flatten, but David held up a hand to stop him.

"Whether it's revenues or earnings or anything else, when I see it and bring it to their attention, these companies always give me a reason why they hit this proverbial wall. Sometimes it's a good reason. But for me, with the benefit of sitting back and having more objectivity and experience with these things, the reasons often just look like excuses."

He paused for a moment to take a sip of the coffee sitting in front of him, watching Ren's reaction.

"I'll tell you how I see it, Ren. From my vantage point, it looks like the underlying issue is that both Dirigat and its leadership need to evolve," David continued. "You either get better or it's a matter of time before the kind of smart, hard-charging people you have are not going to be satisfied and other problems arise.

"I know your revenues haven't flattened *yet*—and I am not describing you *yet*. That is just one of the most obvious signs that I can often see in other companies that need to change and grow," he said, seeming to read Ren's mind. "It is helpful when you can see an empirical indicator like flattening revenues or earnings. Otherwise, you may need to pay attention to be preemptive.

"In your case, I can see another kind of flattening and see some issues looming that could hit hard. Even to you, it feels like your business needs more leadership and direction. Intuitively, you know it. That's why we are having this conversation. Your team isn't set up right. You have a vision that everyone agrees on, but you haven't clearly articulated the next stages of your business in a plan for everyone to work toward, in alignment."

"What do you think I need to do to make the adjustments we need and shepherd things in the right direction?" Ren asked.

"Frankly, Ren, I don't think you're the guy to run this company on a daily basis." David paused, knowing Ren needed time. "It's not that you aren't capable. You know you can grow and improve as a leader. And in the areas where you lack, you could continue to learn," David said firmly. "I'm just saying that, given where you are now, it would be harder and riskier that way than to find the right person to do it. And you owe it to your employees and customers to put it in the best hands possible.

"Look," said David, pausing and then proceeding with more volume, to emphasize his next statement, "in my experience, when you find yourself asking the question 'Why doesn't my company—that I am supposedly in charge of—have better direction?' That, by itself, is enough to indicate that you need to take a hard look in the mirror. You're probably not leading it right."

Ren raised an eyebrow. This felt personal and more than a little hurtful. He didn't necessarily want to step back, but he had enough history with David to temper his knee-jerk response and wait for him to explain. As Ren considered the implications, he realized he was holding his breath under a wave of conflicting considerations washing over him.

"You have the ingredients, and the problem has not started to set you back too much yet." David seemed to be trying to soften the blow as he continued, "Your revenues are still growing, which is helpful. To someone outside looking in, your company might look like it's doing well. People have bought into your long-term vision. They trust you and Tom and your leadership."

David went on to explain that some of his concerns were that the business lacked immediate direction, focus, cohesion, and essential discipline. The company was coming to the point where more consistent processes and systems were vital for day-to-day operations. Now was a critical time to lay the groundwork for those considerations.

David didn't place all of the blame for the current state of affairs at Ren's feet, though.

"Tom's a great guy," he said, "but he's busy delivering and has never been president of a startup before. He's like you—I actually think he might grow and get to that point someday. And you know I don't say that of everyone. This is not a criticism of the kind of person you or Tom are, but an objective perspective on where you are now. I also don't think Tom has the right experience and qualifications for that role right now."

Sitting quietly, Ren tried to digest every word David was saying. He'd learned from their relationship that he didn't want to miss anything David said, no matter how difficult it sometimes was to hear.

"As I and others have told you before, the person to start a company is often a specialist or a visionary, or someone solving a problem or meeting a need. In some cases, that person might be the right one to build a business up to a certain point," David said as he ran a hand through what little remained of his salt-and-pepper hair. "But the person to take a company to say, 8 or 15 million in revenues—depending on the type of business—is usually not the one to take it from there to 80 or 100 million. And, the person to take it there may not be the one to take it to the next stage of 350 to 800 million, and so on. Those jumps just take different skill sets, different types of leadership, and different sets of experiences. Just the fact that they got it to those points makes the person who started the company more entrenched and less effective as a change agent."

Appreciating that David cared enough to speak the truth, Ren heard the absence of judgment or harshness in David's delivery.

"One of the evolution points that I see a lot is when a company is ready to become a real sustainable, replicable business," David said, softening his tone. "I know you are capable of becoming a real businessman. But, why go through all that the hard way, with unnecessary risk and pain? Find the right person, someone who has learned that stuff before and fits it better than you. You can learn it from them and be that guy later!

"And, frankly," he added for a more positive spin, "a lot of times the founder is exactly the right person to drive vision and values. I think you may be that. And you may find that you can still contribute to your business, better than ever, in some ways.

"Look," David said, "all growth businesses need to evolve at some point—usually multiple times. In fact, for many startups, they are just selling their product or service because of the founder. Maybe people buy it just because they trust and want to buy from them. And maybe that's a good reason to buy for now. But it's not a replicable, sustainable business.

"Eventually," he continued, "maybe that business gets to a point where it needs to have more processes and systems and better communication in place.

"Most of the times when I see a company that needs to evolve, I see a company that needs to evolve its leadership. A lot of times, it takes different people and processes and mentality to keep the company moving forward. Even the change itself is important to break momentum in the old direction and serve as a catalyst—you know, things like going from a product or solution to the kind of replicable, sustainable business that you and I have been talking about.

"Or," David said, "going from a startup where you need people to think and work outside the box of their job descriptions, to be proactive, and to solve problems as they arise—almost in survival mode—to then having more rules, processes, and systems that a bigger business may need to reproduce and have a higher survival rate with less risk.

"There is a model we used in our Boy Scout troop, where the Scoutmaster got to be 'above the fray' and lovable. There was a disciplinarian-type assistant Scoutmaster that served as the bad guy. That sort of good-cop, bad-cop model can be very effective.

"And just calling it what it is, you are more suited to be a good cop, Ren."

That last point reminded Ren of Joe Chapman's pointing out about being a pleaser. Ren felt that he had proven, over and over since then, that he could make tough decisions and stand strong in front of anything. He had never minded delivering tough messages, as long as he believed they were in the long-term interest of the person he was sharing them with, or for the improvement of a project or product. But even as he was defending himself in his head, Ren knew David was right.

"Honestly," David continued, "it will also be best for you. Find someone who is a better fit for the next stage of the business than you—or at least that can get past the harm of your affinity and personal feelings for everyone—to make the tough decisions that you are just not objective about. Hopefully you can find someone with the right experiences for where you want to go. You'll almost certainly end up better off too, Ren. When someone is not exactly the right leader, they're often relieved when they end up in a position that is a better fit for them and the organization.

"People seem to love and trust you, Ren. Keep it that way." David smiled. "The other thing is, I think I know a guy . . ."

CHAPTER 34

Baby's New Caregiver

"With the right alignment, everything you want makes its
way into your experience. You are the keeper of your own gate."

—Esther Hicks

David offered a connection to Bart Stanton, and Ren didn't waste any time scheduling a meeting with him. During it, he liked what he saw and learned.

Bart had found some success in prior startups, carving out a reputation for being a hard-driving professional relationship guy who came with the right technical proficiency and with great industry and performance improvement background. Bart knew how to deliver for the companies he represented. A thirty-something with jet-black hair, sharp attire, and a sinewy physique he had honed from hours spent working out and practicing martial arts, his presence screamed, "I'm an achiever!"

While Bart had a young family that he loved more than anything, it was clear that when he was on the job, business was his priority. Those that knew Bart seemed to all appreciate his commitment to delivering results and were impressed by his reputation for great solutions.

When Ren first met him, Bart was working as a consultant in the enterprise performance improvement space for hospitals and had a Rolodex bursting at the seams with valuable relationships. In short, he had loads to offer a company like Dirigat.

For such a critical transition, Ren initially approached Bart to do some consulting work for the company on a three-month contract. It seemed to be the perfect solution. He and the team would get to know Bart before Ren would approach him about becoming the new president. During that time, Bart could get to know the company and the customers, as well as get to know Ren better, too.

———

During his three months as a consultant, Bart really delivered. He brought in actionable leads and advanced them, outlined a compelling new vision for the technology-driven solution, and proved himself to be a strong, dynamic leader. That led to Ren and Bart coming together to discuss expectations, compensation, and what being the president of Dirigat would look like.

Never caring much about titles, Ren always wanted everyone to feel like partners and reasoned that getting the work done—and done well—was more important than the moniker on your business card.

So it came as a bit of a surprise that something about the prospect of naming Bart his company's president bothered him—and, at the same time, the title seemed really important to Bart. Why did he—and others around him—care so much about titles?

Intellectually, Ren could see that there was functional value in Bart having the title, as customers liked dealing directly with a president and employees responded better to a president. But Ren came to realize that, in some cases, it was also about the appreciation and respect that could go with the title. It was something he aimed to make peace with, as he worked toward his goal of advancing the company's agenda, despite any personal emotions. And really, Bart was the right guy and the company needed him in that role.

Ren decided that if there were going to be formal titles to serve a purpose, he would be the CEO and founder. He recognized that making Bart the president, with the responsibility of building and driving the company on a daily basis, would then be the right solution. And depending on *when* he thought of it, there were times when he felt relieved about the new direction—yet at other times it felt inconceivable.

Coming up with a compensation deal with Bart Stanton as president was a real challenge.

While he had often been accused of being a good negotiator, Ren never thought of himself as such. He was always just looking for a win-win deal that made sense for all parties. He had read a lot of books and taken a few short courses on negotiation and had studied the art of persuasion and reading people's expressions, posture, and tone of voice. He knew that most people gave away their intentions, if you paid attention. And he knew about pacing and anchoring and framing his case—and much more that could give an advantage in a negotiation.

But what worked best for Ren was to *not* use what he had learned.

He believed that a great deal of his professional success was because people trusted him. And as Ren learned from his father and often told people, "You can learn all the tricks and try to fool people. But that will never be as effective as just genuinely being straight up with people and trying to do right by them. Hand-in-hand with that is to have empathy, consideration, and respect. And that also helps you better understand what they really want."

Ren didn't always want others to see it—particularly when he needed a tough business poker face for negotiations—but he was actually very empathetic. He made an effort to understand others, to see and feel for their insecurities and challenges, and to genuinely want the best for them.

While he avoided manipulating others, Ren did abide by a few of the rules for negotiation. For one thing, he always sought a win-win. And he was always willing to walk away from any deal after weighing all potential consequences. He established and wrote down firm boundaries for himself—of how far he might be willing to go—before entering any negotiation process. He always tried to understand what the other party really wanted, and prepared a great deal for any different scenario that he thought could come from a negotiation.

What Ren particularly didn't like was the idea of negotiating with key people in his business. He felt like it started a partnership in an uncomfortable way. But he quickly recognized that Bart Stanton was going to be tough to work out a deal with, and that he needed to come up with something reasonable to make it functional for both of them.

Most people wanted to come out of a negotiation feeling as if they had won—or at least that they had not lost. Others seemed to be looking to validate something more about themselves. And of course, there was a lot to be said for making enough money to pay one's bills and to keep the lights on.

Bart Stanton was smart. He started from a perspective that was anchored by the huge salary and compensation he had made before. Ren knew that, in a prior job, Bart had been making almost a million dollars a year, which was way more than Dirigat could afford to offer him. Bart also had a huge ego and a need to win—some of the same things that would make it great to have Bart inside the company, working with Ren and Dirigat.

David had made the point to Ren that all great salespeople—and most great leaders—needed, or maybe even had to have—big egos. Ren just always thought the key was to recognize the good and bad of an ego and to keep it in check. He liked that Bart had an ego, but only until it got in the way.

David noted that many of the greatest historical figures, like Lincoln, Churchill, and Dr. King, had shown great fortitude, overcoming adversity through sheer force of will. And he pointed out his belief that ego was necessary for such strength. So Ren was prepared to have a leader with a huge ego. He just also wanted it wrapped in genuine consideration and respect and humility, as those leaders had.

Ren was a huge fan of compensation based on performance or by commission, as it really served to line up incentives. But Bart made some good points about being motivated to deliver results, most of all, by ownership.

That was the one thing that seemed to light up Bart's eyes: ownership. And Ren liked the idea of that and of Bart having significant ownership, over time. He just found it challenging that Bart wanted so much, so fast.

They did eventually come up with a deal. Bart got a below-market base salary, some uncapped potential upside in commission, and six percent of the company, vesting over five years and beginning with a vesting cliff after his second year, to pick up the amount added up to that point. They agreed they could possibly revisit for more ownership as Bart proved his outperformance.

Moreso even than with the initial negotiation with Tom, Ren felt this must have been a great compromise from both Bart and himself, since both felt so far from what they thought was the right solution.

Ren would have given up more of the company if Bart had been willing to go with less commission and salary. But Bart had a family to feed and bills to pay. And Bart knew he would deliver results. Of course, he didn't see himself as risky.

Bart's big ego, which was such a good thing for sales and driving the business, did often seem to bring challenges for Ren in matters like compensation and acknowledgment. And Ren often wondered if Bart's insatiable expectations on compensation may have been more about appreciation and validation than about money.

At any rate, without much fanfare, Ren largely turned over daily management of his company—his "baby"—to Bart Stanton, along with Tom Strong and the team. That freed up Ren to focus on bigger-picture vision and other matters. And of course, he and Bart "fought their battles up front" on things like Ren staying engaged in hiring and firing and some other essential matters at some level, at least for a time.

———

To any outside observer, Bart Stanton's leadership in the company looked good and made sense. But it's never easy for a founder to step back, even when they know it's for the best. The new setup was hard for Ren to embrace, thanks to his emotional attachment to the company and the lack of objectivity that came with it.

One of the first things that Bart did when he came in was to remove the company values statement from the business plan. He felt it was not serious and professional. Ren tried to respect Bart's reasons. But for some reason, it felt like a personal blow. And Ren kept the values list for himself, to keep in mind for future hires and culture issues that he would still be engaged in.

As hard as it was for Ren, it might have been even harder for Tom Strong. It seemed to catch Tom by surprise to find that he had a new boss. Ren never really thought of it that way. He always felt like everyone in the leadership team at Dirigat were all, to varying degrees, going to be owners/partners in the company, and that the rest just came down to semantics and who was in charge of what. Ren recognized that he must not have prepared the way well enough with Tom, which caused some challenges.

Bart really advanced the important services and consulting component of the solution that needed to drive the business—and started to bring in real, excellent consultants, as the company required, and set them up to succeed as well as possible.

He did an amazing job of pushing the HospitAlign software to where it needed to go. Where they had been selling to departments in hospitals, Bart took it a step further and made it bigger. He evolved Dirigat's software to an enterprise-level solution, resident on the CEO's desktop and throughout the organization. Ren and the team had always envisioned and worked toward that. But of his own volition, Bart took it there in a way that the team previously never would have.

One of the hardest things in health information—that people outside that world could never understand—was getting good information and tying it together in a standardized, usable manner. Dirigat was actually decent at getting good data and using it functionally. The HospitAlign solution became increasingly powerful, usable, and well positioned. The organizations could take operational, financial, and clinical data and tie it all together, and they could drill up and down throughout their institutions, utilizing their organization chart, strategic plan, job descriptions, or any priority or set of objectives.

The hospitals could also easily see if there was a problem with, for instance, C-section rates, reimbursement in a specific department, customer satisfaction, emergency department turnaround times, or with anything else that they chose to measure.

Of course, you improve what you measure. It was great to have this articulated and directed with an objective measurement system, helping hospitals to be more proactive and effective.

Using proven statistical process control methods, the software could indicate if there was a problem that might otherwise be missed—for instance, in surgical supply costs rising gradually over time in a way that would otherwise not have been noticed—and then notify everyone and show a yellow or red light, as appropriate, that could be clicked upon, to see what was going on and where things needed to move.

The HospitAlign software could compare any relevant indicators and notice correlations. So, if bed utilization issues were creeping up, in correlation with customer satisfaction and reimbursement problems, they could see the link. Of course, just because there was a correlation didn't necessitate causality. But just being able to link those things together and combine them with other potential causal or interdependent factors was incredibly powerful.

It was empowering for the team, leaders, and even customers to see exactly where they stood in alignment with everything. When people know how their performance aligns with the organization's goals—and even to their compensation—that can be empowering.

CHAPTER 35

Friction

"It isn't what we don't know that gives us trouble,
it's what we know that ain't so."

—Will Rogers

W hen Bart, Tom, Cindy, and Chip asked to schedule lunch at his earliest opportunity on a busy Monday morning, Ren got a little worried. They all got together regularly, often in groups like this. But if they *scheduled* lunch, there was something big to discuss. More often than not, he thought gloomily, it wasn't anything positive.

When they arrived at the Taco Mac, making small talk along the way, Ren could feel the underlying tension among the team—presumably in anticipation of a tough conversation.

After they all ordered, Ren cut to the chase: "So, what's this about?"

Bart spoke first. "It's Carl Joseph. He's a disaster. We've got to let him go," he said flatly.

This was the first time Ren had ever seen Bart look the least bit apprehensive. He sat for a moment, contemplating this. Ren had already been a little worried about Carl. After more than a year on the job, Carl's results had been mixed, at best. The team had been moving forward pretty well before he got there, but they seemed to be producing less now. What worried Ren perhaps even more was that the morale of the team seemed worse, too.

Carl had said and done some things that had concerned him, but never enough to think he needed to be fired. Ren even felt, at least up to this point, like he had received some good advice from Carl.

Tom and Cindy summarily explained to Ren that Carl had been doing almost nothing productive while crushing morale for several months now.

Ren was dumbfounded. "Why am I just now hearing this?"

"Because we know he's your guy and y'all are such good friends!" Bart replied, sounding exasperated, his usually perfectly combed jet-black hair ruffled a bit as he gestured to make his point.

Ren would have laughed out loud if not for his concern over the situation. Not only was that not the case—in fact, he had always felt much closer to everyone at the table than he ever had to Carl—but it really bothered him that everyone seemed so worried about having this conversation. It was important that Tom, and particularly Bart, didn't fear dealing with these things or at least addressing them frankly and directly with him as they arose. Ren wanted them to feel empowered to take action where they needed to.

He wanted everyone at Dirigat to feel authorized to do their jobs, including dealing with all coworkers, whether as a boss, a peer, or a subordinate.

Since Ren was completely behind his team, he felt he just needed to share any disagreements he had with Bart and Tom behind the scenes and then simply get out of their way and let them do their jobs. It was important to show a unified front and support whatever they did.

Carl had been coming into the office, surfing the internet all day, and convincing everyone that he was working really hard on things that nobody could ever see. Carl had also done a great job of making everyone believe that he and Ren had become best buddies during his time there. Hence, everyone was afraid to say anything to Ren along the way, which explained their trepidation going into this conversation. It really would have been funny if it had not been so troubling.

Of course, Ren *did* go to lunch with Carl regularly. After that harrowing first ride during Carl's interview, though, Ren never rode with him again. But they had a lot of fun conversations and Ren really liked Carl. Although he learned a few things from him, the two often disagreed. Sometimes Ren worried about certain things that Carl said. And he certainly never thought of Carl as a good friend, like the others at this table.

It didn't take long for Ren to figure out what needed to happen. *I've gotta fire Mr. Magoo!*

Later that afternoon, Ren and Bart gathered privately to work through the best way to handle the matter. Ren made it clear that he trusted Bart and would normally have deferred this one to him, but that he wanted to do the firing himself, in this case.

Ren felt he had a reason to deal with Carl directly. Part of it was because Carl had used him as a kind of shield—misleading others about his overstated relationship with him. Most of all, though, Ren wanted to flatly demonstrate that he was fully supportive of Bart as he did it. Bart seemed to understand and agree with the reasoning.

With Tom and Bart in the office, Ren brought Carl in and delivered the news. Carl did not take it well. He said he was insulted and that he couldn't wait to get away from "this circus." He said that he was disappointed, most of all, that Ren had "let Tom and Bart push you around like this."

It was interesting to Ren that the most obvious people to fire were often also the ones who were most likely to be a problem when let go. You would think they would be the most likely to expect it and know they deserved it, and therefore would have taken it more reasonably. But it was usually the opposite—perhaps due to their insecurities and deficiencies that caused the problems in the first place.

Ren noticed how much the mood and tone in the office improved when Carl was removed and kicked himself for not noticing Carl's detrimental effects on the office culture before he was gone.

In hindsight, Ren could see how Carl had "hidden" in a big corporation in his prior job. He was great at seeming good—and would have been terrific at company politics in a large business. But some of the advice Carl had given Ren demonstrated how bad he was. At times, his advice contained elements of value and was built around some truth, which made it believable but especially dangerous. Ren felt he could have realized this, had he paid better attention.

For instance, Carl had once advised Ren not to ever speak frankly and directly with employees. It was only many years later that Ren looked back and regretted heeding that errant advice so fully.

Before Carl's admonition to never do so, Ren always wanted to have direct and candid dialogue with everyone on the team. Whenever he spoke with Tom or Bart, they could disagree respectfully among themselves, make their points, and present their reasoning. In most of those cases, it was easy enough for all parties to see which position was better—and in that way it was often surprisingly easy to arrive at an answer.

Ren had been treating people the way he wanted to be treated, with honest feedback. He always loved to know where he stood and felt grateful to anyone that could show him where he was mistaken or doing wrong.

"But," Carl had made the point, "you need to pick your battles. You need to soften your tone. And you need to back off from ever speaking so frankly."

Of course, that was good advice in many cases. Ren did need to get better about picking his battles. So, for all the bad of Carl's advice, there was also some truth and good in it. The real trick was just knowing when to be straight and when to hold back and bite his tongue.

Carl had explained his case, at the time: "I know that you need to let people do their job. You've said as much to me before. If you have the right person, get out of their way. If you don't have the right person, you fire them.

"But," and this is the part that Carl added, twisting the truth into bad advice, "don't insult people by speaking directly with them, the way you do."

Aside from the irony that Carl was—for the only time, ever—doing to Ren what he had told him to never do to others, Ren looked back later and realized that what Carl said was dangerous because it *was* partly true. Sometimes you did need to bite your tongue and let people do their jobs and make mistakes. And sometimes you did need to pick your battles or position your message to be less severe and more effective.

But as Ren later reflected and measured against all of his experiences, it was usually okay to give the sincere, constructive, and well-meant feedback that Carl despised so much. In thinking about it later, Ren realized that his direct feedback had almost always gone over well. People needed to know where they stood—that seemed obvious. It just wasn't Carl's way. Ren was bothered that he had let Carl convince him otherwise for a time.

Ren also recognized that the people who he could not speak frankly with—and who handled honest, well-intentioned, and professionally delivered feedback poorly—were the same ones that he was most likely to have other problems with. From everything that Ren knew, it was best to foster a direct, well-intentioned, constructive dialogue of professional feedback among respected teammates.

In looking at his life, Ren may have occasionally regretted having been direct with others—but felt much worse for all of the times when he should have spoken straight to people and instead had held his tongue as a result of that bad advice.

———

After letting Carl go as director of R&D, it was mission critical to find the right person for that essential position. Most technology companies would have put a technical expert with plenty of experience heading technical teams in charge of leading their software. But with Bart in place now, Ren—with guidance and endorsement from David and Bart—made Tom Strong the COO of the company and director of R&D.

With his engineering and syllogistic background, Ren was almost obsessive about setting up processes and systems for success. But in a small business— maybe in most businesses or organizations, period—he had found that the right answer is really putting the right person in charge. That person was typically the best one to set up the systems and processes.

From Ren's conversations with David, he knew that his experienced mentor felt like there was a better solution to drive the development. Of course, Tom needed a solid understanding of the technologies being used. But, David had convinced Ren that what he really wanted was someone who understood the customer and was not biased by being overly technical, running R&D. David also felt, as Ren did, that Tom had the kind of personality and integrity that the company could count on to deliver.

The change wasn't drastic, because Tom had basically already been a key part of running R&D, albeit less formally, as he had largely been involved with Cindy and others in getting everything done at the company. But with the formal delineation of those responsibilities, Tom admitted to Ren that he was less certain of himself for the new role, particularly as the company was growing and evolving so quickly.

Tom knew the market and had a decent, highest-level understanding of the development technologies involved and, even more so, of the techniques being utilized. He was also a good manager, a skill born from years of experience and hard lessons in and out of hospitals. But he was not a hard core architect or developer or technology guy, and he didn't have any experience with managing this sort of effort on this scale.

So that was the new daily leadership structure of Dirigat, Bart as president and Tom as COO and director of R&D. And the titles made plenty of sense, structurally. Bart was the right guy to drive the solution and the business forward now. And Tom finally had the right title for all he had already been doing in the company. Given their personalities and backgrounds, they were the appropriate leaders for each position.

Bart was driving growth and vision. Tom was in charge of delivering. That put them at odds at times.

It helped that Tom, Bart, and Ren all really respected one another. They maintained a good enough relationship through most times. While friction was to be expected, it was still a problem Ren tried to deal with and learn from. It was the topic on Ren's mind during his long overdue visit with David, over bacon and eggs and hash browns at "their" Waffle House.

Ren shared with David that he had noticed more tension than usual between Tom and Bart, as Bart was out selling and Tom was charged with delivering. They just seemed to be pushing on each other: Bart pressing Tom to deliver and Tom wanting Bart to apply some brakes at times.

As Ren explained, "I think Tom's having a hard time with Bart selling things that he is not certain he can deliver."

Or, as David summarized it after the explanation—trying to illustrate his point in a facetious, humorous way—"It's Tom's job to make Bart 'not a liar.' And, there's the rub."

David described it as the "healthy friction that you want." But Ren wondered with concern, at the time, if it was really that healthy and whether he really wanted it.

"Most good sales guys," David noted, "are going to push the limits of what you can deliver. I know that might bother guys like you and Tom. But if Bart was not like that, he'd be the wrong guy for your company. To be honest," he added, "I think Dirigat needs a lot more of that.

"Some of the best companies I know of were built by selling more than what they had and then just finding a way to deliver. I, for one, don't feel so bad about the situation here, because I trust Tom and his team to find a way. That's the kind of people they are: They live on merit and substance and can't bear the idea of not delivering."

——

There continued to be some friction in Bart and Tom's dealings, but it seemed that they both, along with Ren, may have been learning to live with it. At least, they all were showing plenty of respect and appreciation at the time.

Maybe part of the friction was also their contrasting personalities. Among other things, you could say they were smart in different ways. Bart was quick and almost brash. Tom would eventually see through a wall—but whatever the opposite of brash was, that was Tom.

David told Ren that he didn't believe that either was doing anything wrong. They were just positioned that way: between Bart wanting to push the limits in selling—something the business really needed then—and Tom feeling deeply, morally convicted to deliver great results but being asked to stretch beyond his comfort.

With the growth and the new deals that Bart was bringing to the table, the company needed to bring more people on board, yet again. It felt as if Ren had suddenly looked up to find that there were dozens of employees running around the office. With that came another set of challenges. As David put it, "If you have a good business and everything aligned, then the challenge becomes about having employees and all of the drama that comes with them."

CHAPTER 36

Freedom! Or Not So Much!

"Work ON your business, not IN your business."

—Michael Gerber

As Bart Stanton engaged with Tom Strong and the team and they took more and more ownership of running the company daily, Ren felt some freedom—at least at first. He felt increasingly "off the hook" for the lion's share of the day-to-day obligations, which helped him step back and look at the forest, rather than just getting caught up in the trees in front of him. Looking back, it seemed strange to him now that this had not been an obvious move to him before David suggested it.

One major change was that Ren was actually getting better about working *on* the business more than *in* it. This felt like a huge relief as he realized that he was better at being a generalist businessman than a specialist anyway. And it felt right for him to be able to focus on the big picture and where the company needed to go. Ren used to lie awake worrying about a specific customer or hiring issue or contract. Or his yard work, whenever he was trying not to think of those things. Now, he was awake worrying about things like compliance and putting more consistency in the way the company did business, for protection and survival. Or still more yard work.

He started thinking more about possibly putting together an outside board of directors, raising capital for growth and driving the vision of the business and solution, at the highest level. Although Bart and Tom were running the company on a daily basis and driving the software and solution, Ren felt more empowered and perhaps more entrepreneurial than ever. And he could still help drive the vision and the culture of Dirigat, potentially better than ever.

Ren was also available to help Bart, Tom, and the team put out proverbial fires as they cropped up—whenever there was an employee problem, an unhappy customer, a bill that didn't get paid, or any of the other minor crises that pop up every day in a growing small business. The Villain was still out there, fighting as insidiously as ever.

But Ren also found himself, at times, feeling helpless. He still felt the same deep obligation to his customers. After all, it was still ultimately his business with his name, at least figuratively, above the door. He also felt a deep responsibility to the team and their families and a need to be there when people had to be fired or reprimanded. Even if the employee clearly deserved to be let go, Ren always felt an overwhelming sense of compassion for their family. It was even harder to let an employee go when they had done nothing wrong but just weren't a fit for what the company needed any longer.

It was difficult to feel responsible for so many things that Ren no longer directly controlled, when Bart, Tom, and others were making the decisions, but he still felt like he owned a lot of the consequences.

What Ren didn't see, at the time, was the other side of it. Bart and Tom did feel a lot of empowerment and high-level responsibility and ownership of the business. But, at times, they treated Ren's expectations with more deference than he realized.

———

Collecting wisdom from mentors since he began his journey, Ren considered himself exceedingly fortunate to have cultivated so many strong relationships with people he respected and trusted, people whose lives and careers he would be happy to emulate and learn from. And these mentors and advisors were a great part of the growth and success of Dirigat.

So, when Ren began to create an informal board of advisors, he brought in a number of successful friends on a quarterly basis and updated them on the company. The friends included David, Jon Weiser, Sid Richardson, a local hospital CEO, and a few others with potentially relevant perspectives.

Ren didn't expect—or even try to solicit—meaningful feedback or guidance at these group gatherings, given that everyone's questions and perspectives would be too much for one sitting. The salesperson would get caught up on development or the funnel. The technology person might ask less informed questions on sales, and the industry people would spend too much time addressing issues that were germane to them. Instead, he held brief, directed, and informational meetings that were relatively short and always ended on time, in deference to everyone's busy schedules. He gave updates to everyone at once, and then invited each of them to a separate breakfast, where he would then ask his targeted questions. Everyone seemed to like that approach. And he would often send them home with his wife's chocolate chip cookies (with plenty of pecans!), jelly, or her other homemade treats.

He knew that he would never be able to pay Weiser and David back for all they had done. But he decided that someday he would find a way to pay forward their investment in him by helping others the way they had helped him.

Ren did provide David and Weiser a little ownership in the company by way of options that could turn into equity, whenever they chose to exercise them. It was a token and never added up to much, but they seemed really touched by the gesture. David, the "giver" who never asked for or wanted money for his help, even seemed to tear up a little.

CHAPTER 37

Morphability

"If you had asked people what they wanted,
they would have said a faster horse."

—Henry Ford

"What's *eva pollution*, daddy?" asked RJ, mouth open and head sideways in inquiry.

"Evolution. That's when you change, RJ," said Ren.

"Like when Mommy changes Christopher's diaper?"

Ren had been trying to explain that the family was evolving, with Christopher and Caulie. And now RJ had a new role in the family, with new responsibilities as a big brother.

"That isn't what I was thinking of. Usually an evolution is a change that will last," Ren responded. "And evolution is supposed to somehow develop things, to make them better than before."

Seeing the puzzled expression on RJ's face, Ren added, "You want to get better at things and sometimes bigger, like our family did when Caulie joined us. That was evolution."

Napping in her bed across the room, Caulie raised her head and looked around on hearing her name.

RJ nodded and smiled. "Caulie is a funny doggy. She runs around in circles so much."

She must have heard him, as she rose from her bed and approached the couch where Ren and RJ were sitting, looking for a ball to chase or an opportunity to play.

"She sure is . . ." Ren responded as his thoughts brought the conversation back to ongoing issues he was wrestling with at Dirigat.

RJ looked at him sideways again. "So how do you know when to do the eva pollution?"

If I only knew the answer to that, Ren thought, *and how to make sure to do it the right way when you do.*

———

One of the greatest challenges that the Dirigat team constantly faced was knowing when and how to change their solution and when to stay the course. And it felt like The Villain was lurking out there to trip them up at every opportunity.

It would be impossible to keep up with every idea for the HospitAlign software and how to deliver it, so the Dirigat team kept a prioritized list. And to the point of David's funded development model, they liked to favor the solutions that customers paid them to create.

In a catch-up breakfast, after one of Ren's Dirigat advisor meetings, Sid Richardson offered yet a deeper dive on some new things to consider.

As usual, Richardson spoke more about selling customers what they want to buy, what they know how to buy, and what is easy for them to buy—rather than just what Dirigat wanted to sell them. The most important and essential advice from that exchange, and something Ren heard from others, too, was a concept that Richardson described.

"Morphability," Richardson said, "goes hand in hand with evolution, for your product and ultimately your business. If you get the morphability right, you will get the evolution right."

He said it was the quintessential issue all businesses eventually face—to know when to change and when not to change. If the company needed to evolve in order to grow, being good at this morphability, with adaptations driven by the market, was the key to evolving in the right way at the right time.

"When do you go with what the market is telling you?" Richardson asked, rhetorically. "How do you know if your innovative idea will be adopted? When do you stick with what you believe? How does the company afford to transform? And what about when it can't afford not to? How does a company change in order to give itself the best chance to innovate in the best way and stay ahead of the market?"

Richardson noted that businesses had to evolve and that changing quickly was more important than ever. But at the same time, changing too much was also a recipe for disaster.

As he put it, "Maybe the surest way to struggle is to change too often—but the second surest may be to not change when it is time to do so. Knowing when to keep doing what you have believed in versus when to alter course with your business or product or people is a constant, massive, inevitable weight.

"Of course, you want to be a good business, serving a promising opportunity," Richardson said. "But, one key is to remain mindful, because if you're a creative entrepreneurial type, you can have all kinds of new ideas and possibilities arise that tempt you to change course. And the market will always offer opportunities for you to change.

"I know David has told you this *ad nauseam*, and he is right: Really understanding your customer's needs and problems and why they buy, paired with the right customer-driven business model—hopefully where they pay you to build a solution for them—forces you toward where you need to go, better and more reliably than anything else. It is then that things like luck, intuition, and such are more likely to be able to help."

Richardson also noted that "You may find that, in many cases, you are better served if you don't build your business for exit. In many cases, you should just build the best, most profitable business you can, as fits your goals and circumstances. If you ever start making shortsighted decisions for things like your model or expenditures, you will struggle if a recession or a pandemic or some other disaster happens.

"We notice all of the good exits when the economy is good or everyone seems to be buying companies. But we don't notice how many other times businesses crash because their timing didn't work out."

Richardson added, wryly, "This may sound funny or as if I am contradicting myself, but I suggest you don't ever *want* to sell your company until ten weeks after the check clears for it. But if you get a good deal that makes sense from both sides—from someone that will give your company a better chance to be a better business—then you take it.

"And a company that is set up with the right model for that morphability—the right setup to be forced to evolve your solution and your business in the right way at the right place at the right time—also has the best chance to be at the right place at the right time for an exit. And," he threw in, "is less likely to need to exit. You give yourself the best opportunity to stay ahead."

———

Maybe the business wasn't the only thing that needed morphability. Arriving at his house in the evening, in the wake of his conversations with Richardson and RJ, Ren was thinking more about evolution at home, too.

Although he was helping more at home, there still was not enough of Tiffany to go around. RJ was very active now. Christopher needed a lot of TLC. And even Caulie needed attention. But it seemed like every time one of them needed something, Ren was off with another business commitment or responsibility.

Ren's mother had given RJ one of those fancy new video game boxes, which RJ loved. But Ren didn't want it to become RJ's babysitter. *I won't be that parent.* It was easy for him to say, Ren realized, since it was Tiffany who was stuck with so much new responsibility.

I need to get some of that morphability for my family as we also evolve. How do I find the right balance and get us doing the right things around here? In this case, I guess our family is the customer. Is there some sort of customer-driven model to make us a better-functioning family?

CHAPTER 38

Finding a Tribe

"When we live in alignment with who we are and how we want to live, we will attract and find like-minded individuals."

—Akiroq Brost

When Ren began his journey as an entrepreneur, he had often felt alone. And now, in his new role within his company, he experienced that again. He scheduled a visit with his old mentor Joe Chapman to discuss the struggles and evolution that he was going through.

As always, Joe had great advice, telling Ren, "There are almost too many resources for you, as an entrepreneur. You don't have the bandwidth for all of them. But if you pick the right ones, you'll find a great payback on your time invested. As you probably know, there are a lot of mentoring groups, business forums, discount providers, incubators of any kind you can think of, and a ton of others.

"The first thing you need to check out is the Entrepreneurs Organization, or EO, as everyone calls it. It is similar to another group, the Young Presidents Organization, or YPO, that you also need to check out when your business gets a little bigger."

Ren noted that he had heard of EO before and already knew about YPO. Now that Bart was on board, Ren had more bandwidth to get involved in that sort of thing. But it still sounded like a big potential time drain for a busy businessman with a family.

That's probably why Joe pushed him to it so much: "In my strong opinion, Ren, if you join EO, you need to make it a priority. It's like everything else— you will get out of it what you put in. You have to invest time to make time, and it will pay back down the road. There is no place you will find more value, as an entrepreneur, than EO. I know you already have an assortment of mentors and advisors, but EO does have a good mentoring program and you will find plenty of education, networking, and benefits.

"For you and your business right now, the first thing you are going to love is something called a forum. You need to make sure you get in the right forum that fits you best. If you do, it will change your life." Joe went on to explain that membership involved monthly meetings with seven to nine other business leaders with whom Ren was sure to feel a kinship.

"Whatever is wrong with me is wrong with you and a lot of other entrepreneurs and CEOs," Joe said with a wry smile. "We are all members of a special club of sorts. We can be stubborn, impatient, contrarian, mercurial at times, hardheaded, *never* satisfied, impatient, and have our own set of problems that are common among those leading a business like yours or mine. For better and for worse, maybe that's part of the deal.

"When you see others like you, you'll start to observe and understand things about yourself you haven't before. You can share problems and solve them together. Once you get in the right forum and build trust, you'll find it very empowering. You'll often walk out of your forum meeting with more certainty about the tough decisions you have to make. And that will help you in all of your interactions, business and personal.

"The beauty of these forums," said Joe, "is that you discuss your issues in complete confidence. The people in your forum are not supposed to do business with you or solicit from you. That's important—to have people that are not allowed to want something from you."

Joe looked satisfied, just from saying it, as he elaborated why that meant so much. "For you, as a successful guy, it always feels like everyone wants something from you. I don't begrudge them for it. But it's nice to have a group of real peers that allow you a break from it," he added, with the same relieved look on his face.

"I really like people," Joe said, "but I've learned the hard way not to trust them. It sure seems like a lot of them eventually want money or political help or whatever. Don't get me wrong, I sincerely appreciate that they usually want it for a good cause or for their family or some good reason. But I have learned, the hard way, to be careful about it."

Ren noted that he was becoming a little cynical about people himself. He would often be approached to provide advice or join a board, and in the end he could see what they really wanted was money or for him to do a big favor.

"I also think EO can be good for your marriage," Joe said. "Being married to people like us is not easy. They have lots of opportunities for spouses, including their own forums. Being around others like us helps them to look at *whatever's wrong with us* a little differently—maybe helps them to possibly accept it better as a part of what helps with our successes, too." He made a great case. Ren had seen firsthand how his entrepreneur's mentality had taken a toll on Tiffany, though she had learned to handle it like a champ.

On Joe Chapman's strong endorsement, Ren checked out the Entrepreneurs Organization website, called one of his friends for a connection, and then joined the organization and a forum. It proved to be even better than Joe suggested.

Joining was relatively quick and easy. For his first event with the group, the local NFL team owner had hosted the local chapter, including spouses and guests, before a game. And he shared many of the things he had learned in business.

The NFL owner's feedback on pricing was especially helpful. He shared with the entrepreneurs that when he had bought the team, he had noticed a lot of empty seats in the upper deck of the stadium. He noted that everyone was advising them to price those seats at a certain level—in that case it was forty dollars per seat, per game.

But this new owner ignored that advice and went out on the streets and just asked people what they would pay. The best answer to fill those seats was three dollars. So that was what he charged. The seats filled up.

Later, once people started enjoying their seats and the games and the value proposition, he was able to increase the price, eventually coming up to where it needed to be to be profitable. It was a dynamic, real-time example of business in action.

And then, after that learning opportunity, the entire group went to the football game together and had a blast!

———

With his forum, Ren felt less lonely as a business leader. And the forum meetings were incredibly empowering with what Joe had described as the power of certainty. He would come in with a problem that was burdening him because he wasn't sure of the best answer and leave with the blessing of assuredness about how to deal with it.

At one of his early forum meetings, Ren surprised himself by sharing a compensation issue he was having at the time with Bart Stanton—a new iteration of an old recurring problem that Bart, as always, wanted more.

It was weird to feel so much trust for these new people in his life. And it was reassuring to know that everything was in absolute confidence.

Ren was already getting good advice from mentors. By now, he often felt like he knew what David and the others would say about a lot of things before he even brought them up. But it wasn't the same as these others that were mired in the same issues now. So Ren laid it all out for his new forum.

When he shared his issue, the other members then offered their own experiences and what had come of their decisions. The process of everyone's experience sharing was powerful. The forum didn't tell one another what to do in their meetings—they simply shared what they had gone through and what had come of it. Others could then, equipped with the lessons, make their own, more informed, decisions.

This reinforced Ren's feeling that if he wrote a book someday, it might be a fiction story, based on sharing his experiences and what came of them. Others could learn from his journey and make their own decisions on what was right or wrong.

Ren loved watching as his forum mates found their successes. One of the greatest, most fulfilling sensations in his life was when he felt like he was able to help them, even a little, to get there.

Joe was right. Decisions are easy if you have assuredness. What kills you is if you're not sure. Combined with the directional value of his WAYAWAYG exercises, the tactical value of the forum experience was invaluable and worth every minute of time Ren invested.

CHAPTER 39

Recipe for Success

"Life is not about finding yourself. Life is about creating yourself."

—Lolly Daskal

The individuals who made up Ren's EO forum group—Ernesto, Annie, Daveon, Lee, Jeff, Steve, Laura, and Sammy—became some of his most trusted lifelong friends.

Ren noted that they had a number of traits in common. He kept a mental list and would ask himself, *How does that correlate with their successes and what can I learn from it?*

Many of the forum members were remarkably stubborn. Maybe that tied to the tenacity and perseverance that could be such an important success factor?

Most of them also had a fierce, independent nature—they were adamant about wanting to earn their success on merit. "I'm going to make it on my own!" was a typical implied mantra among group members.

It seemed like many of the members in the group had built their successes on being trusted. Trusting them was easy for Ren, since he himself had no suspicions about their intentions. But it also helped that, in a very genuine manner, it seemed that these people wanted to do right by others.

One member expressed how he hated to ever ask anyone for anything. And if he ultimately ever did have to ask for anything, at least he *had* to assure that he provided more back in exchange. Perhaps this was a big success factor for each of them, because of the trust it engendered from others?

To that point, another forum member complained about how people had been able to take advantage of him before he learned to be so careful. The member explained, "I feel like I genuinely, almost manically want to try to do right by others at every opportunity. As weird as it seems, I always only want the best for everyone—even my competitors and even sometimes for others who have done me wrong."

He meant it as a complaint. But Ren felt there was a compliment hidden behind it. That sincere wish for the best for others seemed like it could be powerful, as a foundation for trust. It might have sounded phony or at least disingenuous coming from anyone else in any other setting. But from this forum member, confessing to this group that knew and trusted him so well, Ren knew it was true. This forum member had been phenomenally successful and had a huge following. And Ren felt like he had just heard a key reason for it.

There was one comment made by a member that really hit home with Ren. It reminded him of his friend's statement from years back, about how some entrepreneurs who would go from all over the place, to hyper-focused, and then back to scattered again.

Of course, most of them were fragmented and felt spread thin in their busy lives, with so many priorities demanding their attention at all times. But some of them could also have that sort of superpower focus to force through any barriers and get a lot done. This behavior could create distance between themselves and others, including their family members and coworkers.

This came up when Ren was sharing how he was having some problems with others around him. A couple of his closest friends were acting weird, at a time when he had been really focused and trying to do some important work.

After he finished explaining that and the meeting ended, one of his forum mates pulled him aside and gave him some powerful guidance.

"Look, Ren," Annie said, "you know I care about you. I think you may need to take a hard look in the mirror about this."

She was giving an opinion now that didn't fit within the rules of their forum. But he trusted her and wanted to hear her guidance. "When you get really locked in and going on something that you believe in, Ren, you are a force of nature! We all think you are like a focused, directed explosion. It's exciting to watch and empowering just to know you and see it. It really can be a gift.

"I've heard you speak of what you call The Villain," Annie continued. "How you sort of personify all of the bad fortune and resistance and barriers and circumstances that arise as you build a business. As a business leader, I can see him, too. He normally looks daunting and scary. But you have grown so much in wisdom and purpose and strength as a leader that when you talk about him, I mostly just feel sorry for him being in your way!"

Ren registered that vote of confidence with a measure of salt. He didn't feel comfortable with compliments. But he wasn't sure where this was going and just took it in stride for now, listening intently.

"Of course," Annie pressed on, "as you like to point out, that kind of focus can be a superpower. And, in theory, maybe we all should just accept the consequences of it as part of the deal, what helps make you so successful—and just be grateful for the results.

"The results of your extreme focus," Annie continued, "are helping hospitals provide better care, helping create jobs and value. I want you to know I'm really glad you are that way. If you asked your wife or coworkers, or anyone that is acting 'weird' now, if they were glad you were building this business that helps so many people, every one of them would say 'yes.' And if you asked them if they would be willing to live with you being impersonal and focused for periods of a few hours or days or occasionally even weeks, in order to do so, they would take that, too."

Ren could feel the punch line coming.

"*But*," Annie said, "what you need to know is that there *are* consequences to those around you. What you think is *them* acting weird is really caused by *you*, setting them up to be that way, as you are so caught up in what you're doing and so focused and directed about it that you have blinders on.

"They don't know what's happening with your extreme focus," she said. "And they've never considered the trade-off for the results that come from it. If we could just help them understand that is what they bought with us, as a high-focus achiever, it might help them. We might find they actually help and support us more."

Annie was really digging in now, as she kept going, "You don't mean it personally and you are barely even aware that they—or anything else, except what you are working on—*exist* while it is happening. But they *do* still exist, and they *do* still have feelings, and they *don't* understand what is happening. I would just about bet that most of the problems you have with people come during those times, from people who don't understand what's going on with you.

"What is happening," she emphasized, "is that they're wondering what's going on. Why are you suddenly being less friendly or less considerate to them? Why did you walk right by them without acknowledging them, as you otherwise often do? Did they do something wrong?"

She continued, softening her tone a little now and positioning her delivery, "I want to be very clear. I don't necessarily think you need to apologize for being that way. As you can see, I think it is a good thing that helps all of us. I want you to keep doing the good work that you do. And if feeling regretful makes us even the tiniest bit less focused and therefore less powerful for all of us, then I want you to not feel apologetic.

"*But*," Annie told him, "what you *do* owe all of these people around you is to help them understand, in advance, and buy into what is happening during those times.

"Recognizing and learning to accept this focus thing is a good example of what our spouses and coworkers and friends can get from being around other entrepreneurs," she said, her head tilted to the side in empathy. "I realize you don't always know when these hyper-focused times are coming on, so I don't think it is fair to ask you to warn us when they start. But I can't tell you how much I want Tiffany and everyone around you to understand and be prepared for them."

Ren appreciated this enlightening feedback from Annie. And he came to believe that every spouse, partner, friend, or close coworker really needed to understand and buy—or choose not to buy, if they are unwilling—the good and bad that came with an entrepreneur. He increasingly felt this commonality with other entrepreneurs, CEOs, and organization leaders that shared similar issues and traits. And he wanted others around them to at least understand, going in, that their contributions to the world could come with some costs, at times.

Experiences with the forum also ended up altering, a bit, Ren's idea of himself and other leaders as contrarians that others erroneously thought were optimists. It turned out that most people in this forum of successful business leaders *did* have positive expectations and tend to dwell more on constructive and laudable ideals. More than half of the forum were big believers in the power of positive thinking.

Maybe a better way to say it was that most of these terrific entrepreneurs and leaders were "contrarians with an optimistic twist." Perhaps that was a factor in helping them keep a constructive, consistent mindset through all of the ups and downs of the roller coaster of leading any organization.

Of course, they were all persistent and tenacious. There were some side effects of those characteristics that he noticed and recognized in himself. For instance, he could use the same weak humor—what his sons later described as "dad humor"—over and over again. One of his favorites was when he walked in a store and a salesperson asked, "Do you need help?" He would automatically answer, "Well, my therapist thinks I do." Or when anyone asked, "How are you?" he had a number of canned answers that he would use repeatedly, such as "Well, I just keep getting older and fatter and balder—but otherwise pretty good."

Such lines might get old to a normal person, but they stayed every bit as amusing to Ren, every time. What made this interesting now, in consideration of his forum and success traits, was his thought that it came from a personality fault: the same positive/contrarian and persistent nature that was an important success factor in business. Maybe the trait that helped David and Sid and Ren and others repeat themselves so much, until someone fully took their point, also helped them to keep banging their heads against a proverbial wall until they hit a door in their businesses and ideas. And that seemed like one of the most common traits among this successful group.

Another complementary characteristic Ren often noted was the entrepreneurs' pervasive mindset around success. They used the word "success" a lot and some seemed almost obsessed with it. It was as if everyone in the group truly expected to find their success—and in many cases could tell you, with specific metrics, what they considered it to be. Was that a strong factor in getting there?

And, for this group, everything seemed to look like both a threat and an opportunity. Ren felt that this must have been another defense mechanism. For example, many of them had a passive-aggressive perspective on competition. For Ren and some others, they thought of every similar business in their industry as both a competitor and prospective partner. If one of their competitors started to beat another, they were then a prospective acquirer. For anyone that had never experienced it, it was strange how some of them were ready to go to war against the competition and still be pulling for them, or sometimes even working with them, at the same time. Some called it "coopetition."

Noting this perspective among so many of these entrepreneurs and CEOs helped Ren to frame not only how he approached some decisions regarding competitors but also to understand why he tended to trust other leaders and the value they could bring back to his team. They could compete one day and combine forces the next. Sincere interest in one another's success helped them through that.

At one of the forum meetings, one member went on a rant about how he despised the idea of anyone ever feeling sorry for themselves—and how it hurt him to see a family member almost becoming "addicted" to doing so. Over half the group nodded, as they clearly felt the same way. Ren thought, *What does that say about the force driving this group? Was that underlying some of the tenacity and drive?*

One concept that Ren introduced to the group was his own deep-seated mantra that "the only important thing about the past is what you learn from it." He wanted to never carry a grudge or hold on to any hard feelings. That never seemed to help anything. Normally it took people a long time to understand and appreciate that about him. But most of this group got it immediately—and some were already that way.

Ren also noticed how most, but certainly not all, had a real, genuine, compelling confidence about them.

One of them expressed it aloud: "*Real, true* confidence can be powerful and useful in leadership. But that is very different from fake confidence, cockiness, or dangerous arrogance born from insecurity. With genuine confidence, it's easier to feel humility and respect, too. And it's easier to change and evolve and admit mistakes and learn from them when you have it."

This came from one of the nicest people in that group—really one of the nicest people that Ren ever knew—despite the fact that his company saw him as a "hard-ass," as he described it.

This forum member was now building his third business. His first company had underperformed. He had been lax in enforcing necessary rules and ended up with a disastrous culture. He had to exit before it died. His second venture ended up going out of business because he had been too tolerant of one employee's unethical behavior and waited too long to call him on it—out of empathy but also out of fear of making a change. But he knew better now! He owed it to his employees and customers and shareholders to be forceful when he needed to. So now, when called for, he was the tough guy!

Ren felt that a lot of entrepreneurs and business leaders he had observed were incredibly nice, at least until it came time not to be. Then many could be as tough as they needed to be. The results bore that out, time and again.

The group seemed to agree on things like leadership through integrity and accountability and so much more. It was really encouraging to be among these amazing, fast-trusted new friends. In reflecting on all of the traits these entrepreneurs had in common, Ren suspected that many of these ingredients were a great part of the recipe for their success!

CHAPTER 40

Defining Dirigat

"One key to successful leadership is continuous personal change. Personal change is a reflection of our inner growth and empowerment."

—Robert E. Quinn

E ven with all of the issues and employee challenges that came with a growing and evolving business, Ren felt that Bart, Tom, and the Dirigat team increasingly shared in the ownership of the responsibilities. They also eagerly tackled problems and looked for opportunities. Though Ren felt that the buck ultimately stopped with him, he knew that the team also shared the weight. It felt good.

The team seemed to look at Ren differently. Perhaps part of it was with the success the business was finding. And they must have picked up on his newfound assuredness from his WAYAWAYG exercises and forum, to make decisions with more confidence and certainty. The change was a paradigm shift that served him well. Of course, there were still always going to be necessary tough decisions. And he learned a number of lessons in dealing with the team, as their perception of him changed.

Ren expected, of course, that every situation is different. How a founder and leader should interact in the company must surely depend on the stage and type of business and people. So, there was probably no discrete right or wrong in this. But there were plenty of new opportunities to make mistakes.

Disciplining employees and having tough conversations was never fun, but it had probably been easier for Ren than for most managers. Other than a period of time when he had followed the bad advice from Carl, he had always found it easy to speak frankly to others.

He learned, though, to be careful when going to lunch and having seemingly harmless conversations with the team. Sometimes, over a meal at a nearby restaurant, Ren would say something to the team that he thought was small and innocuous—a suggestion for development, for instance. But the development team would take it as a new imperative: For example, "the founder said to do that incremental recalculate feature." And they would drop what they were supposed to be working on to do it, to the chagrin of their development manager, who had his own priorities and objectives, with good reasons.

Ren also found that he needed to be careful about humor and how he spoke with any members of the team, at lunch or otherwise. Despite thinking of himself as a peer who interacted in a familial manner with everyone, he learned that anything he said was received completely differently when it came from the guy they perceived as the "big boss," in a more removed and sensitive environment.

In fact, Ren discovered that he needed to be careful not just about humor or suggestions for development but about everything he said to the team. As one of his mentors, Doug Banister, had described it, "You might think you are casting a pebble, but it is often received as a boulder."

Ren realized that when he expressed any personal appreciation for someone at Dirigat, or even acknowledged their birthday, it seemed to mean a lot. He really liked being nice to everyone. And he saw that it could be motivating to them—that is, at least until he forgot or missed someone's big day, or if he seemingly made a bigger deal over one person than another. And it was hard to handle such things consistently, if the birthday or occasion came at a bad time, maybe when there was a customer problem or had just been a layoff, and it seemed inappropriate to be celebrative. In some cases, the harm of it seemed to outweigh any prior benefit or warm feelings.

Even just being friends with team members and going to lunch with them—without necessarily saying or doing anything colorful or of note—caused problems. Some people at Dirigat, whether with good intentions or not, would represent themselves as being the founder's "buddy," as Carl Joseph had done, or would presume a derivative authority and knowledge from their friendship or visits with him that caused problems for their team leaders or team.

———

As Dirigat grew, the culture and demeanor in the office evolved. Where Bart injected energy and velocity to the team, it seemed like the company still had a lot of the "even keel" personality that Tom and Ren had established early. The focus on being professional when you walked in the door but staying positive—and hopefully having fun—seemed to work. Along with all of the culture and compensation lessons, Ren noticed that people seemed to love working at Dirigat.

The fun and energy in the office had just morphed into a more professional direction as they learned to be more careful. Instead of engaging in people's birthdays or anniversaries, the company celebrated successes in solving customer problems, development milestones, and big new sales. Over time, at least for the circumstances of Dirigat, it seemed to be a win.

During one of his great lessons on culture, Sid Richardson had told him, "Employees won't say as much to you with their words, but you can usually tell if you pay attention. And of course, you can tell if you are doing right by your team if people almost never leave, as opposed to if they leave in waves."

Almost no one ever left Dirigat of their own volition. When they did, it was only for a bigger, much better-paying offer. When that happened a couple of times, the recruited team member had come to Ren or Bart or Tom and expressed an interest in staying, if Dirigat could even come close to the higher-paying offer. After Dirigat couldn't and had to let them depart, they each came back and expressed later how great it had been and what a mistake it had been to leave.

David also offered some worthwhile guidance on delivering tough messages, like to "never tell a man his kid is ugly." By that, he meant that you needed to be wary anytime you spoke to anyone about anything that would be emotional to them.

The way he explained it to Ren was "Look, your developers are like you. They also think in goals and constraints and logical progressions—like their algorithms. And really this company is mostly filled with people that are like you. Y'all may have similar personality types and will normally be more likely to hear and recall past conversations the same way.

"That is, until—" and he waited a full second for emphasis, "you trigger them with anything that may be emotional to them. So, whenever you talk to anyone about their compensation or job performance or anything that might be close to them, you can bet they shift to 'emotion thinker' mode and hear and think and remember differently than they otherwise would. And you can just about bet that what they take from your conversation, from that point forward, will be different from what you recall being said.

"That's why I like to have 'em write down everything you both agree to, on a piece of paper, in their handwriting—and keep the original and give them a copy. It helps when they see the original," the older man continued. "It's surprising how often, when they recollect things differently, and you come back and show them the page they wrote, and they just go, 'Oh!'

"Of course they didn't remember it right, clouded by so much vested interest. Our human minds tend to misperceive and edit history. And you can only have one 'come to Jesus' at a time."

His point was that you should only address one impactful subject at a time with an employee. They were going to have a hard enough time just dealing with one big issue—much less anything else that came after that.

Those were the good ol' days at Dirigat. Most feedback was constructive, and people were aligned and doing great. It helped that everyone was so busy and enthusiastic because of all of the rapid growth and happy customers.

Of course, that affinity and happiness didn't last forever. The bigger issues came not when people wanted to leave but when the company needed to let people go.

No one likes to fire people. Or at least, no one Ren ever knew did. But Ren could see, at least intellectually, that he had an obligation to his other employees, his customers, anyone that had ownership in the business, and even to his own family, to let employees go when they clearly weren't doing their job or when they were dragging the company down.

The Villain was always there, battling incessantly against you!

Some of the problems came when people no longer fit as the company evolved. Others came when people took advantage of the latitude they had and didn't live up to the responsibilities, consequences, and accountability that came with it.

Even if the firing decision itself was completely clear—which was the case when someone did something dishonest or unethical or destructive—it was never fun or easy.

With Ren's new purposefulness, it was easier now, at least intellectually, to make the call to fire people when they really deserved it.

In many cases, the decision to let someone go came down to knowing that they were not a fit and were very unlikely to ever become one. Those cases were much harder than in the case of malfeasance because they were less cut-and-dried.

What really got Ren conflicted—even when the person clearly merited firing, which was really most of the time—was that he still felt bad for their families. The families hadn't done anything wrong and yet were still hurt when a team member was let go.

Ren had to acknowledge this potential soft spot in order to be the leader that his company needed and deserved. He could act with kindness and compassion but still make decisions that were right for the business at large. By making those tough decisions, he preserved his ability to have a company that could care well for its growing roster of high-functioning employees and their families, and thereby do what was right for their customers.

He also took heart in knowing that in most cases, the person he fired ended up finding a better fit wherever they landed.

Ren had always wanted to be a company that erred on the side of being overly loyal and patient with team members, as long as there was no ethical, legal, or character problem and there was potential to work past the issue. Bart, Tom, and the leadership throughout Dirigat were of the same mind-set, as the personnel and other tough daily operating decisions increasingly fell to them.

David was surprisingly on board with them in many cases. As he put it, "Maybe in some types of businesses, it's okay to have a firmer, 'tough love' culture and in others a frequent firing and commodity-hiring culture. But whatever your boundaries, employees and customers should be sold what they are getting.

"And Ren, I know your thoughts on the negatives of having a tough, 'fire-fast' culture, so it doesn't fit you or the kind of business you are building. Your employees signed on for a different culture and are living it. And that is what best suits who you are and where you are going now."

Then, he had to add, with a little bit of a warm smile, "Just as long as you have adequate, firm boundaries and don't let them take advantage of your big heart and sunny disposition!"

Ren already knew that his biggest failing as a businessperson was that he would see people for what they could be, not what they were.

He learned the hard way that people can change, but rarely do. The optimist-twist and devout loyalist in him always wanted to wait too long to fire people. But there was also plenty of good that came from that.

Ren would never expect loyalty from the team without offering it first, and he knew that no one was ever as bad as they seemed on their worst day nor as good as they seemed on their best day. He decided that he would rather wait too long than the other way around, as long as he could afford to do so.

This fed into Ren's concern with the risks and costs associated with every major change that a startup took on. He recalled when Sid Richardson had noted that one of the surest ways to struggle is to change too frequently. That included changing your team. Letting people go always seemed to have a lot of cost. It was expensive, painful, and risky, and should preferably only be done when there was no longer much hope of getting the employee in line and moving forward.

The other side of that was when a company got increasingly sloppy or increasingly had a reckless or dangerous culture as a result of the team getting too comfortable and not honoring firm boundaries.

David, Sid, and others encouraged Ren to expect some honest mistakes of effort—and maybe even to reward those sometimes, or at least not to punish those honest-effort mistakes too much at first.

But sometimes you had to draw firm lines, too.

In most cases, letting people go was cut-and-dried. If someone did something illegal or unethical, it was fast and easy.

———

One surprising incident got Ren's attention. Dirigat had signed up for ultra-fast internet. Serving up intensive amounts of data and large files should not have been a problem. But increasingly often, the internet speed seemed to slow down considerably.

At one point, as Ren walked into the company's server room to find Tom, Cindy, and Chip working away, he noticed an expensively housed new server that looked a little out of place in the busy set of racks. "What is that fancy new box for?"

Tom responded, "We thought it was yours."

After some exploration, they realized that no one knew what the new server was for. Curious, they went out into the development room.

"Does anyone know anything about that new box in the third rack over?" asked Ren.

Everyone on the team looked around, but no one responded. Ren did notice that one of the new contract developers, Arn, looked down at his feet and seemed particularly apprehensive.

Sure enough, later that afternoon, Ren heard a meek knock on his open door. As expected, it was Arn. On entering the room, the now-sheepish developer admitted to having set up a porn operation back there. He said, with a pained expression, "You had all of this high-speed bandwidth and didn't seem to need it."

Ren and Tom ended up consulting with their attorneys before taking action about this, and the lawyers advised that the server needed to come down right away. Particularly if it had been serving revenge porn or anything illegal, there could have been significant exposure for the company if they allowed it to continue.

With Arn's contract expiring soon anyway, the attorneys advised them to end the relationship immediately, as set forth in the agreement he served under.

This incident cost Dirigat time, a developer with needed skills, and some expense, although it could have turned out worse.

That was just one of many circumstances that couldn't have been predicted but seemed to incessantly arise from the team and often cost the company in various ways. The Villain seemed to have a sadistic sense of humor, at times.

———

Ren had learned, when possible, to give others a chance to get better. In order to make sure there was no ambiguity, he would use David's advice to have them write down what they needed to do to keep their job. That way, it was on them to keep going or not. As Jack Welch noted, people should not be surprised when they lost their jobs.

When it came to personnel and other critical decisions, certainty and clarity and empowerment could come from having a trusted, objective forum group or advisors, from the WAYAWAYG exercise, or from objective, aligned measurement. But even with all that, there always seemed to be more employee drama.

CHAPTER 41

Boundaries

"Hires refine culture. Fires define culture."

—Shane Jackson

After the experience with firing Carl, Ren could see that Bart felt more comfortable bringing employee issues to him. And the relationship between them improved greatly as Bart discovered that the founder had his back.

One day, he came to Ren with a challenging problem. Ren was already aware of it, but this conversation finally helped him to understand the challenge better.

"You see," Bart said, "I don't know what to do with Carter."

Ren could tell from Bart's expression that he was pretty torqued up about this one. Carter was an employee, embedded and working full-time on site, with Dirigat's largest and most important customer.

"For one thing, Carter's being all *cowboy*." Bart emphasized that word, explaining, "He's doing things in an unorthodox way and it's concerning. He's playing by his own rules rather than the company's. He's doing nonstandard things with the HospitAlign software: building scripts and basically adding on things with what I'd call 'bubblegum and duct tape.'

"Carter's a super-smart guy, and he's trying to give the customers what they want. I get it. It's a smart way to sell. But he wants to do it quickly. And the development team just can't support and deliver like that."

He slowed down for a moment to bring it home: "It's causing problems. When Carter's tweaks break, it's a painful or impossible challenge for our development team to fix them, much less make them replicable throughout our other customer implementations, which can lead to huge problems down the road."

Carter was causing other problems, too. Of course, every instance of an employee-related issue is different—but this one was weird and hard for Bart to figure out how best to deal with.

He let Ren know that he preferred not to fire Carter. In fact, Bart had hired Carter and was pulling for him more than anyone. It was just challenging. And if nothing else, Bart seemed to be venting a lot of pent-up frustration to Ren.

"Carter does a lot of extra work and puts in a ton of effort and creates great value. But it's also like he wants to do everything except what's in his job description.

"One example of this," Bart elaborated, "is that Carter's supposed to send status reports every week. Our team needs them for tracking and addressing issues, and they help me to stay on top of what is going on. But he just won't send them regularly like he's supposed to. I've addressed this with him repeatedly."

Bart had even offered that Carter could come up with a better solution or at least reasons to not send the reports that outweighed Bart's reasons for needing them. And, in each case, Carter agreed that he didn't have such reasons and agreed to get better. But he continued, time after time, to skip weeks of the important reports.

In fact, Carter would get better about that and other similar issues, for a while, every time Bart addressed them. But, in many of those instances, Carter would get really weird for a time and then eventually go back to the same problems. And that seemed to bother Bart most of all.

"Looking at it objectively, his positive results with the customer give a good answer. And I hate to fire someone for not sending updates. But when you consider what that means—not doing something essential to his job description—and weigh it with all the other things he does that add up to a greater problem . . . well, maybe I have to?" Bart asked as a rhetorical question. Ren knew that Bart didn't often solicit advice—and didn't want to be told what to do.

Bart's frustrations seemed mostly about the strange behavior that came after discussing any of this with Carter. According to Bart, as Carter's work would improve for a time after they addressed these matters, he also would act like an admonished child. He never responded directly to counter Bart's feedback as it was delivered. In fact, Bart would have welcomed any disagreement or opportunity for discussion. But he would leave their conversations thinking he and Carter were copacetic and then a couple of days later, Carter would fire off a long "butthurt," as Bart described it, email about how insulted he was that Bart was addressing these issues with him.

Then, when Bart reached out, Carter would apologize and explain how it was due to some personal matters in his life. He'd get better for a time before going back to his old behavior.

In one case, after Bart had offered some constructive feedback to Carter, he got an obvious cold shoulder from him for weeks. Of course, Bart was ready to live with that part, by itself. But the potential consequences were what worried him. For a couple of months after that, Carter would not look at Bart. In meetings, he would only look to Tom and speak to Tom, rather than Bart, his boss—even when Bart was speaking directly to him.

This was completely foreign to Bart and Ren, as they both always appreciated direct feedback and always wanted to know where they stood. Ren could see that it really bothered Bart that he couldn't provide that to Carter. Of course, it hurt Carter most of all. How could Carter improve and save his job when Bart couldn't provide feedback to him? But what got Bart most was the potential harm of the weirdness in regards to team dynamics.

"Do I call him on it there in front of everyone? Should I just go ahead and fire him to set a healthier dynamic among everyone?" Bart speculated out loud to Ren. "As much as I like him and see potential there, can I afford to set an expectation and precedent for this immature interaction in the company? What else can this lead to, behind the scenes, with employees or customers or the solution we provide?"

It was only after venting all of this that Bart finally confessed, "I actually did go up to meet with Carter to fire him, at one point, fairly recently. But, when I showed up, he proactively reached out, apologized sincerely. He said all of the right things, and explained yet again how the behavior came from events in his personal life and how it wouldn't happen again." Wanting the best for Carter so strongly, Bart took this to hopefully mean Carter would change, yet again.

But of course, Carter was already gravitating to his issues again, at least to a degree. Bart and Ren both knew the danger of this repeating cycle.

"Look," said Bart, "I still want to be his biggest fan. He does a lot of great things. Sometimes lately he even does valuable things that are *actually on* his job description. I can't tell you how much I am pulling for him and how much I want it to work out. But you need to be aware of this, and that I may need to make a change."

The amateur psychologist in Ren thought he could see what some of Carter's problems might be. But he had learned to pick his battles. And he knew that Bart had the better perspective and the right to deal with him.

Ren also had a good idea of what he would do. He knew that most of his forum, David, and most of his mentors would have told him, unequivocally, "Fire him." To them, the idea that someone would willfully, indefensibly do things that were counterproductive and in other cases to just refuse to do part of their job was unacceptable, as the underlying problem would recur and manifest elsewhere. But Ren thought he would probably have done as Bart did and continued to give Carter more chances, at least as long as there was hope that he could improve and better live up to his great potential.

For one matter, Carter was remotely deployed. So, letting him continue with being so immature was not going to hurt precedent and the dynamic in the team as much as it might have, had he been stationed in the office. And Carter had a ton of potential upside. As long as he didn't do anything unethical, he was worth a great deal of patience.

Ren also recalled David's guidance that there was always risk in any change. For one, whomever they replaced Carter with would assuredly have some other, different issue. And there would be time and expense lost in bringing them up to speed.

Most of all, Ren and Bart believed in empathy and loyalty, at least as long as they could afford it. Bart ended up keeping Carter on and continued to work with him, in the hope that he could live up to his great potential.

A different matter arose involving Aric. He was one of the early team members and best developers. Ren really liked and appreciated him, personally. Aric was good at his job, with a few exceptions: There were some things he did that concerned the team at times. But, at least to Ren, you sometimes need to take some bad—and hopefully work to address it, constructively—to get the good.

A critical time arose when the company needed Aric to complete a development project. It was a project that only he was immersed in and that he was most proficient in. The company was dependent on him for that period in a unique way. Aric took this situation as an opportunity to demand a completely unreasonable amount of bonus and ownership in the company. He made it clear that he wouldn't finish the project on time for this critical implementation if they didn't pay up.

Ren thought this ultimatum must have been coming from someone else. Maybe a family member was talking in Aric's ear and brought him to do this? It didn't seem like him to hold the company over a barrel in such an obviously out-of-line manner.

At any rate, when faced with no other choice, the company ended up increasing Aric's compensation spectacularly. Ren held out and refused to go with the untenable ownership stake Aric asked for. So, they just had to pay that much more in cash.

David and all of the company's management team and advisors were unanimous and unequivocal: This guy holding the company hostage had to go. If he did it once, he would do it again. They could never depend on him in the critical path again. Keeping him on the team was a new kind of poison that had started with the ultimatum and would only fester and grow from there.

Bart and Tom and Ren huddled with their attorneys and advisors before letting Aric go—as soon as he finished his project and they were in a comfortable position to do so. The attorneys and advisors were very helpful in working through all exposures and potential risks, measured against compliance and case law.

And ultimately Dirigat ended up much better for making the move and upgrading the position.

These were only a couple in a litany of troubling things that constantly happened with having employees—manifestations of The Villain that only continued to become more acute as the company grew.

When his forum and advisors, any empirical measures, and the clearly articulated plan for getting from *Who You Are* to *Where You Are Going* gave conflicting or insufficient answers, that might have been when Ren started to lean more on intuition and his gut—but that was only after a lot of situational experiences and getting his gut right with proven experience.

Ren felt that there were three sides to almost everything, and every circumstance was different. But his takeaway from all of his various experiences was this: As you set up for success, you also need to establish the right boundaries.

As Sid Richardson once said, "Firing draws a line. Sets a tone. Establishes boundaries. Shows everyone who you are."

Sometimes it just needed to happen, and it had a positive impact.

Really, in every case where Dirigat let someone go, the person deserved it for more reasons than the circumstance that brought the firing to a head. The team almost always recognized it as the right move and appreciated the boundaries, at least over time.

In every case where it needed to happen—be it Aric or Carl or anyone else—it had been so obvious to everyone that the person needed to go, that everyone else only felt better and performed better after.

CHAPTER 42

Loyalty to Royalty

"Effective leadership is not about making speeches or being liked."

—Peter Drucker

Bart Stanton always seemed so confident on the surface. He carried himself as if he was the king of the world, striding purposefully through the office with shoulders back and chin forward. Ren regularly studied people and noted their insecurities, but he had to look hard to see some of Bart's apprehensiveness simmering below his polished and affable veneer.

The brashness seemed to Ren as if it may have been one of those things where people sometimes seek to overcome their insecurities by going the other way.

He would not have said that Bart was arrogant or that it was even necessarily a bad thing. But Bart *was* one of the people who always had to be out front. Some of the best leaders were able to lead effectively from behind, in the middle, or wherever they needed to be, as the situation called for it. That was not Bart. He wanted to be in charge. He *needed* to be in charge. And he certainly deserved to be in charge of what he was going to be held accountable for.

Of course, Bart had done a great job in evolving the technology into more of an enterprise solution with all of an organization's clinical, financial, and operational data. The solution would sit on a CEO's desktop and would be pervasive throughout the organization, serving to align all indicators with the organization's mission.

The business seemed to take off with this broader solution. New consulting and funded development opportunities kept coming up.

And things had become more fun for Ren, at least for a time. He was now freed up from getting caught up in the weeds and he could spend more time thinking in greater terms, such as big-picture things like disease management. He came up with what David, wearing his Cheshire cat grin, facetiously described as "the megalomaniacal plot to take over the world."

Getting and effectively utilizing good data in hospitals had always been a problem. Ren believed that Dirigat was the best company, at the time, at collecting and marrying all of the data—and organizing it and using it well on a macro and micro scale. So what if they were looking at *all of* healthcare in a greater sense?

Basically, he wanted to get HospitAlign—or something that would evolve from it for the broader industry—into practices, clinics, and other provider settings, beyond just hospitals. Maybe they could have a larger solution called HealthAlign, as it evolved to cover a comprehensive population and help the entire industry?

They could enable clinicians to do a better and earlier job of, for instance, noticing a pandemic and pinpointing it. Or they could help to develop better clinical methods or operational efficiencies across all platforms. And they could save payors a fortune—ultimately passed on to everyone else—in being proactive in so many ways.

Of course, all of that was pie in the sky, for now.

———

The company kept growing and everyone else was really too busy to think far ahead yet. Even Ren tried to keep himself to a "two-minute rule" where he only allowed himself a couple of minutes on grandiose plans for the future. He still often needed to focus on putting out fires.

With the company advancing and becoming a good small business, there was always the seemingly incessant employee drama—the most common manifestations of The Villain, at the time. None of it was fun, and some of it was intensely painful. But none of it was as concerning as when Tom Strong became upset.

Friction had continued to brew at times between Tom, who was in charge of delivering and was the "heart" of Dirigat, and Bart, who drove the solution and sales and was the "head" of the company, as Ren saw it.

Bart Stanton, like many sharp, competent, take-charge people, wanted to be in command and didn't like accountability. He showed decent deference to Ren, which Ren took as a huge compliment, and he greatly respected and appreciated Tom. But he was not consistently forthcoming with information. Bart increasingly demonstrated that he liked to drive things on his own.

Realizing how counterproductive it was to dwell too much over Bart and his decisions, Ren did the best he could to bite his tongue and stay out of the way, fighting any battles with Bart internally and then supporting whatever choice his president made—and only showing a unified front and full support for him to everyone else. Even when interacting with Tom and David, he felt the need to have Bart's back.

As for the catalyst for the big disruption with Tom, Ren never fully understood what went on. He thought that it was probably one of those situations where neither guy did anything wrong—but that, framed with different perspectives, they saw things differently.

Whatever the case, Ren could tell that Tom Strong was not happy. He also knew that Tom was hard to piss off—and was going to be hard to placate, once he got angry.

Ren learned about the problem when Tom came into his office late one stormy morning. The lightning and thunder had mostly given way to a heavy rain. And almost in keeping with the darkness and downpour, he could tell how much Tom was fuming by his expressions and bearing. But he could also see that Tom was trying to be in control.

"Let's just say that I have an issue," Tom said. He wouldn't provide any more specifics, but the matter must have been very egregious to him. "Honestly, Ren, I may have to move on."

Those words were a dagger in Ren's heart. A dark blow to his soul. Ren knew that Tom was not one to threaten or take advantage lightly. His statement—which felt like an ultimatum, even if not intended that way—brought the realization that the company still depended tremendously on Tom.

In a startup, everything feels deeply personal to the entrepreneur. Ren felt the weight of all of the employees and their families, as well as the essential obligation to the customers. And Tom still meant so much to many of the customers that his leaving could be a grave threat to Dirigat. Ren also carried some deeper hurt because he had probably set up the circumstances for this problem. If he had been a better leader and done a better job of setting up roles and resolving problems, this would not have happened.

It took some questions and reading between the lines to realize that Tom felt like Bart had not been straight with him on something. And Tom was all about trust. Ren always wondered—but neither guy ever confessed—what the controversy had been.

It seemed like there were three sides to most every contentious matter. The old saying noted this as "your version, theirs, and the truth." Ren tried very hard to consider any such case from the disparate perspectives.

He had been in enough circumstances to know that the rub between Tom and Bart was probably a misunderstanding. Ren's only issues with trust had seemed to come when people misunderstood or took words and meanings differently, in some cases due to manners of speaking or different perspectives.

Maybe if Tom were more objective about it, he might have thought the same thing.

There was more to be said about the matter—but, it was also a culmination of pent-up frustration and issues.

Ren had to support Bart in doing his job. At the same time, he considered Tom to be essential and at the center of the company. As he told Tom, "If Bart is now the head of the company, you need to be the heart. Bart has the right experience and positioning to drive and guide the company. But the substance and personality of the company need to be built around you."

Tom seemed to appreciate the genuineness and sentiment, and seemed flattered enough to take a step back from the ledge. He told Ren that he still believed in Dirigat and its opportunity—and didn't know that he would find as much enthusiasm in doing anything else now.

He ended up giving it a little time and processing everything. Tom was great in doing things that way. He ultimately came back and worked through the misunderstanding and made things right with Ren and Bart.

But even with all of that, it seemed to Ren as if Tom was never quite the same about Dirigat again, or Bart, or even him, from that point forward.

Tom seemed to still respect both of them. But maybe it became less personal and more of a business to him, going forward.

The shift in dynamics framed everything differently. For Ren, it highlighted the importance for the company to never be too dependent on any one person and to be prepared for anything, as unpleasant as some of the implications of that were.

Ren brought Tom and Bart together to personally apologize and to take responsibility for originally setting them up for problems. He walked through their issues collaboratively with them and worked toward a reconciliation, including with expectations about communication going forward, that they both seemed comfortable with. And it was in this process that Ren seemed to have earned a different kind of respect from Tom and Bart as he took responsibility. After all of the mistakes and all of the growing and lessons that he had experienced, it was probably from this moment that Ren felt that they, and really most of the team, started to see him as more of a true leader, as if they saw him as closer to having more genuine strength and courage and purpose for his role.

CHAPTER 43

Wins and Losses

*"My favorite part of a roller-coaster ride is when you're
going up and you're slightly scared and really excited."*

—Gina Gershon

Just a couple of weeks after the concerning situation with Tom, Bart Stanton came to Ren's office. He knocked politely on the open door as he walked in, with the regal posture of conquering royalty and a huge smile on his face. "We closed the GHS deal!" he said, nearly skipping as he walked across the room and slid into one of the secondhand leather club chairs across from Ren's desk.

This came as a great surprise to Ren. It took him a moment to respond.

This deal was something Bart had been working on for as long as he had been at the company. Ren still didn't know very much about the deal, but he found that Bart had now sold a significant, multimillion-dollar deal to the government health system.

Bart had sort of kept Ren posted. But Ren had intentionally discounted the opportunity until it materialized. Now that it had actually happened, it was obviously a game changer!

"So, as you know, we are working through a GSA provider, Terrissett," Bart started. The General Services Administration serves as the acquisition and procurement arm of the federal government. Many small businesses contract through GSA-approved organizations to work with the federal government.

"I'll need some up-front capital to make a key hire in the system and to bring in some development specialists." It was easy to see that Bart was very caught up in this.

Ren was still processing the size and importance of this deal. He was enthusiastic and glad for Bart, and wanted to show support.

Then, Bart told him how much money he would need to make it work.

"800K?!?!" Ren questioned, stunned. "Really?" That was an expensive investment.

He always wanted to hire behind a need, but, after walking through it all in greater detail with Bart, the math on this deal made sense. So, Ren agreed to come up with the money. Bart, Tom, and the team made the deal work. And it ended up being a great thing.

———

The company continued to evolve, as did new challenges served up by The Villain.

One day, Tom Strong knocked on Ren's door. Tom's serious expression gave Ren pause. "Hey," Tom said, "can you come to the conference room?"

Curious as he followed Tom down the hall to the meeting space, Ren entered the room, where he found six of his key company leaders waiting with serious expressions. Tom joined Bart, their three top developers, and the company's key services guy.

Tom was the one to break the silence: "Martin Neep has got to go."

Martin had been one of the first employees at Dirigat; in fact, he came on board right after Tom joined the company. He was one of Ren's good friends. He, Martin, and Tom had been fraternity brothers in college, and they had stood in one another's weddings. Their wives were friends and their kids played together. All of this was racing through Ren's mind as Bart continued where Tom left off.

"Martin is technically proficient with technologies that we no longer use or need," Bart explained. "And he's becoming a negative influence in the development team now."

Cindy shrugged her shoulders. "He's really pissing everyone off, including our customers."

"What is he doing?" Ren asked. He wanted to really understand, since his inclination was to err on the side of waiting too long to terminate an employee rather than jumping to fire someone too quickly. And this was quite personal to him, with someone he respected and cared about.

Everyone in the room seemed to answer at once, before he even finished asking.

It boiled down to a near-universal sentiment about Martin: "He always seems to need to prove that he's the smartest guy in the room," Tom summarized. The other team members nodded.

"To be honest, he probably *is* the smartest guy, or at least one of them, but he needs to let his coworkers, and even any customer he interacts with, be right sometimes," Tom went on. "He needs to worry less about proving himself to them and more about solving their problems and even letting them feel good about themselves."

Ren wanted to be thoughtful about how to respond and not jump to conclusions. "It sounds like Martin must be insecure about something," he said to the team.

In hindsight, he realized that Martin's issues probably went back to the point when the company evolved its technologies away from Martin's expertise. He was great at a set of specialized skills, but their needs had evolved. As Dirigat no longer utilized the same development technologies they used at Avery University Health System, Martin was no longer a fit. It was a credit to him that he was still creating some value. He just was acting out from feeling the mismatch in his skills with the company's most pressing needs.

Rather than agreeing to take immediate action, Ren told the team that he appreciated them bringing the issue with Martin to his attention, and he promised to carefully consider how to handle it.

He walked out of that impromptu six-on-one conference room meeting and asked to get together with David to talk through the issues that his staff brought up.

They got together at their favorite coffee shop later that afternoon. Over steaming cups of black coffee, Ren poured out the conversation and shared how he felt a bit blindsided by their assessment of Martin's performance and attitude.

David listened thoughtfully, asking detailed questions to make sure he understood the issues at play before offering his perspective.

"Most of your development team are a lot like you, Ren," he began. "They probably have similar Myers-Briggs and personality factors as you do. They're objective-type engineers. And, you will find that, unlike some others, they will tend to see and hear and remember things like you do.

"That is, at least until you talk to them about their job performance or compensation or anything significant to them on a personal level," he continued. "Then, they will likely shift to be more emotion-driven. You can almost expect that what they hear and recollect after that will be different than what you hear and remember."

This idea was something they had discussed in the past, but he wasn't sure how to prevent it from happening. He said as much.

As much as he was reticent to do it, he had the challenging conversation with Martin at the earliest opportunity. And he utilized David's method of having Martin write down what he needed to do to keep his job, in order to assure they were communicating clearly. It wasn't fun, especially since Martin and Ren had such a long personal history, but it was necessary.

It was just after his conversation with Ren that David went to Martin and told him, "Just so you know: I am telling Ren that he should fire you."

David was that good of a friend—he stepped in as the "bad guy" so Ren didn't have to be, or at least not as much.

Ren worked out a deal with the team to move Martin into responsibilities and special projects, where he had less direct contact with customers and less regular interaction with the rest of the development team. That move alleviated some of the most urgent pain points his staff felt on a day-to-day basis.

It would be several months of travails with the team before Ren finally capitulated and let Martin go, after all of the conversations and shifting roles didn't have the desired effect. But when it was time to pull the trigger and cut Martin loose, Ren was grateful for David's wisdom, that handwritten piece of paper, and having a friend who was so caring that he would take the rap for him.

Martin was a great guy and friend. But he wasn't a fit for where Dirigat was anymore. And Ren felt increasingly sure that was what brought about all the problems with Tom and the team.

While driving home after letting his friend go, it was hard to think of his friend Martin going home to his own family. When Ren arrived at his house, he noticed Caulie's excited greeting more than he typically would, anymore. He looked at Tiffany a little differently, thinking of Martin's wife, who was also a friend and a great person. And he hugged RJ a little longer than usual.

CHAPTER 44

Clean Your Closet

"Productivity is never an accident. It is always the result of a commitment to excellence, intelligent planning, and focused effort."

—Paul J. Meyer

Belinda Harden called Ren, out of the blue, and said she wanted to connect and catch up. Ren wasn't sure if Belinda quite fit the "mentor" moniker, since she didn't instruct or lecture him as others did. But if not an official mentor, she was pretty close. A longtime friend and someone that Ren looked up to, she was the CEO of a very successful energy and transportation logistics business that she had helped to build from its early stages.

Ren had met Belinda years before when she spoke to one of his college classes. They crossed paths again through a civic leadership development organization, where they both volunteered. He stayed in touch with her over the years, and she was often on his short list of people to consult with about big decisions and challenges.

A fifty-something executive who had moved to Chicago for the company, Belinda was smart and savvy. She was one of the most warm, gracious, genuinely likable, and easy-to-respect people that Ren knew. She often sent articles to Ren when she thought of him. He was blown away and humbled with how she still reached out at times and kept their relationship going despite her incredibly demanding schedule.

Belinda had asked to come back to Atlanta to visit with Ren, a few weeks out, suggesting dates in the latter part of the second week in April.

Ren would have moved just about anything to accommodate her—but unfortunately, he couldn't shift his schedule that one particular week. When Ren told Belinda that Dirigat was hosting their annual customer forum near Las Vegas on those dates, he was surprised when she asked if she could see him there instead.

"I really just want to catch up. The closest thing I have to an agenda is finding out how you and your family and business are doing. That sounds like a great opportunity to do just that," said Belinda.

"The only thing I ask is that you don't make a fuss over me or take much time away from your customers and the forum," she added in her friendly manner. "I can learn what I want from hiding in the back of your conference and watching what's going on!"

Ren accepted. It bothered him not to "fuss" over her. But he agreed, as he would have plenty of other priorities and responsibilities during the customer forum.

———

Bart Stanton had a great many shrewd ideas, including a philosophy that it was smart to host his customer forums near—but not too close to—fun destinations.

Bart knew that if you have a customer forum on the Vegas Strip, South Beach, the French Quarter in New Orleans, or in some other destination known for tourism and entertainment, the customers would all want to sign up for the conference and stay at the venue for the days you are there, but attendance would be sparse at your sessions, as everyone was out having fun or would be too hungover from the night before.

Instead, he set his meetings for Wednesday through Friday, in some more tame location, maybe about an hour away from such exciting places. Customers would take time from work for a trip where they could expense part of the travel, attend the sessions, and *then* they could tack on time to the Vegas Strip, beach, or other fun spot for the adjacent weekend. Everybody wins!

For the third annual Dirigat customer forum, a few hundred dedicated customers and employees showed up at a resort in a community that was several miles outside of Vegas, to share best practices, network among similarly minded leaders in their industry, have fun, pick up swag, and show off how they were using the company's solutions.

Ren enjoyed the first day of the forum but was looking forward to the second day, when Belinda would join them. He liked knowing that one of his favorite role models would be hiding away in the back of the room, watching the proceedings with great interest.

That day finally arrived and wore on. And while he really wanted to spend time with his customers and the Dirigat team, Ren wanted even more to speak with Belinda to see what she thought of his company and what they were doing.

She was not giving anything away with her expressions. Ren wondered why Belinda—normally enthusiastic with praise—hadn't offered any feedback yet. That is, until, increasingly apprehensive for her opinion, he finally cornered her during a break.

Belinda, dressed in a casual navy dress and sweater, her sandy blond hair tucked behind her ears, was selecting a green apple and a bottle of sparkling water when he approached. "Well," he said hopefully, "what do you think?"

Belinda finally gave up her poker face. Her stern look gave way to her signature heartwarming smile—only now punctuated with excitement and enthusiasm.

While Belinda was often encouraging and effusive, Ren could always count on her to be honest and to deliver a hard message if she needed to. So, it meant a lot when Belinda said, "That is one of the most impressive things I have *ever* seen!" she said, patting him on the shoulder. "I *love* your software and solutions. I *love* your people and their competence. And, I *love* how your customers are using this to provide better care, make the world a better place, and save lives!"

Ren could feel his emotion rising, as Belinda continued, "But the thing I am most impressed with is how much your *customers love it*. They are like a cult!"

Not often given to showing what he considered "sappy" emotions, Ren started to tear up. To have one of his heroes see his hard work come to fruition and to truthfully and objectively validate what he wanted to believe was just too much! He felt his heart expanding with happiness.

Trying to be cool, Ren told Belinda that he "must have got something in my eye," and promptly excused himself, telling Belinda to plan for dinner with a couple of his customers and team members. They agreed to meet back in the lobby in an hour.

———

Just ninety minutes after the fulfilling episode with the tears, Ren and Belinda were at dinner at the most-recommended local Italian restaurant, with Tom Strong and two of Dirigat's best customers: Terry Harrell and Claire Bishop.

Bart had been unable to join—busy working his magic with prospects and keeping things in line at the conference. But Ren was proud of himself for putting this dinner group together. He knew Belinda would hit it off with Tom, Terry, and Claire. He expected the food and drinks to lay the groundwork for a fun and constructive evening.

Ren considered Terry Harrell to be a friend and an inspiration. He had an immaculately groomed beard and always looked cool, competent, and well attired. He was also one of those rare people who always seemed in charge but not in your face. You hardly noticed him, at times. But whenever everyone laughed at a joke or needed to make a tough decision, it seemed like they all looked right at Terry.

If Ren had to guess Terry's age at the time, he would have speculated early fifties, mostly because Terry had graying hair and had accomplished so much in different opportunities.

From what Ren knew, Terry had started his career as a psychologist before transitioning into hospital operations, becoming a hospital performance improvement consultant. He then moved into hospital administration, where he was now the Chief Improvement Officer of a very successful, progressive multi-facility hospital system in the Seattle area.

Ren enjoyed spending time with Terry immensely. Terry was also a "foodie" like Ren but with a much more sophisticated palate. Where Ren could enjoy Waffle House or a Chick-fil-A sandwich as much as anything, Terry knew fine food and wine pairings.

Claire, on the other hand, was mostly about business. Sure, she was fun. But she always seemed to incisively cut to her point, spoke quickly, and even treated many of her conversations as if they were business transactions that she wanted to complete and then move on. Ren found it remarkable that she could be like that and still seem so likable. Under that tough, businesslike exterior, she was genuinely caring, thoughtful, and empathetic.

And Claire had achieved considerable success, as well. She also came into hospital administration from a consulting background. It seemed to Ren that more people seemed to go the other way—to start out working in hospitals and make the move into consulting or services. But the reverse had worked very well for Claire. Ren guessed she was probably in her mid-forties now, and she had already been the COO of two of the most-respected hospital systems in the country, with a great reputation as a constructive change agent.

Claire was powerful. Ren's biggest—really only—problem with Claire was that whenever he and Terry were talking about food, Claire didn't seem to notice or care—she was good with whatever they ate and didn't seem to have much opinion on the topic.

Over what Terry declared to be a "pretty good" Italian meal, the jovial conversation moved from how Ren originally connected with Belinda, to Dirigat's increasing successes, to shared admiration and appreciation for Bart Stanton, Tom, and the team.

A modest guy, Tom looked embarrassed as they all bragged about his exemplary work, but he managed to add a little humor when he looked at Ren and said, with a smile, "I'd just like to thank all the little people . . ." and then used that to segue into a change of subject.

"I'm proud of what we are doing," he said. "But I'm in one of those seasons now where I'm struggling to be more productive."

This caught Ren's attention. "I'm surprised to hear you say that, Tom," Ren said. "I've learned a lot of what I know about productivity and being effective in getting things done from you. What's going on?"

The rest of the table listened with similar interest and curiosity.

"Well, I think I'm just getting too fragmented. And I feel too close to what we are doing. I almost feel some resistance and baggage around our software and dealing with the people in our development team. Random challenges always seem to pop up, from a grown adult employee showing up late to an important meeting with a note from their doctor, to a customer changing what they want after you did it already, to an employee experiencing a life challenge when you need them most. And everything else, too. Ren calls it The Villain. It feels personal sometimes and adds up to a barrier."

Tom surprised everyone at the table, perhaps himself most of all, as he continued, venting to people he respected, after a few glasses of wine, in a way that he normally wouldn't have.

"I even feel some of the same pressures building around my family. Don't get me wrong, everyone's happy and healthy and our relationships are great. I just don't feel satisfied with what I am putting into—or, frankly, getting from—our business, my family, and all the responsibilities around me."

Terry managed to both listen intently and savor every bit of the desserts he had ordered for the table. He could somehow intercede in a conversation without anyone minding. After a pause, he interjected, "You can tell a really good Italian restaurant by its crème brûlée," as he used his spoon to crack the caramelized sugar crust on top. "This one is good. The cheesecake is pretty tasty, too." Then he looked at Tom thoughtfully.

"I really identify with what you're saying, Tom," Terry said. Ren and everyone else nodded agreement and understanding, their own challenges coming to mind during this frank, intimate conversation.

"My CTO at the hospital system is very sharp and competent," Terry said. "In fact, she reminds me a little of you, Claire. She's one of the sharpest people I know."

Claire blushed a little, in response.

"At any rate," he said, taking a sip of his espresso, "maybe because she knew of my psychology background, she recently came up to me and confessed that she was unhappy. I'd never heard her say anything like that before, but I came up with a suggestion for her.

"I told her to go home and clean her closet. I told her that while she was cleaning, she would have distractions come up. She would think of how she needed to get her son's closet straightened, as well. She would get a phone call. She would think of other things that she needed to do," he said. Terry was such an effective storyteller, everyone leaned forward, hanging on every word.

"But I told her to just keep cleaning it until she finished," Terry recounted. "I told her that it didn't need to be perfect, or even all that great. It just needed to be done."

"You know, Tom," Ren interjected, "you're the one who told me the Voltaire quote that 'perfect is the enemy of good.' And I often go into projects feeling a lot more empowered in thinking that."

Ren was glad to have made that point, hoping to make Tom feel a little better. But he quickly recognized that Terry was feigning patience—not used to being interrupted. When Terry could see that Ren was done with his interruption, he continued, "She came back to me a couple of days later. She said, 'It happened exactly as you predicted. I thought of ten other things that I needed to do. I got a couple of those phone calls that you said would come, pulling me to more urgent matters. But I got it done. My closet is clean!' She put an emphasis on 'done' and 'clean.' Then she added, 'And I just feel better!'"

Terry kept going, "She felt better in getting closure on something. We can get so fragmented in our lives. Often, we have a place—maybe a closet or even a drawer—that basically represents our state of mind.

"More than that, sometimes breaking through our barriers opens a logjam for us—when we didn't even know we were constrained," Terry said. "Solving that one problem may have freed her up a little for some other things. In fact, she seemed to do better in many ways for some time after that."

Ren felt a little gun-shy, knowing now that his last interruption had been a distraction. He waited until he felt relatively sure that Terry was finished before jumping in again. "That makes me think of a close friend who told me, some years ago, that he was unhappy at the time. This friend was healthy and successful, with a great family and a thriving, profitable business in the insurance industry. But he just felt unfulfilled," Ren recalled, adding that his friend had sought out a psychologist for help.

"The psychologist he met with noted that, throughout history, our ancestors would do things that were tangible and constructive: They would build a home for their families and use it. They would slay a bear and use the meat to feed themselves and make clothing from the skin. They would grow crops, harvest them, and feed their tribes with it.

"She gave my friend a book called *Flow* that talks about the flow state that we get into when we work out, go for a run, or get engrossed in a project," Ren continued. "I think research shows that we need to get into that state at times. But the psychologist added that we particularly needed to get into the flow state while accomplishing something constructive, and particularly something tactile and observable. It's important that we can see and touch and feel and use those things for constructive purposes, just as our ancestors have done throughout human history.

"This psychologist explained that my friend couldn't even see all the money he was making from his business. It was all moving around behind a computer screen," he said. With a couple of glasses of wine loosening his tongue a bit, Ren was on a roll now. "So, my friend took up woodworking. He told me that it was like eating healthy: He didn't necessarily feel better immediately, but he felt a lot better soon. He said he would build a cabinet, and when he was finished, he just felt good."

Finally starting to run out of steam, Ren said, "I know I sometimes need to do something constructive and tactile in order to feel good. I can go out into my yard and build a yard feature or do some work, getting exercise and getting in that flow state, as I do so. It really does make me happier and feel better."

Looking at Terry, Ren concluded, "That sometimes seems to break through logjams around productivity too. A few weeks ago, I was getting bogged down in a project at Dirigat and went out in the yard, built a stone retaining wall, and came back to the office all fired up. I was able to knock out some of the best, most productive work I had done for some time."

Belinda jumped in next. "That is such good feedback, Ren and Terry. When I get home, I'm going to clean my closet." She smiled her winning, warm smile that put everyone around her at ease.

"For my part, I read a lot of books on productivity hacks," she continued, "but I still get bogged down sometimes. I sometimes change out techniques to freshen up my approach, but I do have some practices that I have been using for years. I've become decent at using technology, including blocking time on my calendar for tasks and holding myself to it. I also love checklists.

"For instance, I have my own task list template that I like to print out every night. It only has eleven lines on it—that keeps me from getting overly ambitious with what's realistic to accomplish in a day. I handwrite each task list item on it before I go to bed," she explained, gaining momentum as she shared what worked for her.

"I've read that you are more likely to do something if you write it in your own handwriting," Belinda said as Ren nodded, recalling how he'd learned the same principle from David. "I believe in the power of the subconscious mind. And I think most people, when they go to sleep, their minds are probably working on whatever they were watching on TV when they fell asleep.

"But, for me, when I make my list right before bed, I'm putting my subconscious mind to work on what I am going to do the next day." Ren had heard the same thing from a couple of self-help speakers.

"And while we are being honest among friends, over a delicious dinner and wine," Belinda said, raising her glass for emphasis, "I will confess that I love to physically check off each item with a blue ink pen, as I go down the list. I get this real satisfaction when I have ticked off every item on my list for the day. That check mark actually motivates."

Claire had been listening quietly, taking in everyone's stories with interest. "I have my own system, as well," she interjected. "I just juggle a lot these days, and was finding myself getting less effective, so my assistant took on my task list and my calendar. He assigns times in my calendar to take care of most of my priorities. We use an interactive task list that I can use from my cell phone and laptop. It keeps me on track by allocating my time and helping me stay accountable. So, a ton of my tasks look like calendar appointments that I get done when I set aside time to do them. That way, I don't let resistance get me off track."

"What do you mean by resistance?" Tom asked with interest.

"Ah," said Claire, "resistance has been a huge concept for me to understand. Knowing it's there is half the battle. For me, it's about powering through any resistance, without allowing or considering any other option. And it may be one of the tricks from Ren's Villain.

"Resistance seems to arise from all the barriers that build up. As a per-fectionist entrepreneur, you want to do everything perfectly, right?" Claire's rhetorical question was met with subtle nods around the table. "And, when you can't, you feel this disempowering pressure to get it done well enough with the time you have, competing with pressure to do it perfectly.

"I love Stephen Covey and Tony Robbins—really most of the productivity and self-help gurus," she added with a smile, knowing she was fleshing out her answer to Tom's question. "I use a lot of their suggestions for managing priori-ties and aligning my schedule and emphasis. And, all of that is great . . . but I once read a book by Steven Pressfield called *The War of Art*. It basically says the same thing that Tony Robbins and Nike say: 'Just Do It!' You don't need tricks. You just need to blow it up!

"I know I can use a lot of productivity hacks and tricks and games. Or I can take the book's advice and just attack what needs to be done—and get it done without even considering that not getting it done is an option," Claire contin-ued, her forearms resting gingerly on the white tablecloth in front of her.

"Pressfield writes about that same resistance that we're talking about. For example, for hard-charging, successful people with perfectionist tendencies—you guys all qualify!—it becomes like a thickening wall in front of us," she explained. "I think particularly with our children, our jobs, projects—things that mean something to us—we build up this emotion and strong conflicted feelings. When I get frustrated or feel resistance, it's like I have a little voice in the back of my head that says to 'attack and lay waste' to anything that needs to be done. Or even more simply 'blow it up!'"

Claire continued, passion infusing her voice and pink coming to her cheeks,

"With those mantras in the back of my head, I just power through things. When I'm finished, I always feel empowered."

Ren found himself thinking that, other than closing deals, this was the most emphatically he'd ever heard Claire speak. He liked it, and he felt that he'd gotten a valuable window into her psyche during this conversation.

"I am big on delegating, too," Claire added. "Some of the things I'm best at aren't necessarily the best investments of my time. Like, I've found that I'm good at the financials, but, once I start diving into them, I get bogged down. I invest time in the details that someone else can address better than I can. There are a couple of trusted people on my team who can review and provide the most vital information, to keep me engaged, without ruining my day."

Ren and Tom looked at each other, each knowing the other was thinking that Claire was describing most decent CEOs, when Claire added, "I do go into the financials at times, for my sake, as well as to send a message to everyone that the details in the financials are important. And if we watch the pennies, we'll be a better organization for it, even beyond the value of those pennies, which do add up."

They sat at the table, enjoying the last of the wine, until they could see the restaurant staff was closing down. Out of respect for the servers' time, they knew it was time to call it a night.

Ren didn't just like to learn philosophy and high-minded concepts from his role models. He also derived a ton of value, including practical and tactical and mechanical guidance, from that dinner conversation.

For instance, he learned from Tom that the best trick for self-discipline and getting things done is making it a habit. He could invest a few weeks in making something a constructive habit and then never need to fret as much about it again.

He already knew that diet and exercise and sleep and mindfulness matter. But the reminder, applicable in this conversation, helped him to take action toward watching his diet better, with good results. He even eventually switched from sweet tea to unsweetened!

Belinda really inspired Ren with her morning routine, built around gratitude and prayer and preparation for a constructive and energetic day.

And there were so many other useful effectiveness and productivity tips.

Ren hung on the group's advice for keeping a time diary and weighing priorities, fostering an attitude of *wanting* to do what he *needed* to do, utilizing his most productive times of day, setting up a distraction-free workspace, turning off his phone when he needed to, tackling one small difficult task first, breaking up lengthy tasks, rewarding completion of difficult tasks, eliminating unproductive bad habits, taking some free time for exercise or breaking away each week, sleeping healthily, standing at times while working, and much more.

Ren never asked Tom what he took away from that dinner that had turned into an impromptu productivity forum. But he did notice that Tom seemed a little happier and more at ease after that conversation. Even though he couldn't say for sure, Ren wondered if Tom had simply cleaned his closet.

CHAPTER 45

Paying It Forward

"Immortality is to live your life doing good things,
and leaving your mark behind."

—Brandon Lee

Ren felt a compelling sense of purpose to do something meaningful with the wealth and wherewithal that the exit from Standard Link and now, prospectively, Dirigat was building for him.

Earlier on the company's journey, he had met Doug Banister through an introduction by a mutual friend. Banister had been successful, first as the leader of one of the best-known national consulting firms and then as the CEO of a multibillion-dollar technology company that he had taken public. He was also engaged and instrumental in a number of local charitable and civic causes. He served on boards, hosted fundraisers, and quietly made impactful donations. Ren found Banister to be incredibly insightful. Among other matters, he emphasized doing genuinely meaningful work—and the importance of human factors and emotional intelligence in business.

In one conversation, Ren relayed to him some of David's warnings about starting a business and all the circumstances that line up to oppose you.

Banister shared that he, too, had experienced The Villain. He noted that these travails were not just the case with startups: "As businesses become more successful, the roller coaster continues in some different ways. It helps sometimes to have cash and resources. But the closer you get to the center of the hurricane, the more it almost always feels like it is held together with bubblegum and duct tape. The types of problems and margin of error are always changing. But The Villain never stops."

And he advanced more from another point that Ren had heard from David before, "When you get through all the challenges, you're always glad you did it. And really, there was value in the journey. You grew from the adversity and affected others constructively along the way.

"Life is not supposed to be easy," Banister said, looking directly into Ren's eyes. "It can be meaningful and fun and rewarding. But one thing I believe is that people who look for an easy life will never find it. At least in my experience, it's the people that want to work and innovate and pay their dues that may get there. And often when they arrive at a point where they could take it easy, they go out and find the next challenge, for good reason."

Banister was an inspirational leader who liked to put his money where his mouth was. Many wealthy people *pretend* to give away their wealth, using tax-avoidance tricks to avoid truly giving as much of it away. Banister actually *was* giving away most of his wealth. He was doing almost all of it anonymously. And he was doing it in a wise "venture philanthropy" way, to many worthy, actionable causes. Ren understood from their conversations that Banister's primary motivation in his successes had been to be able to give it away in a sustainable manner.

And he suggested that often, the best way to give back was not even as much in money as in time and in the wisdom gained from the journey.

———

RJ turned five years old the same year that Dirigat turned four. With his one-year-old son Christopher, as well, Ren and his family sometimes joked that he had three kids. It felt like that most of the time!

As much as Ren had been caught up in his business—and even before he turned most of the daily responsibility over to Bart Stanton and Tom Strong—he had always wanted to do more with his own family, particularly his young sons.

Ren was pulling his weight, at least a little more, around the home now, even helping with cleaning, looking after Caulie a bit more, and occasionally with cooking.

Tiffany must have finally figured out how terrible the "hockey puck" was— or at least moved on to other dishes, as she never made it anymore. In fact, now her cooking was great—and there was lots of bacon involved.

Christopher was still too young to go out and play as much, but Ren was taking RJ down to the creek more often. Caulie had matured a lot but was still very excitable and absolutely loved to go with them. And he found a church basketball league, where the kids could start playing at four and five years old.

When Ren went to sign RJ up for basketball, he learned that the league was struggling to find coaches, to a point where they might not be able to field enough teams. Ren had plenty of other things going on, but he found himself volunteering for the job—it was a good opportunity to be RJ's first coach and spend more quality time with him at this formative period in his son's life.

Ren may have started this for the opportunity with his son and from a sense of obligation to pull his weight for the greater good of the team. But from that point forward, coaching youth sports became a huge part of his life.

Volunteering in youth sports was a labor of love that certainly would have its challenges over the coming years. But few things ever gave Ren as much joy as coaching that first basketball team of four- and five-year-olds. They played on a regular court, but with a basket that was only six feet high. Every team, including Ren's, had at least one player that couldn't throw the ball high enough to get it in the basket, as well as a few kids that couldn't really dribble.

But all of the kids had great fun with it. Ren felt like it was his job, as coach, to send the kids home happy and tired.

Half-jokingly, Ren always told his players that when they went up on the stage at the NBA draft someday, they needed to at least acknowledge their first coach, even if they couldn't remember his name!

———

The basketball team's practices were after preschool on Tuesdays and Thursdays, each week, from 2:30 to 4:00 p.m.

Ren was walking out of his team's practice one evening, with RJ holding his hand, when he noticed an older-model Toyota in the parking lot behind the building. He thought he had seen the same car there before, a couple of times.

It always got his attention because it looked exactly like David's fifteen-year-old Land Cruiser.

This time, Ren pulled around for a closer look. It *was* David's Land Cruiser! Maybe he had *finally solved the mystery* of where David had been sneaking away to, a couple of days every week!

RJ seemed confused by Ren's eagerness, as his father took him by the hand and hurriedly led him into the building, where they wandered the halls, looking for David.

After a few minutes, Ren noticed some noise coming from a classroom in one of the back hallways in the church recreation building. As they approached the door, he slowed down. Maybe he didn't want David to know that he was on to him? *Was David in an AA meeting or something he might want to keep to himself?*

As Ren sneaked up to the door, RJ in tow, he could hear David's drawling, gravelly voice: ". . . and so, I'm not going to presume to tell you what all of your values and principles should be, but just that you need to have them and to know what they are. And you need to measure your life and decisions against them."

Ren had heard this from David before!

He peered in carefully from behind the door to see a classroom of perhaps twenty-five students—Ren was guessing mostly around ninth or tenth graders—sitting attentively in their seats as David spoke to them from the front of the room.

Ren watched for a few more minutes as David led a discussion on values and leadership—and where they can tie together with entrepreneurship or even intrapreneurship within an existing organization.

He could see that David was selling it, and the kids were really buying it, and—judging by their posture and expressions on their faces—*owning* it!

Pulling his son along, Ren retreated before David could see him. He took RJ to his favorite restaurant for a little daddy-son dinner, as they often did after practice. But he was already formulating his plan to "catch" David!

The following Thursday, as David walked out toward the parking lot, Ren was waiting, leaning on the hood of his Land Cruiser.

"Excuse me, sir! You can't park here!" Ren said, with a smile on his face.

It took a second for David to process the scene, seeing Ren out of context like this. "What are you doing here?" he asked.

"I'm on to you!" Ren answered. "You're teaching a class to those kids!"

David got an odd look on his face and blushed a bit. Then he confessed. "I've been teaching principle-based leadership to a group of kids here for the past few years. It isn't a Sunday school class, but rather a business and life-coaching session for these young people.

"And, yes, I've been leaving the office at times and teaching this class. I feel passionate about helping these kids. Some of them come from challenging backgrounds. They're intrigued by the opportunities and lessons I'm doing my best to share with them. Really, I even feel like I'm learning as much from them as they are from me."

It turned out that David had experienced some frustration with teaching in schools, libraries, and other institutions where, it seemed to him, there was always paperwork, hassles, and bureaucracy in the way. Then a staff member at this church had become aware of David, as they were helping some of the same kids that he was teaching, and their families. They had offered him this classroom.

David had started out with a few kids but had quickly gained so much interest from participants telling their friends that he had to cap participation when the classroom became full. Now he was looking for a bigger venue to bring in more of the youth that wanted to join in.

At some point, the kids he was teaching had started doing service projects together. Some of them had started their own businesses—dog-sitting, raking leaves, or providing other services in the community.

Through all of this, David had been frustrated with some of the challenges. In one recent case, two of the kids had skipped David's class and were caught making out in another room in the church. A senior staffer had caught them and was reasonably furious. He had threatened to kick David's class out of the building.

As he was getting more worked up, and venting, about his many frustrations, Ren reminded him, "It makes me think of something you once said to me a few years ago, David—'Good deeds don't go unpunished. But it doesn't mean you don't do them.' You told me that you do the good deeds anyway!"

CHAPTER 46

Bringing It All Together

"No one knows what you have been through or what your pretty little eyes have seen, but I can reassure you—whatever you have conquered, it shines through your mind."

—Nikki Rowe

Eventually sitting through one of David's courses on entrepreneurship, management, leadership, and character, Ren loved the infectious energy of these young students. And the course seemed to incorporate a great deal of what Ren had learned over the years, from David and elsewhere in building Dirigat.

It was at the end of that course that Ren got perhaps the best summary for starting and building a business that he had ever experienced. He took notes.

David liked to qualify all of the lessons that he was sharing with these young people. He told them that all of this was just his opinion, based on his experiences, and he hoped they would come up with their own views of it. Then he launched into summarizing a lot of what he thought might help them in being entrepreneurs.

"You should start with the end in sight, and drill down and work from there to serve your greater goal. Begin by defining and articulating your goals and vision and priorities—your purpose—and work toward that.

"Based on this big picture, clearly articulate who you are and where you are going. Maybe work for a fifteen-year horizon for yourself, and really understand your circumstances and visualize and believe in your goals. Take action, with force and commitment, in terms of always moving in that direction.

"If you are the right leader with the right, clearly articulated plan, people will want to follow you over any mountain.

"Truly take responsibility and ownership of your business and life.

"If you are starting a business for yourself, as the entrepreneur—doing what you believe is meaningful—also articulate a 'who you are and where you are going' for your venture. Maybe use a five-year horizon for that, since the world changes so fast now that five years is usually plenty for a business.

"And particularly if you have partners in your venture or just want to be *intra*preneurial in someone else's organization, as opposed to *entre*preneurial in your own, then reconcile your fit with any other applicable values, purposes, or goals that may come from other stakeholders. Do that before going too far along the way. Better to get it out of the way up front than to set up for problems later.

"And seek wisdom and knowledge. Find mentors with relevant experience, who care enough to tell you what you need to hear rather than what you want to hear. Try to heed them and use their guidance. They don't see your business like you do and don't know all you know about it. But you lack the objectivity and wisdom they have. If you struggle to trust their credibility and intentions, they may not be the right ones. Find the right ones.

"Learn all you can from reading and from others about culture, success factors, leadership, management, aligning incentives, positioning for success, and everything else that can be constructive.

"You also need to fundamentally understand your market and what your customer is *really* buying.

"Based on what your customer is really buying, find the right model to serve them and to force you to be a great business.

"People will advise you to have a great idea, be at the right place at the right time, work hard, put the right team in the right place, come up with the capital to execute, and so forth, as well as deciding when and how to evolve the business and solution—and make decisions on investment and everything else. All of that stuff is important, but with so much on the line, the right model will drive you to all of that and give you a much greater chance to find the way to success.

"Make it a priority to be great at serving your customers and selling to them.

"Also key is to get the right leadership and team in the right position to serve the model and everything else that came before it.

"Of course, it helps for *you* to have the right success factors in yourself, like integrity, purposefulness, intelligence, and the wisdom that comes with experience. Like tenacity and persistence. I think a positive and constructive mindset can be compelling. I hope you will look at leaders you admire and model their traits that work for you. Keep a list of these success factors. Be like them. Your company will probably become like you. Or if you are not what your company needs to be, find someone else to drive your business that's a better fit. You can learn from them along the way. And you owe it to your customers and team and shareholders, and yourself and your family, to make sure your business is in the best hands at all times.

"Of course, you want to build your venture with the right people. Those success factors you noted also apply to your team, throughout the organization. The people you hire to build your business with are essential and should be treated as an absolute priority. In addition to qualifications and competences, focus on their personalities and cultural fit, depending on their roles. In this way, you can help to set up and foster a culture for success.

"Look for the characteristics in your team that are aligned with your vision and values. Those might include things like integrity, work ethic, honesty, perseverance, diversity, competence, and other considerations that best serve your customers, model, and type of business.

"Make sure your people are in the right roles in the organization with the right accountability. And once you have the right people, settled into the right business and opportunity, it becomes about aligning incentives, including how their compensation and appreciation line up with your goals.

"At some point, you want to work toward putting systems and processes and rules and resources that fit, internally and externally, in place: to structure and serve it all, and make your business increasingly replicable and sustainable.

"Be sure to arm and empower your team with clearly articulated expectations and sufficient authority and resources, internal and external, to get there.

"Whatever model you have in place, keep tweaking it and letting it evolve into something better, perhaps leveraging your strengths and weaknesses and opportunities that arrive.

"It's good to have the right infrastructure and providers around you, as well. For example, the best-fit lawyer, accountant, and banker can make a significant difference. If it makes sense, make sure you have the right value-add investors, funding, and resources to enable your best chance.

"Ensure that your organization and cost structure serve your model and customers. Make sure your team fits appropriately in it. Wherever you can, consider mitigating risk and giving yourself a better chance to be a great business by leaning more on incremental models and minimizing obligated overhead. If you do that, you might find that your income statement and balance sheet also better take care of themselves.

"Follow your customer-driven model and any objective guidance to give yourself the best morphability: the best setup to cause you to change when you need to, or to keep pressing forward when you should not change. With so much on the line for you and your team, you have to give yourself the best opportunity to stay ahead with your innovation.

"And the right model will help you to better evolve your business structure and protocols and leadership team, and to best know when it is time to do so.

"In most cases, objectivity is your friend and subjectivity can get in your way. You may want to be careful about following your intuition for big decisions, particularly at first, at least until your gut has validated itself repeatedly.

"When you do find success in your efforts, I hope you will consider your values and priorities and hopefully find a way to give back or pay forward or do what works for you to make the world a better place.

"While all of this may sound overwhelming, you may actually find that every element of this all ties together—in an almost elegant way, with alignment throughout. Of course, this is just the beginning of the process. Every circumstance is different, and I'd rather focus on ideas and philosophies than tell you what specific decisions to make.

"For most of what I've shared with you," David said, "you may just have to live it. It will always be better if you come to it, yourself—if you own it and the consequences. If I ever told you to fire someone or sell your company, or do anything that could go badly, you would still be the one that had to live with it. So, I might share my experiences and what I learned, but you need to come to your decisions for yourself and own them."

David wrapped up the summary to his class with a final piece of advice: "Through all of this, it helps if you believe in what you are doing. If you love what you are doing and are passionate about it, you'll do a better job and it won't feel so much like work. It will be more fun and rewarding."

CHAPTER 47

Cowboy Culmination

"The best parts of any story to me are the unexpected things."

—Kirsten Vangsness

Bart Stanton dropped by Ren's office, enthusiasm on his face and in his bearing, after lunch on a Tuesday. The office was still quiet, since most of the sales team was out at client meetings and the developers were focused on working on a new solution.

"The new deal with Terrissett is working pretty well," said Bart, as he slid into one of the sturdy but relatively inexpensive leather chairs in Ren's office. The contract through Terrissett was a very big deal for Dirigat. And dealing with them, and the government contracts through them, was different from working with any of the other customers. With several hundred million dollars in revenue, hundreds of federal contracts, and thousands of employees, Terrissett was an established company.

From what Ren could tell, the end customer, GHS, was happy with the contract and the solution that Dirigat was providing, contracted through Terrissett. There may have been opportunity for considerable expansion and growth in the system. Terrissett had taken acute notice.

Ren had not been very engaged in this. It was hard for him to stay out of it and give Bart space on such a big opportunity, but this was completely Bart's deal. He was taking the opportunity to let Bart do his thing and own this success. Bart had always kept him informed at a high level, and was now getting better at providing more details on how things were going.

"Our biggest issue, as you know, is Carter. He does great work. I think more than ever now that he is the right guy. The customers love him . . ." The way Bart's voice trailed off gave Ren pause.

Carter was now the main guy whom Dirigat had working full-time within the huge GHS provider organization, through Terrissett. Ren could feel the *but* coming.

"*But* he is still concerning me." Bart's voice had gone up and he had a wry expression on his face. "He still gets a little 'cowboy' at times." There it was.

It sounded like Carter's issues were ongoing, but Ren needed more specifics now.

"What is he doing now?" Ren asked, wondering what the consequence and cost might be.

Bart referenced some headaches from how Carter was still building scripts and using fragile, nonstandard techniques to do things that were not stable and that the development team couldn't support or replicate. And the consequences were really starting to add up now, with the HealthAlign software having more problems.

"Oh, and, our guy at Terrissett, Mike Messer, wants to meet you." Bart said it almost as an afterthought—but Ren got the sense that last point was a bigger deal to him.

Bart's expression and delivery seemed pretty positive, but Ren suspected that Terrissett must have been concerned or displeased about something—presumably the consequences of whatever Carter was doing.

He rarely got pulled into client meetings anymore, at least as a matter of regular course, so he worried that something was amiss. *What is The Villain up to now?* Were they upset about whatever Carter was doing? He hoped for the best but wanted to be prepared for the worst, if it came to it.

Per Bart's entreaty, Ren booked a day trip to Washington, DC, and set up a meeting with Mike Messer at the Terrissett headquarters there.

———

Just four days later, Ren arrived at Terrissett's headquarters, almost an hour early for his 9:30 a.m. appointment. He grabbed a newspaper and waited over an iced tea in a nearby coffee shop. Fifteen minutes before the appointed meeting time, he headed up to the Terrissett office.

Ren had expected swank accommodations from this large government contracting firm, perhaps marble floors, mahogany desks, and oil paintings—even though such things never impressed him. Instead, he was pleasantly surprised to find a practical, professional environment, buzzing with activity but without frills. The floors were covered in Berber carpet squares (that Ren loved for their functionality, practicality, and cost-effectiveness!), many of the desks were cherry laminate veneer, and there were only a few sparse paintings of nature scenes. Ren kind of liked these guys!

He was welcomed into Mike Messer's corner office, where they exchanged warm greetings as he entered. They had a friendly conversation that wound about for a few hours, about their businesses and combined efforts. They talked about Bart and Carter with mutual appreciation and discussed the upside and opportunity of the relationship.

From what he had taken from the last conversation with Bart, Ren had feared that Terrissett must have been unhappy with how Carter was doing, but Messer didn't seem to care about that at all. If anything, he seemed to really like and value Carter.

Throughout the exchange, as much as possible, Ren carefully stuck to constructive ideas and opportunities. He listened to Messer's points, which seemed to be circling around a purpose, but Ren never really connected to where Messer was going with the conversation or what he was looking for. Maybe he was just feeling out Ren's commitment to the relationship with Terrissett.

At some point, Ren looked up and realized that it was mid-afternoon. The day was disappearing, and he needed to get to his flight home.

Messer walked him out, through a parking deck, to the area where Ren would catch his ride back to the airport. They came through a dark area in the parking deck, when Messer surprised Ren:

"So, would you sell Dirigat?"

Ren wasn't sure that he had heard correctly. He was struggling to process the question, as Messer continued.

"Would you take thirty million for the company?"

Full Circle

"Always two there are, a Master and an Apprentice."

—Yoda

As Ren was in a better position to do so, from finally being able to cash in from the exits of his prior business, he started angel-investing in other companies. At times, he would take David to meet with, and help evaluate, these companies.

In one case, Ren and David went to meet a couple of bright young technologists, right out of college. The pair had innovated a new solution to sell to hospitals and radiology practices. Ren felt a soft spot for Whitney and Andy— they reminded him of himself, and of the time he had his own idea for a hospital technology solution.

A few of his friends had invested in this startup, and Ren was impressed with how smart, creative, and savvy these new entrepreneurs were. He knew they also had a lot to learn. Even in a best-case scenario, they were going to have a hard time turning their excellent innovation into a replicable business. But Ren wanted to see them succeed and have the best chance at making it work.

He was about to share some of his concerns with these young entrepreneurs, to tell them that perhaps they could find the right model and bring in a management team to help turn their technology into a business. Or maybe they could sell their solution to an existing business that could get it out there.

But David spoke up before Ren could. "You have no chance at making a go of this. You're not going to make it."

Much like Ren had done on hearing a similar message in his first meeting with David, years earlier, Andy and Whitney both froze, each with a deer-in-the-headlights expression on their face.

"You have no understanding of the industry you are going into and have no idea what it will be like to sell to your potential customers," David continued. "You'll struggle for credibility in a world where any customer will be afraid they might get fired for hiring a startup, if you don't deliver. And you don't know anything about business models or putting the right team together in the right way or any of the things you need to do to give yourself a realistic chance of success."

Ren could see the shocked look on the young faces. They had never heard this message before, and it was easy to see that this was a tough pill for them to swallow. But, as Ren knew now, David was right.

To their credit, Whitney and Andy were gracious and asked a few follow-up questions, trying to clarify the message that David was firmly delivering. The kids—for that's how they seemed to Ren—thanked them for their time and feedback and reiterated their determination to proceed with their plan. Ren found himself taking a deep breath once the meeting was over.

The sun was shining, and the day felt full of promise as he and David left the building that housed the communal workspaces now so popular with budding entrepreneurs and tech startups. David paused to take in the fresh spring air.

"You know, those kids may be on to something," David said. "There's a big need for what they're planning. I like their technology, and I think their market might be willing and able to pay for it now. The best thing they have going may be that they don't know what they don't know. Since they don't know any better, they might go out there and keep working at it until they find their way."

He added, "If they're crazy enough to keep going, you should try to help them."

Ren was dumbfounded. "What do you mean?" he asked, his voice elevated. "You just told them they had *no chance*! You said, unequivocally, that they were not going to make it!"

This time it was David who showed a hint of surprise and perhaps a touch of disappointment, as if he had expected Ren to have already figured him out.

"Yes," David said slowly, with a knowing smile. "If I can talk them out of it, they have no business doing it. Building a business is hard and they will need to be persistent. But if they are going to do it anyway, it's only then that you should try to encourage and help them."

As Ren watched David walk to his car, he felt suddenly flooded with a warm rush of gratitude to have had both youthful determination *and* someone like David to help show him the way. And, he knew that he would pay it forward for the next generation of entrepreneurs, adopting many of the mentorship techniques he'd learned from his experiences and mentors, including one David Olden.

Experience Sharing

"You're going to fail," he had told me. And even though it happened a very long time ago, I remember that statement like it was yesterday. I prefer positive, constructive language. So, at the beginning of this book, I changed it to "You're not going to make it." But the real-life mentor on whom I primarily patterned the fictional David Olden was trying to talk me out of starting my business. After all, if he could talk me out of it, I shouldn't be doing it. But when he couldn't talk me out of it, my own David then decided to do what he could to help me.

For anyone that is a prospective entrepreneur, I want to scare you and thereby prepare you, as well as I reasonably can, before *you* commit to so much risk and work. Then, if you still decide to proceed, I just want to help, as David and others did for me. The purpose of this book is to honor and pay forward the great service that my dad and David and Jon Weiser and so many mentors and role models and others did for me.

And I really feel genuinely humbled and grateful to you, for your willingness to put up with my writing and give consideration to any of it. Even if you just pick up a nugget that helps a little in your life or efforts, that seems like a victory.

I started this book with entrepreneurs in mind, but I hope it can also help others. One of my friends that read the first draft, a retired CEO of a huge, successful company, said, "This book is really for *everyone*." I hope so.

Of course, I have done the WAYAWAYG (Who Are You and Where Are You Going) exercise with a number of people from all walks of life, including many entrepreneurs and CEOs from a handful of Russell 2000 companies, as well as many that are not involved professionally in leading any business or organization. And many of them have said it was very useful or even life-changing. It seems to me that in most cases, the more successful leaders have also tended to be the ones that put the most into the exercise—and then, by their own accounts, it follows that they got the most out of it.

Many of the concepts and material in this book have come from conversations with CEOs and other leaders of organizations ranging from startups to not-for-profits to several of the largest corporations in the world. And hopefully, a sequel about the next stage of the company will have even more relevant experience-sharing for bigger and transitioning business leaders, other organizations, and general life matters.

Of course, hopefully some entrepreneurs will read this book. My first goal is to essentially give them a sort of handbook to help prepare them for what their journey might look like, based on some of my own experiences and lessons learned.

Hopefully some entrepreneurs' family members and friends may also read this book and better understand and deal with "what is wrong with all of us." Another friend who read an advance version of this book felt that it might be helpful for her key employees to read it so that they can better understand what she is trying to accomplish and why she acts as she does.

I also love engaging with people that are being entrepreneurial in their nonprofit and philanthropic work. Maybe this can provide some value to them, as well.

There were a number of reasons for making this a work of fiction. For one matter, for a lot of lessons, some would say that you almost have to live through them to learn from them. Of course, there is no way to replace that experiential learning. But if you can almost feel like you are in the story and living it, perhaps you may learn from it, at least to a small degree, as if it is your own.

I also have learned the advantage of sharing experiences—from the business forums that I have done—where you gather with a small group of other leaders and share your experiences, rather than give direct advice. I have always been wary about direct advice—telling people what they need to do—particularly in giving broad platitudes to guide people through their unique circumstances.

Each situation may call for a different decision. And the entrepreneur needs to arrive at the answers for themselves—particularly since they have to live with their own decisions and consequences.

So, hopefully any reader can see a little of what we did and learned and then weigh that experience, the outcome, and the learning against each decision.

I am publishing the book under a pen name for a number of reasons. This is about paying it forward and trying to help others, as so many people helped me.

It made sense to put these experiences in a book. Since the time described in this manuscript, I have tried to help a large number of businesses and leaders, as an investor and/or advisor, to varying degrees. Over the years, I have seen the same issues come up over and over. And as David and others did for me through the experience of my business, I keep repeating myself, like a broken record, until things advance. So, it made sense to put them in here, to hopefully illustrate until it hopefully comes together for the reader.

I also wanted to prioritize some items that are not covered as well by others. There are already a lot of great books and online videos out there, with a great deal of guidance for an entrepreneur. What I wanted to create was something different. I wanted a story that would touch on some of the same things that other books and videos cover—but that would also help people to engage and focus on the most important things that those others don't address as much, such as business model and understanding what their customer is really buying, among other examples.

And there are plenty of other reasons this is a work of fiction. If any reader thinks they recognize the business or any of the characters—don't. While this book is loosely based on a real company that was sold long ago, it incorporates lessons from a number of other businesses that I have been around or involved in, as well as wisdom and a few anecdotes from elsewhere.

I also took liberties with the stories and characters to accomplish my goals. All of the characters were composed of traits and experiences from more than one person. So it would be wrong and unfair to assign responsibility for anything in this book to anyone. And I only feel love and warmth and affection and gratitude for *everyone* from the times that inspired this book.

Although a lot of the events described in the book are derived from matters that happened more than two decades ago, I tried to make it at least somewhat timeless. And it intentionally incorporates many companies and references that are more recent.

In explaining points, I tried to credit a few of the books and resources that I like to recommend. I mostly stuck with classic or older books here, although some of them were published well after I experienced or learned their lessons.

And of course, the goal is to make this useful for different types of businesses and organizations and individuals. So, I mostly tried to address the specific industry, business model, technologies, and techniques of my company, at the time, in a way that is still relevant for other circumstances, in a hope that entrepreneurs might reflect on them and apply their learning to their own businesses. Any more details added were at the request of my editors and friends who thought they might be interesting.

And if my readers can somehow bear it, I want to write more. I expect to get conflicting feedback on some things in this book. And even I don't agree with everything in it. Some of the mistakes and lessons are there to help you experience, to a degree, and deliberate as I did. Hopefully you will derive your own perspective from doing so.

I also really appreciate anyone willing to read through all of this. Thanks very much for your time and consideration!

Acknowledgments

There is no way I will sufficiently thank or acknowledge everyone. And I fear that I will miss a lot of very important contributors to this effort. Here are a few: Mr. Darrell, Brenda, Horton, Joe B, Boppa, Nonna, the Chief, the Boss, Mom, Morgan, Maggie, Jennifer, Bill, Kell, Ellie, Maria, Cynthia, and many others made this possible!

The truly great teams at the company and from my other businesses were a huge part of this. I appreciate and care for you more than I even know how to say.

Rick, Jim, Joe, Joe, Sid, Don, Cindy, Ernest, Pat, Tom, Ko, Dave, John, Shane, Ken, Doug, Niles, Barbara, Dink, Linda, Sig, Jim, Carly, Chris, Jody, Matt, Blair, Brenda, Katie, David, Juan/Arn, Bill, Russ, Tom, Rick, Doug, Charlie, Frank, and many others were inspirations for mentors and role models and outside characters in the book.

My Boomerang and TGM family were amazingly important in this journey. And I have to thank the Green Yogis, Tue Live Crew, and now Forum 7 for their patience and consideration as they put up with me while I was writing it.

Huge appreciation to the hundreds of other entrepreneurs that I have worked with, tried to help, invested in, and otherwise learned from, including Stephen, Terry, and David.

Frank, Kara, Russell, Jeff, Jeff, Lisa again, Susan, Matthew, Cliff, and so many more were awesome!!! (Extra exclamation points for the second Jeff.)

Thanks also very much to Brian, David, Doug, Terry, Chan, Sonny, and many others who helped me better express what I wanted to say or provided useful analogies or ideas.

Of course, there are way too many others that I strongly need to acknowledge. A lot of you are going to appear in future books.

WAYAWAYG™

Who Are You and Where Are You Going?

YOUR LIFE IN THE FUTURE

Write down, in as much detail as you reasonably can, what you would like your life to look like in fifteen years. Be sure to visualize all of this as clearly as possible—the details really bring it to life! Don't let current circumstances impact or limit your vision too much. Customize as best helps you see your life then. You might draw detailed pictures or create a vision board. You can—and probably should—add whole pages.

Write and describe—preferably by hand, rather than typing on a computer—the following, as well as any other lifestyle details you can think of:

- **How you live**, including your relationship with your family, exercise habits, daily or weekly rituals, hobbies, and any other relevant details. It may help to draw or download pictures.

- **Describe "A Day in the Life"** that represents a typical day in the future time period.

- **What you look like**, incorporating your physical health, weight, posture, attire, and so on.

- **What your job/vocation is**. This could include what you produce, how many hours you work, how much vacation time and what benefits you receive, what your coworkers are like and how they treat you, and so on. Again, use as much detail as you can.

- **Where you live.** Describe your house, yard, swimming pool, and anything else you can imagine, as vividly as you can. If you have a beach house or mountain house, describe those too. It may again be helpful to draw or download pictures to give yourself a visual.

- **How much money** you make and have in the bank, as well as where it came from and where it's going. It's also important to note what your personal balance sheet looks like.

- **Every other useful detail** you can come up with and visualize. For example, if you are a student, you could list what kind of grades you are making, achievements in your sports or activities, and so on. This could also include your church, friends you hang out with, what car you drive, how and where you travel, what type of investments you are in, and so on.

Once you've completed the fifteen-year exercise, repeat it for ten years from now—keeping in mind that you should then be two-thirds of the way to the vision you cast for fifteen years.

When you have your vision for fifteen years and ten years, complete the same exercise for five years from now. You may be a third of the way there toward your fifteen-year goals, or at least marching in the right direction. Describe and record it all as vividly and in as much detail as possible.

Now, do the same exercise again for three years from now. Finally, do the same thing for a year from now. You might feel some urgency at this point, as you visualize yourself a year and three years from now.

The more clearly you can picture and record details for each stage, the better. This exercise is designed to be completed over a few weeks, so be sure to give yourself plenty of time and space to do this. If you get stuck, take a break and come back to it. Finish what you can for now. It doesn't have to be perfect (remember: Perfect is the enemy of good!). You can always come back and add details later.

Once you have a clear-as-possible picture of your life in fifteen, ten, five, and three years and one year from now, put the papers aside and move on to the next section.

YOUR LIFE NOW

The next part of this exercise is to clearly evaluate yourself and your life in its current state. This is a frank look at who you are now, including your constraints and circumstances. Think of this as a personal "SWOT" analysis. Look it up: It is a thing! SWOT stands for Strengths, Weaknesses, Opportunities, and Threats. BE HONEST and realistic—even to the point of being self-critical. If you're comfortable, ask friends for some feedback. You don't have to show anyone else what you write down.

STRENGTHS

For strengths, you could start with what you believe others (who know you well and are willing to be honest with you) would say about you. Reconcile this with what you believe to be true. Maybe do another Myers-Briggs-type test or weigh your friends' opinions against how you see yourself. It's sometimes useful to list your passions and/or activities or elements of your life that you love or find empowering.

WEAKNESSES

Now, list your weaknesses. This is a challenging but important part of the exercise. Ask your true friends to name three things that you could improve. Try to listen and hear what they're saying. If something they say hurts your feelings, still put it on the list. You can always remove it later if you think it's unfair or unjustified. If your life isn't exactly what you want, ask yourself "why?" Take responsibility and examine the reason. If necessary, as you consider how you got there, ask yourself "why?" five times or more, for each successive answer.[1] When you get to something that makes you uncomfortable, write it down. It may be helpful to consider activities or tasks you dislike doing or that create resistance in your life (for example, your disorganized closet, never having "enough time in the day," being "disappointed with friends/family members").

---

[1] Developed by Sakichi Toyoda.

THREATS

I changed the order because this is a better place for threats (after weaknesses and before your opportunities). Think big *and* small, internal *and* external. For my part, some of mine are "what I don't know" or "something totally unexpected." This sounds obvious, but I like to write those down, as problems often arise in those unknown or unexpected scenarios. It's important to be aware of your most compelling threats and include them here. As a symbolic gesture that I will overcome these threats, I sometimes physically strike through the threats with a pen when I'm done with the list. This symbolizes my commitment to not allowing these threats to detract from my life.

OPPORTUNITIES

This is the fun part! Make a detailed list of opportunities in your life. Some of your opportunities may be large, while others may be small but meaningful. There is no specified number you need to list. The number of opportunities you choose may be telling in itself. Think about whether you may have too many or too few. Have some fun with it!

TAKE ANOTHER LOOK

Somewhere in the process (perhaps under "strengths," "weaknesses," or both) incorporate what your values are. Most people consider their values and ideals (integrity, honesty, faith, family, etc.) to be strengths. Are yours REALLY a strength? How committed are you to them? Is that a strength or weakness, or even a threat? Weigh them and your commitment to them, quantifying each. You don't have to show this to anyone. You may also want to articulate where your values and commitment should be or will be in the future (perhaps under "opportunities").

Evaluate and articulate how much risk you can take and the resources (time, money, connections, etc.) you have to work with. Add this to the section that feels most appropriate.

Finally, it can be useful to list the things that you hate to do (paperwork?), what you love to do, what you are not willing to do (for example, deal with bureaucracy), what you want to get better at, and other preferences that merit consideration.

WAYAWAYG (WHO ARE YOU AND WHERE ARE YOU GOING?)

When finished, gather your SWOT/the Your Life Now exercise and the vision statements for your life in fifteen, ten, five, three, and one years and put them on a table in front of you. Put your stack of current SWOT pages in front of your left hand and the pages with your vision statements in front of your right hand.

If you haven't figured it out yet, the pages in front of you describe who you are and where you are going.

Your SWOT and the Your Life Now exercise are good evaluations of yourself and where you are at this time. It's designed to provide a snapshot of your constraints and goals. If not, go back and add details as necessary.

Your vision should show a pretty good picture of where you are going over the next fifteen years, with milestone points along the way.

As one of my great friends once said:

"Always know who you are and where you are going . . .
Then, at least go in that direction!"

Armed with the knowledge from these exercises, you can articulate and weigh your values and priorities. And, you can measure your life expectation against these values and priorities to assure that they are consistent.

This exercise might take anywhere from six to twenty (or more) hours. Work to a goal of completing it in four weeks. Set deadlines and accountability (maybe an accountability coach) to get this done in a timely manner.

There are also some key questions at the end of this exercise that you may wish to utilize. And, you can weigh all of these exercises to assure that all of it aligns, empowering you to discover who you are and where you want to go, and to march in that direction.

This can be very empowering! Most everything is easier and better when you have certainty and clarity.

15 YEARS

How I live (relationship with family, what day is like, exercise habits, daily or weekly rituals, hobbies, etc.):

_____

_____

_____

_____

_____

_____

What I look like (physical health, weight, posture, attire, etc.):

_____

_____

_____

_____

_____

_____

_____

_____

What my job/vocation is (what I produce, hours I work, vacation time and benefits, people I work with and relationship with them, etc.):

_____

_____

_____

_____

_____

_____

_____

_____

Where I live (dwelling, yard, swimming pool, beach house or mountain house, etc.):

_____

_____

_____

_____

_____

_____

_____

_____

How much money I make and have in the bank (where it came from and where it is going, balance sheet):

_____

_____

_____

_____

_____

_____

_____

Other details of my life (achievements in sports or activities, church, friends, car[s], travel, investments, etc.):

_____

_____

_____

_____

_____

_____

_____

Put any pictures, drawings, or additional points or details on the back of this sheet or insert other pages.

10 YEARS

How I live (relationship with family, what day is like, exercise habits, daily or weekly rituals, hobbies, etc.):

_____

_____

_____

_____

_____

_____

_____

What I look like (physical health, weight, posture, attire, etc.):

_____

_____

_____

_____

_____

_____

_____

What my job/vocation is (what I produce, hours I work, vacation time and benefits, people I work with and relationship with them, etc.):

_____

_____

_____

_____

_____

_____

_____

Where I live (dwelling, yard, swimming pool, beach house or mountain house, etc.):

_____

_____

_____

_____

_____

_____

_____

How much money I make and have in the bank (where it came from and where it is going, balance sheet):

_____

_____

_____

_____

_____

_____

_____

Other details of my life (achievements in sports or activities, church, friends, car[s], travel, investments, etc.):

_____

_____

_____

_____

_____

_____

_____

Put any pictures, drawings, or additional points or details on the back of this sheet or insert other pages.

5 YEARS

How I live (relationship with family, what day is like, exercise habits, daily or weekly rituals, hobbies, etc.):

_____

_____

_____

_____

_____

_____

_____

_____

What I look like (physical health, weight, posture, attire, etc.):

_____

_____

_____

_____

_____

_____

_____

_____

What my job/vocation is (what I produce, hours I work, vacation time and benefits, people I work with and relationship with them, etc.):

_____

_____

_____

_____

_____

_____

_____

_____

Where I live (dwelling, yard, swimming pool, beach house or mountain house, etc.):

_____

_____

_____

_____

_____

_____

_____

_____

How much money I make and have in the bank (where it came from and where it is going, balance sheet):

_____

_____

_____

_____

_____

_____

_____

Other details of my life (achievements in sports or activities, church, friends, car[s], travel, investments, etc.):

_____

_____

_____

_____

_____

_____

_____

_____

Put any pictures, drawings, or additional points or details on the back of this sheet or insert other pages.

3 YEARS

How I live (relationship with family, what day is like, exercise habits, daily or weekly rituals, hobbies, etc.):

_____

_____

_____

_____

_____

_____

_____

_____

What I look like (physical health, weight, posture, attire, etc.):

_____

_____

_____

_____

_____

_____

_____

_____

What my job/vocation is (what I produce, hours I work, vacation time and benefits, people I work with and relationship with them, etc.):

_____

_____

_____

_____

_____

_____

_____

Where I live (dwelling, yard, swimming pool, beach house or mountain house, etc.):

_____

_____

_____

_____

_____

_____

_____

_____

How much money I make and have in the bank (where it came from and where it is going, balance sheet):

_____

_____

_____

_____

_____

_____

_____

_____

Other details of my life (achievements in sports or activities, church, friends, car[s], travel, investments, etc.):

_____

_____

_____

_____

_____

_____

_____

_____

Put any pictures, drawings, or additional points or details on the back of this sheet or insert other pages.

1 YEAR

How I live (relationship with family, what day is like, exercise habits, daily or weekly rituals, hobbies, etc.):

_____

_____

_____

_____

_____

_____

_____

_____

What I look like (physical health, weight, posture, attire, etc.):

_____

_____

_____

_____

_____

_____

_____

_____

What my job/vocation is (what I produce, hours I work, vacation time and benefits, people I work with and relationship with them, etc.):

_____

_____

_____

_____

_____

_____

_____

Where I live (dwelling, yard, swimming pool, beach house or mountain house, etc.):

_____

_____

_____

_____

_____

_____

_____

_____

How much money I make and have in the bank (where it came from and where it is going, balance sheet):

_____

_____

_____

_____

_____

_____

_____

Other details of my life (achievements in sports or activities, church, friends, car[s], travel, investments, etc.):

_____

_____

_____

_____

_____

_____

_____

Put any pictures, drawings, or additional points or details on the back of this sheet or insert other pages.

END OF THIS CALENDAR YEAR

This period is optional: Use another time when it helps you.

How I live (relationship with family, what day is like, exercise habits, daily or weekly rituals, hobbies, etc.):

_____

_____

_____

_____

_____

_____

_____

_____

What I look like (physical health, weight, posture, attire, etc.):

_____

_____

_____

_____

_____

_____

_____

_____

What my job/vocation is (what I produce, hours I work, vacation time and benefits, people I work with and relationship with them, etc.):

_____

_____

_____

_____

_____

_____

_____

_____

Where I live (dwelling, yard, swimming pool, beach house or mountain house, etc.):

_____

_____

_____

_____

_____

_____

_____

_____

How much money I make and have in the bank (where it came from and where it is going, balance sheet):

_____

_____

_____

_____

_____

_____

_____

Other details of my life (achievements in sports or activities, church, friends, car[s], travel, investments, etc.):

_____

_____

_____

_____

_____

_____

_____

Put any pictures, drawings, or additional points or details on the back of this sheet or insert other pages.

WHO ARE YOU NOW?

Strengths

_____

_____

_____

_____

_____

_____

_____

_____

Weaknesses, Barriers, Impediments

_____

_____

_____

_____

_____

_____

_____

_____

Threats—Existing and Potential

_____

_____

_____

_____

_____

_____

_____

_____

Opportunities

_____

_____

_____

_____

_____

_____

_____

_____

Other Constraints (including what you hate to do, love to do, are good at, want to improve, etc.)

_____

_____

_____

_____

_____

_____

_____

_____

Put any pictures, drawings, or additional points or details on the back of this sheet or insert other pages.

VALUES AND PRIORITIES

This exercise should help you to articulate and weigh the priorities in your life. Consider anything that has meaning to you: values, priorities, goals, people, and things. Maybe pick anywhere from 8 to 30 words that are most important, to represent what you value. Then, put them on paper, in the order that best represents them to you. They could be ranked and/or set forth in an order of dependence. You could put your highest priority at the top of the paper or the center of the paper and then work from there, as best helps you to visualize what is important to you. See page 338 for an example.

Here are some possibilities to choose from:

Acceptance	Fairness	Kindness	Responsibility
Achievement	Faith	Knowledge	Results
Adventure	Fame	Leadership	Risk-taking
Ambition	Family	Learning	Romance
Appreciation	Flow	Love	Routine
Authenticity	Fitness	Loyalty	Safety
Authority	Focus	Meaningfulness	Science
Autonomy	Fortitude	Mentoring	Security
Balance	Freedom	Nature	Self-expression
Beauty	Friends	Neatness	Self-respect
Belonging	Fulfillment	Nurturing	Service
Challenge	Fun	Opportunity	Sharing
Character	Giving	Order	Solitude
Choice	God	Organizing	Spirituality
Coaching	Growth	Passion	Sports
Collaboration	Happiness	Peace	Status
Commitment	Harmony	Perfection	Success
Community	Health	Personal Growth	Sustainability
Compassion	Helping Others	Philanthropy	Teaching
Competence	Heritage	Power	Teamwork
Competition	History	Preparing	Tenacity
Connection	Honesty	Privacy	Tolerance
Consideration	Humor	Productivity	Tradition
Contribution	Imagination	Property	Travel
Creativity	Inclusiveness	Protection	Trust
Discipline	Independence	Reaching	Value
Education	Influence	Potential	Variety
Empathy	Integrity	Purpose	Wealth
Equality	Intelligence	Reading	Winning
Excellence	Intuition	Recognition	Wisdom
Excitement	Investment	Religion	Work Ethic
Expertise	Justice	Respect	Zeal

EXAMPLES OF EXERCISES AND CREATIVE ARTICULATIONS

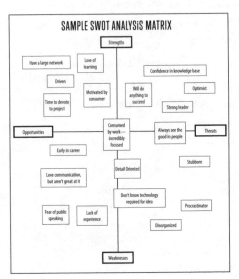

SAMPLE SWOT ANALYSIS MATRIX

Strengths

- Have a large network
- Love of learning
- Confidence in knowledge base
- Driven
- Motivated by consumer
- Will do anything to succeed
- Optimist
- Time to devote to project
- Strong leader

Opportunities — Consumed by work—incredibly focused — Always see the good in people — Threats

- Early in career
- Detail Oriented
- Stubborn
- Love communication, but aren't great at it
- Don't know technology required for idea
- Procrastinator
- Fear of public speaking
- Lack of experience
- Disorganized

Weaknesses

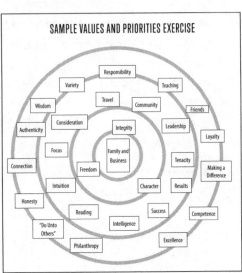

SAMPLE VALUES AND PRIORITIES EXERCISE

Responsibility · Variety · Teaching · Wisdom · Travel · Community · Friends · Consideration · Authenticity · Integrity · Leadership · Loyalty · Focus · Family and Business · Tenacity · Connection · Freedom · Making a Difference · Intuition · Character · Results · Honesty · Reading · Success · Competence · "Do Unto Others" · Intelligence · Excellence · Philanthropy

SAMPLE VALUES AND PRIORITIES EXERCISE

Faith

Immediate Family

Freedom   Integrity   Character

Responsibility   Wisdom

Competence   "Do Unto Others"

My Business/Meaningful   Friends

Work Ethic   Learning   Leadership   Trust   Opportunity   Teaching

Discipline   Respect (Self and Others)   Consideration   Empathy

Tenacity   Reading   Safety   Security   Coaching   Mentoring

Sustainability—Improving self/world in enduring way

Intelligence   Fulfilment   Property   Health   Wealth   External Family   Friends

Knowledge   Growth   Investments   Justice   Value   Loyalty   Kindness

Creativity   Appreciation   Challenge   Competence   Excellence   Nature   Service

Travel   Excitement   Fun   History   Competition

SAMPLE VISION BOARD

VALUES AND PRIORITIES

Organize your priorities and values here, perhaps in an ordered circle or hierarchical chart. Use up to fifty words.

QUESTIONS AND CONSIDERATIONS

What Makes Me Happy and/or Fulfilled?

_____

_____

_____

_____

_____

_____

_____

_____

_____

_____

What Do I Consider Success? Personal? Spiritual? Family? Career?

_____

_____

_____

_____

_____

_____

_____

_____

_____

_____

Why Do I Exist? What Is My Purpose?

_____

_____

_____

_____

_____

_____

_____

_____

_____

Things I Will Change Now

_____

_____

_____

_____

_____

_____

_____

_____

_____

Actions I Will Take Now

_____

_____

_____

_____

_____

_____

_____

_____

_____

What Are My Empowering Factors (Advantages or Opportunities)?

_____

_____

_____

_____

_____

_____

_____

_____

WAYAWAYG™ for Your Business

YOUR BUSINESS IN THE FUTURE

Write down, in as much detail as you reasonably can, what your business is like in five years. Be sure to visualize all of this as clearly as possible—the details really bring it to life! Don't let current circumstances impact or limit your vision too much. Customize as best helps you see your life then. You might articulate your customer list, financial statements and breakdowns by product and customer, key employees' job descriptions, and organization charts.

Write and describe—preferably by hand, rather than typing on a computer—the following, as well as any other details you can think of:

- **What the Business Does**, including the model, customers, management team, solution, and so on.

- **Describe "A Day in the Life"** that represents a typical day in the future time period: maybe with a customer visit, sales meeting, management retreat, staff meeting, or a productive day for everyone in the office.

- **Where the Business Is**, incorporating revenues, earnings, balance sheet, employee count, and other measures.

- **What Your Role/Responsibility Is.** This could include your title, responsibilities, how you primarily interact with your team, and so on. Again, use as much detail as you can.

- **Other Relevant Considerations.** If you expect an exit or change of control event, challenges or opportunities, and so on.

- **Every Other Useful Detail** you can come up with and visualize. For example, customer involvement, insert from your business plan, or pitch deck or pro formas, and so on.

Once you've completed the exercise for five years from now, repeat it for three years from now—keeping in mind that you should then be three-fifths of the way to the vision you cast for five years out.

When you have your vision for five years and three years from now, complete the same exercise for one year from now. You may be a fifth of the way along the path toward your five-year goals, or at least marching in the right direction. Describe and record it all as vividly and in as much detail as possible. You might feel some urgency at this point, as you visualize yourself a year and three years from now.

The more clearly you can picture and record details for each stage, the better. This exercise is designed to be completed over a few weeks, so be sure to give yourself plenty of time and space to do this. If you get stuck, take a break and come back to it. Finish what you can for now. It doesn't have to be perfect (remember: Perfect is the enemy of good!). You can always come back and add details later.

Once you have a clear-as-possible picture of your business in five years, three years, and one year, put the papers aside and move on to the next section.

CURRENT CIRCUMSTANCES

The next part of this exercise is to clearly evaluate your business—and your involvement in it—at this time. If it doesn't exist yet, then do an analysis of yourself, including your constraints and circumstances.

Think of this as a "SWOT" analysis for your business or its genesis. Look it up: It is a thing! SWOT stands for Strengths, Weaknesses, Opportunities, and Threats. BE HONEST and realistic (even to the point of being self-critical). If you're comfortable, ask friends for some feedback. You don't have to show anyone else what you write down.

STRENGTHS

Articulate your advantages. You could start with what you believe others—particularly customers—would say about the business, you, or your solution, if they know it well. Reconcile this with what you believe to be true. Maybe test others' opinions against how you see it.

WEAKNESSES

Now, list your weaknesses. This is a challenging but important part of the exercise. Ask your customers and advisors to name three things that you could improve. Try to listen and hear what they're saying. If something they say hurts your feelings, put it on the list. You can always remove it later if you think it's unfair or unjustified. If your business isn't exactly what you want, ask yourself "why?" Take responsibility and examine the reason. If necessary, as you consider how the company got there, ask yourself "why?" five times or more, for each successive answer.[1]

THREATS

I changed the order because this is a better place for threats (after weaknesses and before your opportunities). Think big *and* small, internal *and* external. For my companies, some of these always include "what we don't know" or "something totally unexpected." This sounds obvious, but I like to write those down, as problems often arise in those unknown or unexpected scenarios. It's important to be aware of your most compelling threats and include them here.

OPPORTUNITIES

This is the fun part! Make a detailed list of opportunities in your business. Some of these opportunities may be large, while others may be small but meaningful. There is no specified number you need to list. The number of opportunities you choose may be telling in itself. Think about whether you may have too many or too few. Have some fun with it!

---

1   Developed by Sakichi Toyoda.

TAKE ANOTHER LOOK

Add anything else that may be relevant to your business. Evaluate and articulate how much risk you can take and the resources (time, money, connections, etc.) you have to work with. Add this to the section that feels most appropriate.

WAYAWAYG (WHO ARE YOU AND WHERE ARE YOU GOING?)

When finished, gather your SWOT/"Current Circumstances" analysis and the vision statements for your business in five, three, and one years and put them on a table in front of you. Put your "Current Circumstances" (including the SWOT) pages in front of your left hand and the pages with your vision statements in front of your right hand.

If you haven't figured it out yet, the pages in front of you describe your business and where you are going with it.

Your SWOT and "Current Circumstances" is a good evaluation of yourself and where you are at this time. It's designed to provide a snapshot of your constraints and goals. If it doesn't do this sufficiently, go back and add details as necessary.

Your vision should show a pretty good picture of where your business will be in five years, with milestone points along the way.

As one of my great friends once said:

> *"Always know who you are and where you are going . . .*
> *Then, at least go in that direction!"*

Armed with the knowledge from these exercises, you can articulate and weigh your goals and values and priorities. And, you can measure your decisions and hiring against these considerations.

You can weigh all of these exercises to assure that all of this aligns for your business and your life, as the entrepreneur, empowering you to discover who you are and where you want to go, and to help make better decisions in going in that direction.

Congratulations! You have just created an internal basis for your business plan!

5 YEARS

Where the Business Is in 5 Years (revenues, earnings, employees, anything else):

_____

_____

_____

_____

_____

_____

_____

Customers (how many, who they are, what the relationships are like):

_____

_____

_____

_____

_____

_____

_____

Business Model (describe the type of business—what the company does to create value and get paid, perhaps including breakdown of recurring revenue percentages or other indicators of the model):

_____

_____

_____

_____

_____

_____

_____

Ownership Structure (Raised equity investment? Brought in partners? Key employees? Who owns the company and percentages?):

_____

_____

_____

_____

_____

_____

_____

Other Relevant Factors (Anything else you need to articulate up front?):

_____

_____

_____

_____

_____

_____

_____

_____

Put any pro forma financials, market research, or relevant information or details on the back of this sheet or insert other pages.

3 YEARS

Where the Business Is in 3 Years (revenues, earnings, employees, anything else):

_____

_____

_____

_____

_____

_____

_____

_____

Customers (how many, who they are, what the relationships are like):

_____

_____

_____

_____

_____

_____

_____

_____

_____

Business Model (describe the type of business—what the company does to create value and get paid, perhaps including breakdown of recurring revenue percentages or other indicators of the model):

_____

_____

_____

_____

_____

_____

_____

_____

Ownership Structure (Raised equity investment? Brought in partners? Key employees? Who owns the company and percentages?):

_____

_____

_____

_____

_____

_____

_____

_____

Other Relevant Factors (Anything else you need to articulate up front?):

_____

_____

_____

_____

_____

_____

_____

_____

Put any pro forma financials, market research, or relevant information or details on the back of this sheet or insert other pages.

1 YEAR

Where the Business Is in a Year (revenues, earnings, employees, anything else):

_____

_____

_____

_____

_____

_____

_____

_____

Customers (how many, who they are, what the relationships are like):

_____

_____

_____

_____

_____

_____

_____

_____

Business Model (describe the type of business—what the company does to create value and get paid, perhaps including breakdown of recurring revenue percentages or other indicators of the model):

_____

_____

_____

_____

_____

_____

_____

Ownership Structure (Raised equity investment? Brought in partners? Key employees? Who owns the company and percentages?):

_____

_____

_____

_____

_____

_____

_____

_____

Other Relevant Factors (Anything else you need to articulate up front?):

Put any pro forma financials, market research, or relevant information or details on the back of this sheet or insert other pages.

WHERE THE BUSINESS OR OPPORTUNITY IS NOW

Strengths

_____

_____

_____

_____

_____

_____

_____

Weaknesses, Barriers, Impediments

_____

_____

_____

_____

_____

_____

_____

Threats

_____

_____

_____

_____

_____

_____

_____

_____

Opportunities

_____

_____

_____

_____

_____

_____

_____

_____

Other Constraints—Anything Else That May Be a Constraint or Factor

_____

_____

_____

_____

_____

_____

_____

_____

Put any financial projections, market expectations, or additional points or details on the back of this sheet or insert other pages.

VALUES AND PRIORITIES

This exercise should help you to articulate and weigh the priorities in your business—that you will build your culture and hiring and customer relationships around. Consider anything that has meaning to you: values, priorities, goals, people, and things. These could include traits like integrity and honesty; emphases like moving fast, being responsive, and outworking your competition; or characteristics like inclusiveness, fairness, or rewarding merit. Articulate them on paper, in the order that best represents them to you. They could be ranked and/or set forth in an order of dependence. You could put your highest priority at the top of the paper or the center of the paper and then work from there, as best helps you to visualize what is important to you.

Organize your Priorities and Values here, perhaps in an ordered circle or hierarchical chart. Use up to fifteen words or statements.

QUESTIONS AND CONSIDERATIONS

What Is the End Goal for the Business? Income and Lifestyle? Rapid Growth? Public or Private Exit?

_____

_____

_____

_____

_____

_____

_____

What Do I Consider Success?

_____

_____

_____

_____

_____

_____

_____

Why Does This Business Exist? What Is Its Purpose?

_____

_____

_____

_____

_____

_____

_____

_____

Actions I Will Take Now

_____

_____

_____

_____

_____

_____

_____

_____

What Are My Empowering Factors (Advantages or Opportunities)?

_____

_____

_____

_____

_____

_____

_____

_____

Recommended Books

For anyone that wants to know how to manage better, I still often give away copies of *The Effective Executive* by Peter Drucker. Some might say it is outdated. But I see it as a timeless classic!

The Goal by Eliyahu Goldratt is a great book, outlining the Theory of Constraints. It also defines a great way of thinking about your business.

How to Master the Art of Selling by Tom Hopkins is outdated, in many ways. But it provides a great foundation for understanding sales. I suggest reading this before the new books.

If you are interested in more on an essential business matter, I advocate *Fostering Culture: A Leader's Guide to Purposefully Shaping Culture* by Shane Jackson.

For anyone that is interested in a frugal, entrepreneurial mindset and the healthy fastidiousness that can come with it, I suggest *Eating Ramen: A Survival Guide for Tough Financial Times* by Ellie Byrd, an entrepreneurial leader, in her own right.

Awaken the Giant Within by Tony Robbins is still the self-help book that I give out most often.

Healthcare Is Killing Us: The Power of Disruptive Innovation to Create a System That Cares More and Costs Less by Terry Howell and Aaron Fausz is a great overview for anyone that wants to learn more about problems in our healthcare system.

Some of the friends that have read this book have seemed interested in how to read people. *You Say More Than You Think* by Janine Driver is one of the better books that I sometimes recommend for that.

The War of Art and *Do the Work* by Steven Pressfield are terrific motivational reads for entrepreneurs, artists, and others for breaking through barriers and resistance.

And now, for anyone that also wants to write a book, I recommend *Ideas, Influence, and Income: Write a Book, Build Your Brand, and Lead Your Industry* by Tanya Hall.

And, last but certainly not least, as a tactical book of considerations for prospective entrepreneurs, I advocate the book *Startup Upstart* by David Cummings.

About the Author

CAP TREEGER is a serial entrepreneur and investor. He has been involved in various roles in building a number of businesses in multiple industries. Treeger has invested directly in several dozen early stage ventures and indirectly in hundreds more through his engagement in angel and venture funds. He enjoys sharing experiences of his own successes and failures to pay forward what he has learned from his mentors and to hopefully assist others in finding their way.